T0365658

HOMER'S SON

An Unusual Life

Jack Watson

iUniverse, Inc.
Bloomington

Homer's Son
An Unusual Life

iUniverse books may be ordered through booksellers or by contacting:

iUniverse
1663 Liberty Drive
Bloomington, IN 47403
www.iuniverse.com
1-800-Authors (1-800-288-4677)

Because of the dynamic nature of the Internet, any web addresses or links contained in this book may have changed since publication and may no longer be valid. The views expressed in this work are solely those of the author and do not necessarily reflect the views of the publisher, and the publisher hereby disclaims any responsibility for them.

Any people depicted in stock imagery provided by Thinkstock are models, and such images are being used for illustrative purposes only.

Certain stock imagery © Thinkstock.

ISBN: 978-1-4620-4213-5 (sc)
ISBN: 978-1-4620-4214-2 (e)
ISBN: 978-1-4620-4215-9 (dj)

Printed in the United States of America

iUniverse rev. date: 10/3/2012

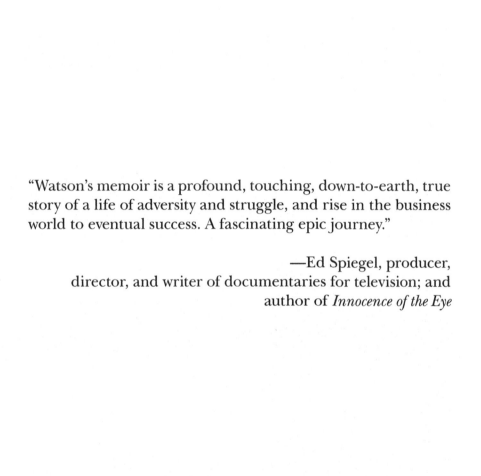

"Watson's memoir is a profound, touching, down-to-earth, true story of a life of adversity and struggle, and rise in the business world to eventual success. A fascinating epic journey."

—Ed Spiegel, producer, director, and writer of documentaries for television; and author of *Innocence of the Eye*

Homer's Son is the story of my life. Perseverance, guts, and *redemption* describes my epic journey from rags to riches.

I hope that my story may inspire others to persevere through their struggles and difficulties and succeed.

Contents

Acknowledgments

Nicole Spiegel—My thanks and gratitude for your support and encouragement in my travails and tribulations in writing this book, as well as in my life, and for your help to keep my sanity in the process. I loved your comment on my memory loss: "You are the freaking best, and all I have to say is thank God you started writing your book before you got so damn old!"

Joanne and Ed Spiegel—My thanks to you both for your generous professional critique of my writings and your wonderful, warm friendship and many hugs! (Ed Spiegel is the author of a number of books and director and publisher of several documentaries.)

My thanks to Martina, the love of my life, who stood behind me in everything I did.

To my children—Ron, Allan, Teresa, Clari, and my beloved David (deceased)—and Martina's children—Maelee and Joel, and her granddaughter Chelsea—who supported me and listened and absorbed the stories I read to them and gave me their comments and assessments.

Deborah Keener—For your insights on life, spirituality, parenting, and happiness. You have had a fascinating life and career. I am amazed at your success as a professional composer and recording artist. I cannot wait to read the book that you are writing of your life.

Barbara Garner—My thanks and gratitude for your advice on how to make a very important change that brought my book around full circle to closure. I am looking forward to reading your book when it is published. You have had a life of joy and pain, as many of us do.

My thanks also to all my other friends and associates who read and commented—good or bad—on my writings.

To Deb Bartlett, sketch artist—"House of Cards," 424 Sunnybrook Drive, Oshkosh, WI 54904—who provided the ink sketches that enrich the stories in my book.

Disclaimer

Homer's Child is true to the characters, situations, times, locations, and knowledge gained from people involved in, or knowledgeable of, the events. Some dialogue, names, and situations have been improvised for story purposes, but are true to the overall understanding of the people and the times.

Chapter 1:
Twilight and Darkness

After a career that spanned forty-six years in the manufacturing industry, I retired to Montecito, California, in 1996.

Our home was a Palladian-style villa. My second wife, Martina, and I had admired Italian architecture since our trips to Italy and Sicily.

Our estate overlooked the Pacific Ocean, the Channel Islands, the Santa Ynez Mountains, and Santa Barbara. We often thought of this as our dream home, but had never actually expected to own one. It had been only a dream. It was worlds apart from my granny's tiny four-room shack in Oregon, where my brother, two girl cousins, and I lived as kids.

I loved being able to provide Martina with the home of her dreams. She had been through difficult times in her life, and we both loved our home and each other.

At the age of seventy-eight, during a routine physical with my doctor, Timothy Leigh Rogers, MD, I swung my legs off the paper-covered examination table and asked him, "What do you think I will die from and how soon?"

After thinking it over, he said, "Nobody knows. You most probably will die from a heart attack; however, it is harder to say when. If I were to guess, I would say in your mid-eighties. But who knows? You could live to ninety—or die next week."

I mentally noted how many years I might have left. *Not bad,* I thought, *everything considered. I never thought I'd live as long as I have anyway.*

A few weeks later, I was alone in our family room, stretched comfortably on my La-Z-Boy lounger, multitasking. The news on CNN International had the sound off and the closed-captioning on. Sentences intermittently streamed silently across the bottom of the large screen. I alternately perused the *Wall Street Journal* and listened to Rush on the radio.

I had just finished an hour and a half jogging on the treadmill, exercising on the weight machine, and doing calisthenics. I lit the first of my "daily dozen"—now my daily three or four—Honduran cigars. I dozed off.

A Dream

Suddenly a sharp spasm gripped my left side.

I leaned forward in my lounger to alleviate the pain and fell forward in slow motion to the floor.

The impact of my head and the floor smashed the cigar in my mouth like an exploded grenade. Blackness.

As my eyes opened, I saw people standing around me. I was surprised to see my great uncles, Kirk and Irv; Granny, who raised me as a kid; Mom; and my great aunts, Co and Eve. They were saying something that I could barely hear.

Uncle Kirk, who in my youth had been like a father to me, was speaking in a soft, low voice. "Don't get up, Boots. Just rest a bit." He had given me that nickname when I was a boy.

Granny said, "Don't sass your uncle. Do as Uncle Kirk says."

Mom said brightly, "You'll be all right, Jerry."

My two great aunts said in chorus, "Jerry, don't go getting the big head—just use your cell phone and call 9-1-1."

I reached up for my phone, wondering how they had found out about cell phones.

Things went dim, and people lifted me awkwardly. Blackness. I heard a murmur of voices in the background. My second wife, Martina, was wearing her white wedding dress—a beautiful, young blonde with blue-green eyes. She was holding the hand of a smiling little girl—Chelsea, our granddaughter—hugging a teddy bear named Corduroy.

Chelsea said, "Hi, Pa!"

Martina gazed at me with her soft, sweet, enigmatic smile and said, "Hi, Bucko" (her nickname for me).

I also saw our combined seven children:

My eldest son, Roland, said with a clipped grin, "Hi, Dad."

Teresa, my eldest daughter, in a sunny voice said, "Hi there, Dad."

David, my second son, who died in Vietnam, wearing his jaunty bush hat, smiled and said, "Good to see you again, Dad."

Allan, my third son, said, "Howdy."

My second daughter, Clarissa, grinned and said, "How ya doing?"

Martina's biological children, Joel and Maelee, whom I adopted, simultaneously said, "Hi, Pa."

Jean, my first wife, looked on pleasantly from the edge of the room. My cousins, Billie and Mackie, smiled tentatively.

Along one wall of the room were all the grandkids, great grandkids, nephews, nieces, and great nephews and nieces, plus several of my best friends—Cal, Rollie, and Tom—and my brother, Perry, in the shadows.

"I love each of you," I said. "This is the happiest moment of my life."

However, no one heard me!

In the far back of the room, I barely made out the silhouette of my father, Homer, whom I never forgave for abandoning Mom and leaving her to care for my brother and me during the middle of the Great Depression.

Gradually, I could see him more clearly. He was tallish and slim, with narrow shoulders, a white, starched, long-sleeved dress shirt with a stiff collar, a thin tie, dark, pleated narrow-leg trousers, and a small, braided silver watch chain fastened to his belt. His thick, graying black, wavy hair was clipped two inches above his ears, like a Mohican cut. His teeth were yellowed and

3

chipped. He was holding a cigarette between the fingers of his right hand, which dangled by his side.

His lips were moving as if he were saying something, but I could not make out the words.

I awoke with a start! A dream—it was just a dream!

Chapter 2:
Looking Back

Reminiscences: San Francisco Bay

It was the summer of 1985. I woke just before dawn, made coffee, and carried the steaming mug outside to the pool deck, awaiting the first flicker of light in the eastern sky, a new day dawning.

My sixtieth birthday was two years away, but I had already lived longer than I had expected to and felt as if I had not lived my life to the fullest.

I was going on a business trip to the East Coast and savored the tranquility of the early morning before preparing to leave for the airport.

It was one of those exceptional mornings. The confluence of cloud formations and the first glimpse of the rising sun in the east created a classic sunrise. The subdued, dark indigo sky turned into a vivid vermilion red dawn. It looked as if the sky were on fire.

In a sense, I was also on fire. My mind was a blaze of present problems mixed with a variety of old memories. I had a feeling in my gut that it was going to be an unforgettable day in my life.

Martina, her two children, and I lived in Kent Woodlands, an enclave of five hundred homes scattered over the green-forested hills of Kentfield in Marin County—across the Golden Gate Bridge from San Francisco.

Our home was a roomy, shake-roof ranch, perched near the top of a steep hillside surrounded by towering redwoods and patches of tall pampas grass. The large deck surrounding the swimming pool was my favorite place to sit alone in the quiet early morning and enjoy a mug of industrial-strength black coffee.

My muscles ached from my weekend jog to the top of Mount Tamalpais, jutting above the Kent Woodlands hills. The mountain's name, derived from its contour, resembled the form of a sleeping Indian maiden. The mountain stood three thousand feet above sea level, but from where I start my jog, it was 2,500 vertical feet to the top.

This weekend, as was my habit, I jogged, ran, and crawled to the top of Mount Tamalpais, and ran back down.

Starting out early on Sunday morning, I slipped on an old familiar T-shirt, pulled on a pair of shorts and well-worn tennis shoes, and finished my cigar. I poured three shots of vodka into a glass tumbler and tossed the clear liquid down in a couple of gulps, thinking that I should cut down on my drinking. However, I like the taste of the vodka and the fiery rush it produces.

Shrugging my shoulders, I pushed the thought aside, proceeded to the gate at the fire road leading up the mountain, and began to jog, the sweat of my body dissipating the alcohol imbibed the previous evening and this morning. I felt alive!

While We Are Alive
Instead of holding forth
Wisely, with great mien,
How much better to drink,
To get drunk, And to shout aloud,
Since it is true
That death comes at last for us all,
Let us be joyful
While we are alive.

—Anonymous

As I climbed up the mountain, I was sweaty and thirsty, and I looked forward to submerging my face in the spring-fed water trough at the bend in the road.

About fifty yards from the spring, I heard in the dead stillness of the mountain, the clomping of horses' hoofs. The horses were a ways behind me and apparently were also heading for the water trough.

I increased my pace to beat the horses to the spring. As I submerged my face in the water trough, two horses, one on either side of me, ignored my presence and stuck their noses in the water. They drank noisily like two buddies at a bar.

After quenching my thirst, I continued up to the lookout tower at the peak of the mountain. As I approached a rock outcropping, I saw a figure running toward me.

I could barely make out the figure's image shimmering like a desert mirage. As he approached, I saw his chest bare to the waist, a loincloth, moccasins, a scarf around his forehead, long dark hair, and skin the color of bronze.

As the running figure and I came closer, I vowed that I would not be forced off the trail and prepared myself for the crashing impact of our bodies, like opposing football linemen.

Nothing happened! Like a phantom, the figure virtually disappeared in front of my eyes. I quickly swung around to look for him behind me. There was no one there. It was as if he had passed right through me and vanished.

I was shocked; an eerie feeling pervaded my body, and the roots of my hair bristled like porcupine quills. For a few moments, I stood bewildered on the trail and wondered if I had been gripped by a sudden paranoia and was seeing things that were not there.

After a short time, I concluded that the illusory episode or preternatural event was from a momentary hallucination— or perhaps just too much alcohol consumed over too long a period.

I shook off my puzzlement and apprehension, made myself a new vow to cut down on my drinking, and resumed jogging at a fast pace up to the peak.

As I rested on the mountaintop, I reminisced about my life.

I had never thought of myself as a dedicated athlete, but I enjoyed physical challenges, the outdoors, and solitude—and I liked to push myself to the limits of my endurance.

I became a boxer in high school—following the lead of my older brother—and fought everyone at my weight class and some above.

At Oregon State College, my boxing coach was demanding. He tamed my wild swings by showing me how to use my feet and posture to leverage my punches.

He motivated me to be aggressive and determined, for which I remain indebted. "Never give up" became my mantra. As a skinny six-footer in the 155-to-165-pound weight class, I succeeded in the boxing ring and fortunately won all my fights in both high school and college.

In one of the exhibition fights in high school, I fought the center of the Klamath high school football team. Lloyd Chidester was shorter than I was, but he outweighed me by at least twenty pounds.

Lloyd was slumped down sitting on the ropes from a hard punch I had thrown. My punches continued to rain down on him like an Oklahoma hailstorm. One of my punches slammed into the back of his neck and he fell forward onto the mat like spilled milk.

The small crowd roared as I stood silently in my corner, my arms resting on the ring's ropes like my boxing idol, Jack Dempsey, the "Manassas Mauler."

I was worried about Lloyd after I knocked him out with a "rabbit punch." I thought that he might be dead and was relieved when he came to several minutes later.

Lloyd and I were to meet again and become friends when we went to boot camp with several other friends. The last I heard of

Lloyd was that he had made it through the war and was driving a taxi in Las Vegas.

I earned a couple of middleweight boxing trophies at Oregon State College. The trophies are in a box somewhere, tarnished and a little worse for wear from our frequent moves from place to place.

I enjoyed fighting; it was exhilarating. However, I did receive my share of damage. I have been stunned, dazed, bloodied, exhausted, and groggy. I have had teeth broken off, sprained thumbs, cracked ribs, an eyeball separated from its socket, and a concussion from a pool cue to my head.

One day in high school, when I was returning my athletic gear for the second-string football practice, I got into an altercation with the crib attendant. The snotty bastard swung at me through the open cage window, caught my nose with a hard blow, and slammed the window shut so I could not reciprocate.

I stemmed the flow of blood as best I could as I rode my bike three miles home, and the bleeding finally stopped. At my front gate, I blew my nose hard, and my right eyeball popped out of its socket. It protruded from my socket, and I could see the ground at my feet without lowering my head. I pushed my eyeball back into its socket with my palm and went about my business with a cloudy eye for a while.

Although proud of my youthful accomplishments, my long-departed Granny Stover, who raised me as a child, would not be happy with the lack of humbleness on my part. She believed that pride and lack of humbleness were against the preaching of the Bible.

Granny portrayed the positive aspects of humbleness, lack of false pride, belief in an Almighty God, and quiet strength, which she taught by her actions and example during her short life. She accepted hardship and life's inequities with equanimity and grace. Although she never had a drink of alcohol in her lifetime, she died of liver cancer at the age of fifty-seven.

She told us kids, "We don't look up to nobody but the Lord, and we don't look down on nobody neither. We are all God's children—no better and no worse. Never pick a fight or strike the first blow, but if someone hits you, hit him back harder! Bullies are generally cowards underneath and do not pick on those who will fight back. But sometimes you just have to take a beating to stand your ground."

For my part, I hated the humble culture, which some condescending people saw as weakness. Perhaps in my case, however, the humbleness pendulum swung too far in the opposite direction. Following the vow I made as a youth, I challenged anything wrongly said against me and was prepared to defend myself against anyone who attacked me.

I remember a conversation about humbleness that I had with Nat Allen, a manager at one of my jobs, whom I respected a great deal.

Nat and I were having a cup of coffee in the company cafeteria when he unexpectedly said, "Jerry, you should be more humble." He was from New Orleans and pronounced it *umble.*

I replied, "Nat, what the heck do you mean? I have eaten humble pie all my life—and I am sick of it."

"Hey!" he exclaimed. "Everybody who knows you, Jerry, knows that you are not the least bit arrogant. Sometimes you may be proud, but a little pride is justifiable when you produce positive results, which you do."

Assuming a benign attitude, I replied, "No offense taken, Nat. You know that I have always respected you and your views— on most things."

Nat nodded, accepting my reply, but continued, "You just don't seem to care what people think about you!"

I thought about his declaration for a moment.

"I used to," I replied, "but I got over it."

I rested in the shadow of the lookout tower on the mountain's pinnacle, admiring the stunning panorama of the San Francisco Bay.

Although I was brought up Baptist by my grandmother, I have my own perspective on God on the mountaintop. I ask myself, "What was before anything—God's hand or just a bunch of smoke and mirrors?" The answer always comes back—"only God."

This place—once the ancient home of the Coastal Miwok Indians—was now a bustling, metropolitan area: the beautiful city of San Francisco, several large towns, and many small villages.

San Francisco was partially obscured by patches of fog. Its steep streets and ticky-tacky houses climbed the hills, and the Transamerica Pyramid and Coit Tower pointed to the sky through puddles of fog.

Berkeley was in the shadow of the Claremont Hotel, perched on a hill. The prestigious, bustling university was populated by egghead professors and scruffy *enfant terrible* geniuses. Emeryville's factories and warehouses are next to Oakland. The company I managed, Grove Valve and Regulator, was located there—a forever come-from-behind city with Mount Diablo looking over its shoulder in the far distance.

Richmond sat at the east end of the long, gangling, caterpillar-like San Raphael-Richmond Bridge wriggling across the bay. Often, on my way to work in the early mornings, I wheeled across the curvy vacant bridge at 120 miles per hour, the top speed for my eight-year-old 1977 Jaguar.

I always liked the phrase "dawn's early light" from the national anthem. I was often reminded of it during hunting camp, sitting by the pool in the quiet early morning, or tooling over the Richmond Bridge, the Jaguar's six cylinders whining, the bridge's huge structural ironwork flashing by like a freight train hell-bent in my direction.

San Quentin Prison—and its lethal gas chamber—was near the west end of the Richmond Bridge, and the city of San Raphael was a mile to the north.

Skirting the edges of the imposing Mount Tamalpais were several villages, including Kentfield and Sausalito. Martina owned the Sausalito Soap Store at the edge of the bay near the Golden Gate Bridge. Otis Redding's song "Sittin' on the Dock of the Bay" epitomized the ambiance of Sausalito and the San Francisco Bay.

11

I admired the towering Golden Gate Bridge, a shining beacon built in the middle of the Great Depression. Its orange paint reflected a golden hue from the sun, its suspension cables draped harmoniously from giant, graceful pylons.

Black, frothy waves lapped at the rock-strewn base of Alcatraz Island near the middle of the San Francisco Bay. "The Rock," as the prison was called, was built to incarcerate the worst criminals and was now a vacant tourist attraction.

To the west, the foaming waves of the Pacific Ocean crashed against the rocks and cliffs of the Marin Headlands. The Farallon Islands basked in the wispy fog twenty-eight miles out in the Pacific Ocean near the continental shelf. Clusters of hungry great white sharks patrolled the cold waters, searching for meals of seals and sea lions—and the occasional wetsuit-clad surfer.

I had a flight to catch that morning. After rising early, I got my things together, packed my carry-on suitcase, and placed the documents that I wanted to study on the flight into my satchel briefcase. I was ready to depart for the airport.

I kissed Martina good-bye and told her I loved her, as I always did when flying somewhere. One never knows for sure what might happen. Did the pilot have a bang-up, knockdown fight with his wife last night? Were his clothes tossed out of the second-story window in a crumpled heap on the lawn? Would our aircraft mechanic have a dizzying headache from a hangover as he made his bleary-eyed inspection of the aircraft's jet engines?

Sliding into my green Jaguar, I drove down the winding road of the wooded Kentfield hills. It was a joy driving this old car, although half the time it seemed to be in the garage for one thing or another.

Continuing to the airport, traffic was light, and I made good time on Highway 101 to the Golden Gate Bridge. I handed three dollar bills to the tollgate attendant, who was smiling at each driver as he or she passed through her tollbooth. She must have been one of those sunny-personality people, or else she was breathing way too much of the carbon monoxide from the thousands of cars passing through the tollbooths.

The 280 Expressway had its usual quota of white-knuckled, wide-eyed, crazed lane jumpers, but I avoided them and exited toward the airport parking garages.

Spotting an unoccupied space, I dodged into it. A runner-up driver shook his fist, glared fiercely at me through his dirty windshield, and drove away slowly. I resisted the impulse to flip him the bird, parked, and proceeded to my gate.

In a meditative mood, I waited in the American Airlines Admirals Club lounge, catching up on the *Wall Street Journal.* An article with the headline "U.S. Energy Industry in Nosedive" discussed the dire conditions of the US petroleum and gas industry. The restructuring taking place reminded me of the seriousness of the task before me. The company I ran was a supplier of pipeline valves to the oil and gas industry and faced the same draconian problems.

Boarding the commercial jet, I greeted the captain and stewardess in the doorway. Both wore crisp uniforms and greeted me cheerfully. Being a pilot myself, I asked, "What's our cruising altitude today, Captain, and how is the weather?"

His broad smile showed his shiny teeth. "It looks good, but there is a weather front north of us with some high winds. We will be flying a little south of our normal course today to avoid the turbulence and have a more comfortable ride for y'all."

Y'all? I thought. *A misplaced Texan, no doubt.*

"Right now, our assigned cruising altitude is twenty-nine thousand feet."

I thanked him and proceeded to my window seat in business class near the front of the plane. I placed my carry-on luggage in the overhead compartment and set my worn leather briefcase on the empty aisle seat beside me.

Looking out the window, I had a ringside seat overlooking the tarmac and the choreographed movements of the baggage carts stowing luggage and freight into the plane's belly.

The food service vans backed up to the plane's galley hatch and transferred soft drinks, ice, and packaged food rations ready for the microwave. Wine, beer, and liquor were loaded onto the plane, offering enjoyment for the connoisseur, courage for the terrified, and relief for the sodden few harboring their unwelcome hangovers.

The stewardess noticed my satchel and my seat back not in a rigid attention position. She spoke in a sweet Southern drawl; she had not had time to be aggravated or get grumpy yet. "Hon, would you please put your seat back in the full upright position and your satchel under the seat in front of you?"

"Sure, ma'am," I answered.

Another Texan, I thought. *They must be all over the place.*

I was born an Okie; most of my older relatives were from Oklahoma or Texas, including my father, who was born and raised in Texas. I liked Southerners; they were generally laid back and friendly. Their soft accents felt familiar to me.

A towing tug pulled our plane back from the gate, and we taxied to the runway. I looked forward to flying in the blue sky above the gray clouds that hovered over the airport.

The control tower cleared our flight to depart. The plane rumbled down the runway, its four jet engines roaring at full throttle, picked up speed, and took off into the gray sky.

For a few days, I was leaving behind the manufacturing company of which I was president. It had survived a fifty-two-week labor strike and faced a plummeting market for its products to the oil and gas industry. The industry was in a downward spiral due to the Arab oil embargo—after a major increase in sales and profitability over the previous several years

During the embargo, OPEC (Organization of the Petroleum-Exporting Countries) stopped all shipments of petroleum to the United States, setting off a flurry of domestic oil and gas exploration. This development eventually produced an excess of capacity and crashed, resulting in major losses to the industry and their suppliers.

There were tough financial, operational, and most importantly, people problems affecting the survival of the company. As CEO of Grove Valve, I would have to confront them all when I returned.

Settling in for the flight, I retrieved my briefcase and removed the documents that my senior executives and I had prepared. I immersed myself in the proposed actions and decisions that were necessary to return the company to profitability and financial stability—and prevent its financial collapse and bankruptcy. Although this business trip was to be only a few days, I was already anxious to return to the action.

I thought, *Being a chief executive officer is not always fun, nor is it what many people think it's cracked up to be.*

The situation demanded strong leadership; the consequences of failure were dire for the survival of the company and the livelihood of many people, not to mention my own professional career and livelihood.

I resolved to take decisive action, make all the necessary changes, and let the chips fall where they may. My management team and I were confident, capable, and prepared to meet the challenge. After a while, I leaned back, stretched, and gazed out the window at the fascinating landscape below.

We crossed the Sierra Nevada Mountain range; the mountains of Nevada extended across the wide landscape to the far horizon.

Scattered clouds looked down on the scene, continuing on their ordained courses, billowing, streaking the sky, and asserting their immortality. The barren landscape had a stark reality and beauty. The vast land was empty of human endeavor—only God's mark was there.

The stewardess approached with a tray of food and served poached Pacific salmon and garden salad with ranch dressing.

I finished the food and a glass of wine, and the smiling young stewardess took the tray away. The pilot announced, "For you folks on the right side of the airplane, if you look down, you will see the Great Salt Lake of Utah."

The Great Salt Lake swept into view below. It was an extraordinary phenomenon—a great salt sea in the middle of a barren desert. Clouds floated like fluffy white cotton balls on an ocean of air. Their shadows trailed on the ground below like a line of orphans in tow.

A railroad track on large wooden trestles snaked across the northern end of the Great Salt Lake in an east-west direction. Memories of a long-ago journey on a train, drawn by a steam-powered locomotive, on this very same railroad track came vividly to my mind. I was flooded with memories and awed when I fully absorbed the gulf between my current circumstances and those when I had been a small child on that train more than a half-century earlier.

It was a memorable day. **This book is the result!**

Artist: Deb Bartelt
Coal mine, Pittsburg, Oklahoma, 1927

Chapter 3:
Homer and Estallee

Coal-Mining Country

My father, Homer King Watson, was born in Dundee, Texas, on February 29, 1900, to Walter and Alma Crutchfield Watson. Homer was of Scot-English ancestry and was, from unverified family accounts, a quarter-blood Cherokee Indian, which dominated his features.

As a young man, Homer sold newspapers on the streets of El Paso, spent his time with Mexican children and adults, and learned to speak fluent Spanish. He also read and wrote the language reasonably well. Homer was a quick learner but he wanted to earn money to support himself, so he left high school in the middle of his second year.

While looking for work, he won money playing pool. He was good at the game and often ran the table on his opponents. He won so often that eventually the locals would not play with him for money. He was a proficient driver and, over the next several years, worked as a truck driver, hack (taxi) driver, and farmhand and laborer when driving jobs were not available.

Working in a coal mine in Gallup, New Mexico, he met Estallee—his future wife and my future mother.

My mother was born in Lexington, Oklahoma Indian Territory, on January 8, 1907, to Edna and Joseph Stover. She had an older brother, Alva, and a younger sister, Ethelene. My grandmother, "Granny" Edna Stover, was raised as a farm girl. Granny, a devout Baptist, was extremely hard working. She parted her dark brown, almost black, hair in the middle and tied it in a roll behind her head. Her eyes were brown with a tinge of sadness, and her face had a beatific quality—like an angel or a saint.

My grandfather, Joseph Stover, was born on June 8, 1879, in Arkansas and died on January 15, 1915. Although healthy and robust, he contracted spinal meningitis from an infected mosquito bite and died. He left a wife, Edna, and three children: Estallee, Alva and Ethelene.

Although Alva was born into farming and was good at it, his sisters did not share the sentiment.

After Joe Stover died, the family could no longer operate the farm. They sold it and moved to Gallup, New Mexico. Alva found a job in a coal mine, and Edna, with the help of her two daughters, ran a boardinghouse for single men.

Alva worked in the same coal mine as Homer, and they became friends. Alva introduced Homer to Estallee and her sister at the boardinghouse.

In 1923, Estallee and Homer became attracted to each other. After a short courtship, Homer proposed, and Estallee, reluctant at first, eventually accepted. They decided to get married in Albuquerque so that they could live with Homer's grandmother.

On October 28, 1924, Estallee and Homer King Watson's first child was born in Albuquerque. His name was Perry King Watson; his middle name came from his father, Homer King Watson.

Later, Estallee and Homer got into an argument, and she decided to leave with her son. She took a train to Purcell, Oklahoma, to stay with her grandparents, Robert Allan and Margaret "Maggie" Coffman. When Homer heard where Estallee had gone, he hopped a freight train and rode the rails to catch up to her.

Hopping trains was nothing new to Homer. If there was work, he hopped a train to get there. Riding the rails was as easy as climbing into an empty boxcar, onto a flatcar, or hanging onto the underside of the train while it was moving slowly out of the railroad yard. It was a free ride unless the railroad bulls grabbed you, beat you up, and threw you off the moving train in some godforsaken place.

Estallee reconciled with Homer after a while, and he got a job at a farm, where he had a freak accident. He was working a plow pulled by a mule when the plow hit a large hidden rock and flipped over. The startled mule bucked, dragging Homer into the plow's sharp blade and badly gouging his leg.

When Homer recuperated, he, Estallee, and Perry headed off to the coalfields of Pittsburg, Oklahoma, where Homer could get a job in a coal mine. The coal mines in Pittsburg were hiring, and he was experienced. It paid pretty well—as long as the mines stayed open.

Pittsburg, Oklahoma

In 1927, there were no computers, Internet, fax machines, televisions, jet airplanes, space flights, satellites, nuclear power plants, or thermonuclear bombs.

On July 29, 1927, I was born in Pittsburg in southeastern Oklahoma. They named me Jerry Jack Watson. As an adult, I changed my official name to J. Jack Watson.

Mom told me later that I was a big baby and it took nearly ten hours to bear me in the suffocating summer heat.

Pittsburg was an insignificant coal-mining town like many others in Oklahoma, with a population of around two hundred. You could walk down any street—end to end—in a few minutes. Half of the town's lots did not have houses.

The houses lacked running water, indoor toilets, electricity, telephones, and radios. The family carried water in buckets or manually pumped the water from a stream or well, used a privy in the backyard, and relied upon kerosene lanterns or candles for light. Without telephones, they conversed with their neighbors in person.

The unpaved streets spouted with dust devils. There were no street signs or streetlights. At night, the town was black except for the moonlight, the flicker of a coal-oil lantern in a dusty window, or the dim headlights of the occasional motor vehicle.

There were a few Model T jalopies in the town; however, transportation was mainly by walking, riding a horse or mule, or on a wagon drawn by a horse or mule. Many of the houses had a cow or goat and sometimes a pig or two in their wire-fenced yards. Rabbits in hutches and chickens were scattered around the yards.

Our house was at the northeast corner of town, on Rea Avenue and Seventh Street. Homer rented the house from the coal company.

The one-room city hall had a part-time mayor and policeman. The town also had a moving picture show, a company store, a general store, a feedstore, a hotel, and two cafes. Estallee worked at the Garden Café.

There was a brick schoolhouse for kindergarten through eighth grade and three churches: Brushy Baptist Church, Choctaw Country Indian Church, and the Catholic Church. In addition, the town had two pool halls and five bars for the coal miners.

Coal miners and their families made up most of Pittsburg's population. A variety of nationalities were represented: Welsh, Scot, Mexican, Russian, Ukrainian, Polish, Italian, Hungarian, and others. There were few Native Americans working in the mines.

The town's population varied, depending on whether the coal mines were hiring or firing. There was a tent city set up north of town that housed from a few to more than a hundred miners, most of whom were single men drifting from one mine job to another. The tent camp was a temporary home for people coming in when there was work—and packing up and moving on when the mines didn't need them anymore.

The town was surrounded by rolling, tall prairie grass and scattered clumps of oak trees. The tall grass swayed with the breeze like an ocean tide. Local farmers grew hay in the small hayfields scattered around the town. Hay fed the mules used in the coal mines to pull the coal cars.

There were four coal mines near Pittsburg: the Hodges Mine and the McAlester Mines #1, #2, and #4 (#3 had shut down). Mine #4 was also called the Storey Mine. Homer worked in the Storey Mine and one or two of the others.

Our one-story house had a two-sided, sloping, shingle roof, two small bedrooms, and a combination kitchen and living room. The furniture included a double bed and two cots, a wooden kitchen table with four chairs, a wood-burning stove, and a well-worn sofa that had come with the house. A pipe into a nearby creek and a hand pump in the kitchen supplied the house with water, and an outhouse sat in back a ways from the house.

Trees surrounded the house on three sides. Across the dirt road from our house was a large meadow, where some of the coal mines were, but you could not see the mines because they were too far away.

Homer walked out to the mine every morning on the road in front of our house. "It's about a three-mile walk to get there, but it's easy walking," Homer said. Sometimes, a group of miners came by in a truck after work and gave him a ride home if there was room.

Mom got up early in the morning to make breakfast and fix Homer's lunch before he left at five-thirty to punch in before the shift started at seven o'clock. If there were any leftovers from supper the night before, she used them to make his lunch. Homer's favorite lunches, though, were two bologna or fried egg sandwiches.

Mom fed Perry and me breakfast and walked to her waitress job. She depended on my brother or a neighbor to look after us, but my brother and I were often alone.

The demand for more coal production brought people of all stripes to the coal mines.

In the coal mines, Indians faced similar prejudices as blacks. Negroes were called "niggers" by some or most whites at that time. Some of these same people similarly looked on Indians as "red niggers." My father's skin was not red; his skin had a bronze hue, like a perpetual suntan.

Mom said, "Homer is lucky to be only a quarter-breed Indian, if he is; otherwise, he would have a troublesome time getting any work in the mines—or anywhere else in this town, for that matter."

Mom told us that Perry and I had Scottish and English blood in our veins from Homer's Watson-Crutchfield side, as well as Estallee's Coffman-Sawycrs side of the family.

Homer was a hard worker, but when he got his hands on a bottle of whiskey, he acted in whatever way suited him. He did not drink every day or every week. Sometimes weeks went by without him touching a drop of whiskey.

However, Mom angrily rejected Homer's amorous advances when he came home and had been drinking or was already drunk. This was the basis for hot arguments between them, which fortunately did not result in violence. Maybe it did, but my brother and I never saw it and Mom never complained about it. When we were older, she said, "That was between your father and me a long time ago. There are always two sides to every argument and he is not here to tell his side, so let us just leave it at that. I will never say anything against your father to you boys. It is not the right thing to do; he is your father, after all."

Mom never knew if Homer would come home from the mine each day. She worried about him all the time that he was underground. He worked fifty or sometimes sixty hours a week when the work was available, most of the time stooping over or on his knees in the detritus on the floor of the low-ceilinged shaft.

He swung his short pick into the coal face, pushing large lumps of coal behind him, or drove long steel drill bits into the coal face with a ten-pound sledgehammer, called a double-jack, for placing sticks of dynamite to crumble the coal and drop it onto the floor. With a muckstick, he shoveled the coal into the coal cars for the mules to pull to the tipple (an apparatus for loading or emptying the coal) high above the surface.

A winch powered by mules pulled the coal cars to the top of the tipple and dumped the coal. The sorting crew screened and sorted the coal, and it was dropped into open railroad gondola cars and transported to coal distribution locations.

"We were barely dragging our asses," Homer said to Mom. He was totally exhausted by the excruciating labor in a hostile and dangerous environment.

In 1900, a US male's life expectancy was forty-seven years. However, for a coal miner, the life expectancy dropped by several years.

Mining was primitive, and accidents were numerous and particularly deadly. There were many different ways for a miner to get killed or maimed: explosions of mine gases, fires, gas asphyxiation from "after-damp" (a lethal carbon monoxide gas from a methane explosion), cave-ins, being run over or crushed between coal cars, falls into hidden pits, elevator mishaps, unauthorized setting off of explosive charges (windy shots), and the black lung.

Many miners died years after they left the mines from black lung. The term described lung diseases brought on by constant exposure to particles of coal dust in the mines. It caused spitting and coughing blood and breathlessness, eventually collapsing their lungs and suffocating them.

On Friday, the mine paymaster, after deducting for a month's house rent, placed the remaining thirty-five dollars in Homer's grubby hand—half in cash and the other half in company script, his pay for the week.

When Homer came home, he walked in the door, smiled, and said, "Hi, have you kids been minding your mother?"

Perry said, "Yes, Dad."

I said, "Uh huh," and concentrated on Dad's coal-dust-stained face.

He placed the company script in Mom's hand, put an arm around her waist, and said, "Give me a little kiss." He placed a glancing kiss on her cheek as she turned her head away from him.

"Stop it—you're filthy dirty," she said.

She knew where he was heading, and Perry and I could tell from the angry sadness on her face that he was going out to the pool hall to play pool, where he could also get a bottle of whiskey.

Mom worked the breakfast and lunch shifts at the Garden Café, Pittsburg's favorite eating place. The four tables were enough to seat a dozen or so people. She often waited on all the tables, but she was home in time to fix supper for Homer and us kids.

Dinner was almost ready. We smelled the chicken sizzling in a skillet on the top of the wood-burning stove and cornbread baking in the oven. Homer took off his tin miner's hat with an acetylene lantern fastened to the top and put it on a shelf by the door, opened his lunch-bucket, set it on the shelf, removed his grubby, sweat-soaked work shirt, and tossed it into the corner.

He stepped across the kitchen to the hand pump and placed a wash pan under the nozzle. He worked the handle vigorously and filled the pan with cold water. Humming to himself, he splashed water on his face and body and dried off with a towel. He put on a pair of clean trousers, pulled on and buttoned a clean, ironed white shirt that Mom had washed that morning, and stuffed the shirttail into his trousers.

Mom spread the red-and-white checkered oilcloth—a birthday present from Homer along with a new cast-iron skillet—on the table. She put down four plates, knives and spoons on the right side of the plates and forks on the left side. She set the table properly to teach us manners and etiquette, which she thought were very important.

"Dinner is ready," Mom called.

We sat down to eat at the table in the kitchen. Hungrily, we ate the fried chicken, boiled okra, and cornbread sweetened with dark, syrupy molasses. We would have licked our plates clean, but we could see in Mom's eyes that it was not the time for any tomfoolery.

Homer brushed a fly away with one hand as he pulled the meat off a bone with his teeth. "There was talk at the mine today that did not sound too good. The company man said that they'll probably have to cut their losses and let the miners go if the buyers don't buy the coal. The railroads and other customers are just not buying much coal because of the Depression, and the company's unsold coal inventories were too high. The bosses are having a meeting next week up in McAlester."

He paused, reached into his shirt pocket, and shook out a cigarette from a pack of Camels. He lit the cigarette with a wooden match, sucked in the tobacco smoke, blew a smoke ring at the ceiling, and turned back to Mom.

"The company man said that we will see what they say before we do anything about the miners, but it doesn't look good."

Homer's speech was longer than usual. When he was done, he concentrated on finishing his food. Mom sat silently with half-closed eyes, looking down, her hands clasped tightly together in her lap.

After a while, she looked up at us and said, "Boys, finish your supper. Perry, when you are finished, I want you to help me with the dishes, and Jerry, when you're done, go outside and play for a while."

We finished our supper quickly. I went to get my stick airplane to play with outside, and Perry helped Mom clear the table and wash and dry the dishes.

Homer got up and, without a word, strode to the door, pulled his cap off the peg on the door, put it on, and walked out.

A short time later, the coal mines in the Pittsburg area fell on hard times, and the mines closed down or worked a skeleton schedule, which supported work for only a few miners. Work ran out for Homer, and our mother lost her job too.

The stock market crashed on October 28, 1929, bringing on the Great Depression, with massive unemployment and misery that lasted for more than a decade.

Our family began a wandering journey, pausing for a while in Oklahoma City, Pueblo, Colorado, and Colorado Springs.

In Oklahoma City, Homer worked at any job he could get: taxi driver, truck driver, cook, or most anything that any working man could do. He also went to the local pool hall to try to make money betting on himself, but nobody had enough money to make it worth his time. When he did win, the money often disappeared into a whiskey bottle.

Homer was good with his hands, and he also was a good cook. The pancakes he fixed for us made our mouths water.

Homer did not speak Spanish around the house, but my mother told us that he spoke fluent Spanish that he learned when he grew up in Texas beside the Rio Grande.

"You could not tell the difference between him talking and the Mexicans." Mom said he got a job once with the government to go down to Central America to do something they thought was important. The government job was before Perry and I were old enough to understand, and we never knew what it was.

Artist: Deb Bartelt
On the Road—The Stock Market Crash

On the Road

My parents were working in the restaurant business in Oklahoma City: he as a cook, and she as a waitress. The restaurant was close to closing its doors due to a lack of customers and had to let someone go. The restaurant had two waitresses and the other waitress had been there longer, so Mom lost her job. The restaurant finally closed its doors, putting Homer out of work as well. New jobs were hard to find.

A little later, Mom said, "Work is scarce in Oklahoma City, and we need to move on again. It will be nicer, kids, you will see."

Through a friend, Homer got a job to drive a car from Oklahoma City to a car dealer in Pueblo, Colorado, where Granny Stover was living. He decided that if we were going to move, Pueblo was as good a place as any. He said, "Now is as good as anytime to find a new home. Pueblo is a nice place, and there may be jobs there. Having a car to get us there is going to make it a lot easier to move."

The four-door sedan had plenty of room to hold our belongings, which mainly consisted of bedding and mattresses, a few pots and pans, and four kitchen chairs. Dad hung a canvas bag of water on the radiator and another one on the bumper on the back end of the car.

We tied the thin mattresses, washtub, and chairs to the roof, padding everything to make sure nothing would scratch the paint. We packed our clothes, sandwiches, and personal stuff in the car and climbed inside.

We were going to Colorado! Perry and I were thrilled. Colorado! Ay-yippy-yi-ki-yea! Visions of cowboys and Indians danced in our heads.

Mom said, "You boys be very careful in this car. Don't make any messes, spill anything on the upholstery, or scratch anything. Homer has to deliver this car clean to the dealer in Pueblo, with no marks or anything."

The journey was longer and bumpier than we had thought it would be. Despite the five hundred miles of rough, dirt roads, Mom felt happy and started singing. All of us followed along.

29

Oh, where have you been, Billy Boy, Billy Boy?
Oh where have you been, charmin' Billy?
I have been to seek a wife, the joy of my life,
She's a young thing and cannot leave her mother.

From this valley, they say you are going.
We will miss your bright eyes and sweet smile.
But remember the Red River Valley
And the one that has loved you so true.

Oh the birds and the bees and the cigarette trees
In the Big Rock Candy Mountain

I went down south for to see myself,
Singing Polly Wolly Doodle all the day

We wound up each group of songs with, "Shave and a haircut, six bits" and broke out in laughter!

Sometimes when we did not know the words, we made up our own. It didn't make any difference because we were happy and together!

We arrived in Pueblo in the afternoon of the fourth day, having done some sightseeing along the way. Homer drove us to Granny's house, and she met us at the door with hugs for everyone. She wanted to know how we were and whether we were hungry.

We were very hungry and ate the bologna sandwiches and drank the clabbered milk. Granny gave us some oatmeal cookies that she had baked, and we ate them too.

After washing and cleaning the car, Homer took it to the car dealer to collect the money he had spent on gas and his thirty-five dollars for delivering the car. He asked the dealer about a good place to live in Pueblo.

The dealer, satisfied with Homer delivering the car on time, clean, and without any damage, thought for a moment and said, "I think Mrs. Minimen has an apartment available in her building over on Albany Avenue. You cannot miss it; it is the three-story building on the hill at the corner. Maybe you should try there first. She is a very nice woman and treats her tenants very well, from what I hear."

Homer went to see Mrs. Minimen's apartment. After looking at the little four-room apartment, he agreed that it would suit our family just fine and gave her eighteen dollars for the first month's rent. We moved in at the end of the month.

Since the apartment was on the second floor, we could look out on the street below. Mrs. Minimen was nice to us—or at least to me. I don't know what she thought about Perry, but she had her eye on him all the time.

Perry's birthday came around, and Mom decided to give him a party. Since it was close to Halloween, she got orange and black crepe paper streamers to decorate the table. Dad got a pumpkin, and he and Perry carved a face on it. They wouldn't let me carve anything because I was too young and might cut off a finger or something.

Mom invited two boys who lived at the Mount Pleasant Apartments. They were nice kids, but we never saw much of them. They brought checkers and dominoes with them to the party, and we had a great time playing with them. They even gave us presents—even if it wasn't my birthday. They gave Perry a metal blue elephant coin bank and me a metal brown dog bank.

They told us that their daddy worked for the government. It must have been an important job for his kids to have checker and domino sets and all. Perry asked the older boy what his father did, and he said he did not know for sure but he thought it had something to do with bookkeeping.

31

We never saw the boys again—they must have moved somewhere else—but they were sure nice kids.

The Great Depression continued strong, with sometimes as many as six out of ten workers out of a job in some places. Men took any job or did anything that would help them feed their families. It was a desperate situation for many people. Those who lived in the country planted gardens to provide food for their tables. Others sold apples or pencils on the street corners in the towns and cities. Long lines of men trying to get jobs were a common sight.

Unemployed men felt like failures when they could not feed and support their families. Having always been self-sufficient, they were ashamed to get relief from the government or to ask for help from friends or relatives. However, in the end, they did anything they could to feed their families.

Homer found himself out of work no matter how hard he tried. He was gone looking for work from morning to evening every day. There were as many as a hundred men lining up for a handful of available jobs. Hardly anybody had the money to go to a restaurant, so there were few waitressing jobs.

It got to be pretty hopeless for Mom to put together a simple meal of cornbread and skim milk, and we were hungry a lot. I thought everything was normal: a father and mother and a bowl of delicious cornbread mush, sometimes with a teaspoon of Brer Rabbit molasses on top.

One evening, I saw a line of silent men standing on the dimly lit street below. They were shuffling their feet and waiting patiently in the cold winter air. I saw my father in the long line, and when he turned his face up and saw me, he turned his eyes away. He was wearing his cap and carrying an empty lard pail by the bail. When his turn came, the woman ladled milk into his pail.

When he returned to our apartment, I saw him in the doorway as he came in, his cap pulled down, partly covering his face.

He said nothing as he handed the pail of milk to Mom and averted his eyes. I did not realize it then, but Homer was not going to be around much longer. They finally broke up and Homer left, leaving her to support and care for herself and us two boys in the middle of the Great Depression. Mom found a waitressing job and moved us to Colorado Springs.

We had gotten over the daydream of cowboys and Indians a long time ago.

We never knew why Homer left us, and Mom would not talk about it. She would not say anything against our father. Perhaps Homer was discouraged by his loss of work, lack of new employment, and his inability to provide for the family. But we never knew for certain what his reasons were for leaving our mother and us two boys.

Jack Watson

Colorado Springs Day Nursery

Chapter 4:
Incarcerated in Colorado Springs and Escape to Oregon

After Homer left, our mother realized that she could not work and care for my brother and me without help. Granny had looked after Perry and me when Mom was working, but Granny had moved to Oregon to care for her mother, Maggie Coffman.

No help was available to Mom, but she found a place that would take care of us, feed us, and give us a place to stay. My brother and I found ourselves in the Colorado Springs Day Nursery, a children's home. We had never seen anything like it.

The wealthy woman who founded and built the Colorado Springs Day Nursery oversaw everything that went on in the home. She had a supervisor for the activities of four or five assistants. The assistants were responsible for all the children in the home.

One of the assistants asked me if I liked my new home.

"Shore do."

The assistant said that "sure"—not "shore"—is the correct pronunciation. "Jerry, you sound just like an Okie."

"I shore am an Okie 'cuz I was born in Oklahoma."

"We'll work on that," she said, a mild disapproval in her voice.

The supervisor and the assistants had their own rooms on the second floor, where they lived and slept. They also had their own small dining room next to the big dining room, where they ate their meals. They ate the same food as us more or less; we had peeked to see what they were eating.

They were available twenty-four hours a day as needed. The assistants were required to be qualified nurses, and for the most part they were—except for the temporary ones. There was also a cook, a helper, and an all-around handyman, gardener, and janitor.

There were seventy or so children enrolled at the home. Less than half were there for day care, and the rest were there for full-time care. The full-time children were at the home twenty-four hours a day, seven days a week—except for approved outings with an authorized relative or guardian. There were boys and girls at the home, but the boys greatly outnumbered the girls.

The younger boys all slept in a large room, with identical white enameled iron beds in long rows, like tombstones in a cemetery. At night, I stared at the shadows on the ceiling and walls and heard the rustling sounds of the kids in the other beds. Sometimes I heard a door open and someone walking around the room between the beds. Sometimes there was a flash from a flashlight in the darkness, and suddenly darkness again. I could hear the building creak and the moaning wind at the windows.

The mattresses had many small cotton balls, with strings connecting them through the mattress to the underside. The cotton balls were my nemesis. One night, a few weeks after arriving at the home, out of sadness or loneliness, I pulled all of the cotton balls off my mattress and threw them on the floor. I had no other way of demonstrating my profound unhappiness.

Later that night, the assistant, Miss Rose, who I thought didn't like me very much, came with a flashlight and saw what I had done. I was asleep in a light nightgown, like all the boys wore, when she grabbed my arm, woke me, and yanked me barefoot across a dim hallway and into a dark, silent shower room.

She told me to sit on a little kid chair without moving until she returned. I shivered and wrapped my arms around my body to keep warm.

I sat quietly in the dark for hours, trying to hear anything. All I could hear was the clinking of the water pipes and creaking of the building as the temperature changed outside. Sometimes I could see the flicker of a light in the hallway and then nothing.

In the early morning, as slivers of light invaded the dark shower room, the assistant, who had slept comfortably in her room nearby, came for me and marched me to the sleeping room. She directed me to pick up and dispose of each cotton ball on the floor by my bed. I did it dutifully.

I was beginning to think to myself, *Some of these people don't seem to like kids—Miss Rose in particular.*

I climbed into my bed, pulled the blanket up to my chin, and fell asleep instantly as the dawn's early light filtered into the room. An hour or so later, the assistant woke me and told me to get ready for kindergarten,

The assistants demonstrated subtle coercion in the daylight, when they were subject to scrutiny, but often exhibited compulsive force in the dark of night.

That morning in kindergarten, we sang "America the Beautiful." The song thrilled me with all that amber waves of grain and stuff, but I wondered what amber was.

After the singing, the teacher said, "Today, we are going to make Indian necklaces. Won't that be fun?"

The kids were excited. I was excited too, but had trouble keeping my eyes open from lack of sleep.

The teacher handed out the balls of clay, watercolors, and string. We rolled small balls of clay for the beads and pierced holes in them with wooden matches for the string. The teacher put the balls of clay in an oven to dry and harden. The assistant took the beads from the oven, and when they were cool, we painted our individual beads in many different colors.

I strung my beads to make a necklace. When I put the necklace around my neck, I felt like an Indian—*just like my father.*

One day Mom came to visit us in the waiting room. Perry asked, "Are we going to go for a ride?"

"No, not today. I am working a split shift at the restaurant and I have to get back to work, but we can talk together for a little while."

Perry was disappointed and put on a long face.

We sat in silence for a while, and then I asked, "Where is Dad?"

"I do not know, but don't worry yourself any because remember, Jerry, you will always be Homer's son."

I asked, "*If I am Homer's son, why doesn't he love me?*"

"Your father loves you, Jerry—in his own way. His way is just different."

"What's different?" I asked.

"Your father is looking for work and he can't sit still in one place for long, but someday he will see you again. Even though he is not here, he loves you still."

I withdrew and angrily blurted out, "I hate him!"

Willing the tears back, I repeated in a subdued voice, "I hate him," and retreated to the opposite bench until it was time for her to leave. She left shortly after, giving each of us a quick kiss on our cheeks.

When she left, I bolted for the door and ran up to the third floor, where I had my own special hidey-hole. I remained hidden while the supervisor and her assistants searched for me. Eventually, they discovered me, took me downstairs, and put me with the other children after admonishing me severely about my behavior.

The days plodded along, and Christmas finally arrived. All of the kids were excited, and we gathered around a big decorated tree in a large semicircle. A man in a Santa Claus suit ho-ho-hoed around the room, set some of the kids on his knee, and asked them what they wanted for Christmas.

The supervisor, in a red cap with white fur, read stories to us. We sang Christmas songs, with the head woman of the day nursery playing the piano. Each of us got a bag of hard peppermint candy and a candy cane.

Later that evening, we stood in a long line. When I reached the front, I was given a real cowboy belt and holsters, with two cap pistols but no caps. That night, my fondest wishes came true!

The assistants picked up all the gifts a week later and moved them to storage to await a future Christmas and future excited kids.

So much for Santa Claus, I thought. *I will never make that mistake again.*

However, I was happier when I thought about how some new kid would feel good when handed the cap pistols and belt. He could play with them too—at least for a while.

In 1933, my brother and I had been living in the day nursery for what seemed a long time. Some of the children went home at night, but we did not. Knowing that they were sleeping in their own beds in their own homes with their moms, dads, brothers, and sisters and we were here made us sad. Perry tried to look out for me as best he could, but he was a kid and could do only so much.

Sometimes I didn't want him to tell me what to do or how to do it. We did not see much of each other anyway. My brother was in the group of older kids, and I was in the group of younger kids. Perry went to school during the day. He walked with the other older kids through a tunnel under the busy Nevada Street to Lowell Elementary School, about three blocks away. I spent every day and night in the home.

They Wanted You, But They Did Not Want Me

One morning, the supervisor came and got Perry and me and had us clean up, comb our hair, and put on some dress-up clothes she had for us. After we were dressed and looked tolerably decent, the supervisor took us to a room with two doors on opposite sides of the room and two benches facing each other in the middle of the room. We had been there a number of times before, waiting for Mom to show up. We had spent hours in the room waiting for Mom—sometimes she didn't come.

"You both wait here and don't you leave this room—some people want to see you."

We waited for what seemed like an hour. *Was Mom coming?* We hoped so, since we had not seen her for quite a while.

Perry walked and ran around the benches several times and said, "Maybe Dad is coming. You remember the time Dad came to see us, don't you? He played and talked to us on the swings in the playground, and we had a picture taken together out in front of the day nursery."

"Dad didn't hold us close, though, and he didn't kiss us on the cheek like Mom does when she leaves us, did he?" I said.

Perry said, "No, he did not—and he didn't tell us that he was never coming back either. When I run around the benches twenty times, Mom will be here!"

He alternately walked and scurried around the benches about twenty times, and Mom was still not there. When he heard the door start to open with a faint creak, he hastily sat down on the bench. A man and woman came into the room, the man's shoes squeaking as he walked. Perry and I stood up; the supervisor had taught us that it was mannerly to stand up when adults come into a room. We looked silently at the strange people before us.

The short man wore a dark blue suit, a tie, shiny black shoes, and glasses with silvery rims. He removed his glasses and cleaned them with a handkerchief. He wiped his sweaty face and returned the handkerchief to his jacket pocket.

The woman was wearing a broad-brimmed hat with flowers on it and had a furry animal wrapped around her neck, its tiny dead eyes looking us over. She was wearing a dress that came down to the top of her large clumpy shoes, which made her look a foot taller than the man and sounded, when she walked on the shiny wood floor, like a horse clomping into its stall. She looked us over carefully with small, piercing eyes, as if she were picking out a piece of meat at the butcher shop.

Neither one spoke directly to us. They were talking softly, as if they were in church. We could only catch pieces of their hushed conversation.

She said quietly, "I don't know about the older boy—he might be difficult—but I like the little one."

The male visitor mumbled as he examined his shoes.

After looking us over and muttering to each other, they left through the door they had come in. The man's shoes squeaked as he walked, and the woman's shoes made a noise as if someone were walking on stilts on a wooden floor. The door closed with a faint creak behind them.

We did not know what to think about the whole thing and waited for the supervisor to return and tell us what had happened.

When the supervisor came back into the room, she said, "It's time to eat. You boys, join your groups and go to dining room for your dinner." She did not say a word about what had happened and left us standing there.

The kids in the dining room were surprised to see us in the dress-up clothes. Some of the bigger boys started kicking the big table legs and teasing us.

"Well, well, lookie who's here. Ya going to church? It's only Friday, ha, ha!"

"Ya going to go live with the uppity-up rich people?"

"And dress up every day?"

"And ride in a big fancy automobile?"

"And live in a big house on Nevada Street?"

"Har-de har, har, hee, hee."

My brother and I kept our eyes on our plates. We did not want to look at their faces or listen to their words. For once, we ate all of the food on our plates—even the customary gristle gravy and stringy asparagus.

Perry found me during playtime and said, "The supervisor told me that those people who looked at us this morning were going to take us away to live with them, but they didn't want me—they just wanted you, Jerry."

I was startled and said, "I'm not going to go anywhere with nobody except if you go too!"

Perry said, "The supervisor told me that she didn't like the idea of splitting the two of us up. She told them that they can't have you without taking me. The woman said that they surely didn't want two boys—especially me, because I'm probably a troublemaker anyway."

I said, "I'm sure glad they didn't take me away 'cause I probably wouldn't ever see you again." An unwelcome tear budded in my eye. With a tiny clenched fist, I said, "They can't make me go!"

"Yes, they can! Who is going to stop them from taking one of us—or both of us?"

I thought about what he said and decided that nobody could stop them.

Perry heard the supervisor talking to the head of the day nursery. She said that it would not be long before the day nursery got serious about getting rid of us because no one was paying them for our keep. It seemed as if we were in line for adoption whenever someone wanted one or both of us.

When we were adults, Perry told me that Mom had told her Aunt Cora, "That son of a bitch Homer left me to take care of those two little bastards. What was I supposed to do?"

Our mother—unbound by the proscriptions of her childhood, a religious mother and brother, and a husband she could not live with—was now free. Now that she had gotten rid of us, she decided to live her life the way she wanted—without two snot-nosed kids like anchors around her neck.

Estallee was a pretty woman, and once unleashed, was wild. She continued working as a waitress, but lived her life as she pleased and did whatever she wanted. She lived fast, drank, danced, had fun—and had as many men friends as she liked! She had a string of men friends—sometimes with automobiles.

When we were older, we found out that she had been raped by an uncle when she was fourteen. She knew her uncle had sexually violated her and was fearful that she might give birth to a child. She was afraid to tell anyone and did not know where to turn for help.

She could not tell her parents because she was too ashamed. There was not any place to go—she had to bear the burden and the shame alone. Estallee was perfectly innocent, and she eventually discovered she was not pregnant. Still, she felt guilty, ashamed, and remorseful, even many years later.

Mom and a gentleman friend picked us up one Saturday and took us for a ride in a big green touring car. Perry was eight years old, and I was five and a half. I could feel the wind in my face, see the trees with their fluttering green leaves, smell the aroma of the pretty flowers along the road, and hear the birds singing. Fancy homes drifted by, with large trees and cars in front and kids playing in the big yards.

We stopped beside a large pond and watched beautiful white swans gliding silently in the water, leaving delicate V's on the surface of the water behind them. Mom brought some bread crumbs with her, and the swans came right up to her and plucked the bread crumbs out of the pond—and sometimes snatched them right out of her fingers. Mom's gentleman friend took our picture. Mom showed off by standing for the picture on a low branch of a tree—just inches above the surface of the water. I still have the picture.

We were sad to end the ride, but we were very happy that we had the chance to go for a ride in a car and feed the swans.

Perry, when he could, wandered around the many corridors and rooms to look for me so that we could talk together.

He once found me playing with a toy car on the third floor.

I asked, "When is Mom coming to see us?"

Perry replied, "We will see her soon—you'll see!"

It turned out to be several weeks between some of her visits.

I went back to playing with the borrowed car that I had been zipping up and down the long hallway and running after. Intently, I wadded up some tinfoil that I had found and stuffed it into the hollow underside of the three-inch toy racer to make it go faster and farther with each push.

I asked my brother, "Are we ever going to get out of here?"

After thinking for a while, he said, "I don't know. I just don't know how we can. If we escape, they'll just bring us back."

Not knowing what our future held, but retaining the hope of rejoining our mother, was an ordeal. We were not sure if we would ever see our father again.

We were sure that our mother and father were alive—at least our mother was—and that we were not orphans. However, we might as well have been. Our sentence in this place was indeterminate, and our release was not to come for more than five hundred days.

Deb Bartelt
Steam Locomotive—On the Way to Oregon

Escape to Oregon

In November 1933, I was six, and my brother Perry was nine. We boarded the train alone in Colorado Springs. Our destination was a small town in southern Oregon—four and a half days away.

Estallee's Uncle Kirk had left Oklahoma, where he had been a train engineer, settled in southern Oregon, and worked for the Southern Pacific Railroad in Klamath Falls. Granny had followed Uncle Kirk to Oregon to help care for her bedridden mother. Mom had no one to care for us while she worked.

Mom wrote a letter to Uncle Kirk since he worked for the railroad in Oregon.

Dear Uncle Kirk.

I need to get my boys out of the children's home in Colorado Springs. Do you think you could arrange for train tickets so the boys can take the train to Oregon? Granny has agreed to take care of Perry and Jerry again in her home in Oregon, but I have to get them to Oregon somehow. I will pay you back the money as soon as I can.

Yours truly, your niece,
Estallee

Uncle Kirk replied in his letter:

Stel,

You don't have to pay me back. I will see if I can arrange something with people I know at the Southern Pacific Office. It might take a while, you have to be patient, but I am sure I can help.

Yours truly,
Kirk Coffman

Uncle Kirk was determined to pay for our trip himself if he could not get help from the Southern Pacific Railroad—even though he was short of money from helping out several relatives who were down on their luck.

Our escape had become a possibility, if not a certainty, but Perry and I did not have a clue that anything was happening to save us.

On November 13, 1933, Perry said, *"We're going on a train!"* I could not believe what I was hearing. "The supervisor told me that we are leaving and we should get our things." We were told that we were going to live with Granny again. I ran upstairs as fast as I could to get my clothes.

The assistant was already there. She was not grouchy and said, "I have all your clothes ready."

She held up each piece of clothing and said, "One pair of pants, one shirt, two underpants, two pairs of socks." She also gave me a keen new jacket.

"You are all ready to go. Take these downstairs to the supervisor." She added, "We will miss you," and gave me a peck on the cheek.

Perry met me downstairs, and we put all of our clothes into a cardboard case. We had plenty of room in the cardboard case since we did not have to pack any toys. We did not have any anyway—except the two banks that the nice boys had given us on Perry's birthday. Perry shook the coins out of the banks and counted them.

"We have thirty-seven cents: one dime, two nickels, and seventeen pennies," he said, showing off his numismatic skills. "This money is going to be for emergencies on our trip. I'll keep it safe," he said. He put the coins in his pocket and slipped the banks gently into the cardboard case.

Sounded good to me.

We waited outside the front door, and someone took our picture in our new jackets. We waited for the car to take us to the train station. After a short time, the car came, and we got in. Perry's voice sounded as if he knew all about cars. "This is a 1930 Buick. Look! It has a radio actually in the car! A Motorola!"

We were both amazed at this. We had hardly seen any radios at all—let alone one in an automobile. The train depot was not far away. Perry announced the names of the streets as the signs slid past his view.

Perry was good at street signs and directions and said, "There is a real short street called Antlers Place about a block that way." He pointed in the direction where Mom used to live at the Acacia Hotel and worked as a waitress at the McRoe Restaurant. Now, we did not know where she was.

47

The depot was way back on a large dirt and gravel parking lot, with only a few cars parked in front. The depot was a big high-ceilinged building, with lots of room on the inside. There were several handcarts outside to move the baggage around the station and onto the train.

Inside, there was a cage with windows where the agent sold tickets. There were benches and a place to buy sandwiches if you had any money. We were not about to spend it except for emergencies on our journey. We explored the depot and could not wait to get on the train and start on our adventure.

The driver who brought us to the train station talked to a man in a blue uniform and a flat-topped hat with a shiny bill.

They came back to where we were waiting, and the driver told us, "This man is the conductor, and you boys are to do as he says."

We told him that it was okay with us. **Then We Saw the Train!**

The massive black steam locomotive engine was hissing, creaking, and belching steam onto the sides of the track. Smoke billowed out of the large smokestack. A headlight as big as a large bucket stuck out in front of the engine, and a massive iron "cow catcher" was mounted in front of the train, ready to scoop up any animal in the way and toss it off to the side of the track.

Hooked to the train's locomotive was a car carrying coal and a line of wooden passenger cars stringing along behind. At the end of the train was the caboose.

A woman from the nursery, whom I did not recognize, gave us a flat cardboard box containing fruit, apples, bananas, oranges, and five Baby Ruth candy bars. Boy, were we happy! She was a nice lady.

A piercing blast from the whistle on top of the locomotive's engine announced the all-aboard signal. We excitedly ran down to the snow-slushy train walkway, up the steps, and into the train.

We proceeded to explore our new surroundings. We ran to one of the passenger cars and claimed two seats facing the depot—in case Mom came to see us off. We could have claimed any of the seats because there was no one else in this particular passenger car. Mom did not come to see us off, but the distractions of being on the train diverted our attention and we forgot about it in a short time.

The conductor stood on the lower step of an open door near the locomotive engine. He swung his lantern slowly back and forth several times to signal the switchman to switch our train onto the main track. The train lurched and started to move—the iron wheels spinning on the sanded steel tracks—and we were on our way. The train chugged out of the station, its locomotive whistle shrieking a series of three long bursts, and picked up speed as houses and fields flashed by.

My brother found a cubbyhole in the rear of the car where the toilet was located. The cubbyhole was very small, but had a real metal flush toilet and washbasin, with faucets for hot and cold water and a metal holder with little paper cups for drinking water. The hot water faucet did not work, but we did not care.

Right outside the toilet compartment was a door that opened to a small open-air platform. Below the platform, big iron couplings and hoses connected the railroad cars together. When the train started, I slipped away from my brother to the open platform and could see all the way down to the tracks below. The steel track's wooden ties were flashing by, and the wind was blowing like a dust devil. The noise of the steel wheels of the train riding over the steel rails was deafening. It was exciting.

Sometime during the trip, we lost the box of fruit and the candy bars. Somebody must have found it and devoured all the goodies—even the three candy bars that we hadn't eaten.

The train traveled about fifty miles southwest to the Royal Gorge near Canon City, Colorado. When we stopped, the conductor invited us to get off the train to see the awesome sight. The train was on a track beside the fast Arkansas River, squeezed between steep mountains of solid gray stone.

We could see the bridge high in the air that spanned the Royal Gorge, a tiny ribbon of steel in the clouds. It was a single span, a quarter of a mile long and 1,053 feet above the Arkansas River and the railroad track. We were amazed that somebody could construct such a miracle.

We gazed with wondrous eyes at the bridge high above and our surroundings until the conductor called us to board the train. He told us that he had seen the bridge during its construction as he passed through the gorge many times. He said that it was almost new—the workers had completed the bridge just four years earlier.

Heading west over the Rocky Mountains, the weather got colder as the train climbed up into the mountains. Snowflakes came down intermittently as the engine labored mightily to pull the train up the mountain passes.

We sometimes were going so slowly up steep stretches of track that it seemed as if we could reach out and touch the towering green Douglas fir and ponderosa pine trees and the piles of snow along the track as we went by. We saw craggy mountains with snow on their tops, like shiny beacons in the distance.

Each night, we were very cold—even with our new jackets on. There was almost no heat coming from the steam radiators, and we huddled together to try to keep warm. Eventually I fell asleep, like a baby in its mother's arms, to the gentle swaying of the car rocking back and forth and the clickety-clackety-clack lullaby of the train's wheels riding over the steel rails.

Hours later, I woke up to a beautiful sunrise peeping through the tree-filled horizon. Rays of sun shone through the snow-laden trees like a rainbow of arrows.

The train was rolling downhill along the sides of mountains and gorges. We saw fast-flowing streams below and waterfalls coming down from the mountains above.

Icicles hung from the branches alongside the train. My brother and I managed to get a window open. We stuck our heads out of the window and let the cool mountain breeze blow on our faces. We filled our lungs with the most wonderful air we had ever breathed. It tasted like a cold mountain stream, with the scent of pine and fir mixed in.

Looking behind, we saw the train's cars and the caboose trailing along in a long curve, like a snake crawling along the mountainside, swirls of smoke from the train's smokestack trailing.

After several more mountain ranges, we came to the high plateau country of Utah. We could see the distant high mountains and the cold hills and lower mountains scattered in most every direction.

We crossed over the Wasatch Range in eastern Utah and headed north. The Great Salt Lake was on our left, and the peaks of the Wasatch Range were on our right. The mountains had a layer of snow on their peaks from an early winter storm.

The train stopped in Salt Lake City. Perry and I started to get off the train to see what was there, but the conductor said, "You boys stay on that train and do not get off. You could get lost, and we would have to leave without you!"

We stayed on, reluctantly, because we sure didn't want to be left in any train depot with slushy snow all over the place.

After the conductor had his passengers safely off the train and the baggage unloaded, he turned us over to a policeman.

I was worried and asked Perry, "Are we going to go to jail?"

Perry said, "Nah, the guy is just a railroad bull. He throws hobos off the train because they do not have any tickets. The conductor has our tickets in his pocket, so we don't have to worry."

The policeman's face was craggy and weathered, and he was lean all over—except for his belly, which hung down over his gun belt as if he were carrying extra grub under his shirt. A shiny silver badge was pinned to his shirt, and he wore a straw cowboy hat and cowboy boots.

He sure looked like a real cowboy to us. All we needed was another cowboy and a couple of Indians for our cowboys and Indians dream to come true.

Looking us over for a minute, the policeman finally asked, "You kids hungry? The conductor told me that you ain't had no vittles since yesterday."

Perry replied, "We sure could use some grub. We would be much obliged."

The policeman took us into the telegrapher's room in the station house, where the telegrapher was busily tapping his finger on a metal switch-like instrument. Perry guessed that he was sending messages to the other stations on the railroad. Perry was very interested in what the telegrapher was doing and asked him many questions.

Perry would have been surprised to know that, many years later, he would come home from a world war, shed his marine corps uniform, and become a telegrapher for the Southern Pacific Railroad.

A few minutes later, the policeman brought us bowls of cereal and a bottle of milk, with rich cream at the top. We promptly emptied our bowls, drank the rest of the milk, and thanked the policeman.

Perry told the policeman that we had learned to respect people who were in charge.

He smiled at my brother's good manners and said, "You're good boys. I've got two young'uns myself, but they're older than you kids and they have never taken a ride on a train! You kids are very lucky."

We thought so too!

In Ogden, Utah, we waited for several hours to change to a Southern Pacific train to take us the rest of the way to Oregon. After changing trains, the passenger cars looked much the same as those we had been riding and were just as empty.

The train started north and then went west across the northern edge of the Great Salt Lake, just south of the Golden Spike Historical Monument. The monument marked the spot where the Central Pacific and Union Pacific Railroads met in May 1869, completing the first transcontinental railroad across the United States.

The train was on a wooden trestle made of many large timbers, with wooden ties and steel railroad tracks on top. It stretched above the water across the north end of the Great Salt

Lake from east to west as far as we could see. When I looked out the window toward the back of the train, the track was curving, and we could see all the passenger cars and the caboose.

Our destination, it turned out, was outside a place called Klamath Falls, a town of about sixteen thousand people, the largest town in southern Oregon. We wondered how long it would be before we saw our new home.

At night, I could see the moon through the frosty window reflecting on the snowy banks along the track, sending off sparkles of light. I spent almost all my waking time—even late on the cold nights—on the hard bench, with my face pressed against the cold window, seeing all the wonders of a new world that I had never imagined.

However, it was not the last new world that I would see in my lifetime.

When we arrived at the depot in Klamath Falls, long after dark of the third day, Uncle Kirk met us at the station. He would become like a surrogate father to Perry and me. Estallee would not arrive in Klamath Falls until one year later.

Uncle Kirk was of average height, but physically strong. His hair was dark and thick, his eyebrows bushy, his eyes brown, his face weathered from sun and wind, and his smile puffed up his high cheekbones like jawbreakers.

A broad smile covered his face as he said, "Hi there, boys! Did you have a good trip?"

We answered excitedly, "Yes, it was fun!"

He was jolly as he tossed our suitcase into the front seat and bundled us into the car. We were tired, but very excited. Our eyes looked out the windows of the 1929 Model A Ford. The town was lit only by a few streetlights.

Uncle Kirk said, "Boys, do you know that cars can have names just like regular people?"

Perry said, "Naw, they don't. Do they?"

Uncle Kirk said, "They sure do. This car's name is Spasm II. I named it after the car that I used to have, Spasm I, that just up and refused to run anymore after over a hundred thousand miles under its hood."

We thought having a name for the car was neat, and we liked the name a lot—even though we did not know exactly what it meant.

We continued through the dark town and were on a two-lane road cut into the side of a hill overlooking Link River.

We were fascinated by the bright moonlight glowing on the shimmering, icy surface of Lake Ewana, outlining Hogsback Mountain and the hills and mountains that ringed half of the horizon in the dim distance.

Our excitement increased as we arrived a little while later at a tiny house in Stewart Lennox Addition, a small community three miles south of Klamath Falls. The population was a hundred or so people, thinly spread on both sides of a narrow, two-lane highway that climbed west over the Green Spring Mountain to Ashland, Medford, Grants Pass, and westward to the Pacific Ocean many miles away.

We were met by a short, plump woman with thick dark hair and silver strands like stray rays of sunlight, sun-darkened complexion, bright, piercing brown eyes, and an angel's smile. We hadn't seen Granny for almost two years. We were happy to see her again, and we were delighted that we were going to live with her.

Granny would leave an indelible mark on our lives, nurturing and teaching us in many ways through her kindness and her admonitions, but most importantly, by her example.

We were all tired, and it was getting late. Granny hugged us, put us on the worn couch in the small living room lit by a kerosene lantern, and brought us blankets and hot cocoa to warm us. She filled our hungry stomachs with bowls of hot chicken soup and pieces of cornbread spread generously with margarine.

We were home!

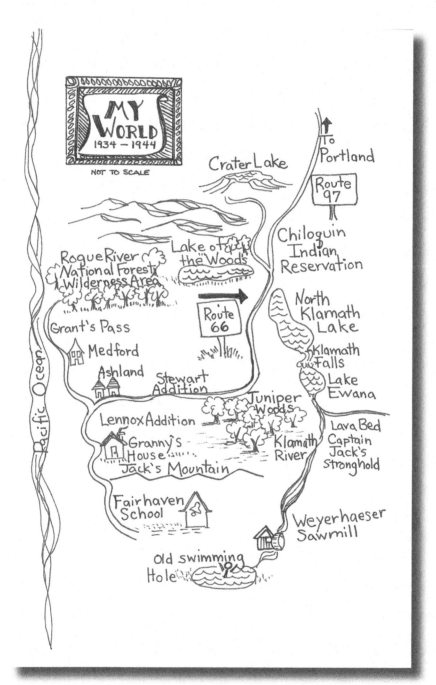

Artist: Deb Bartelt
My World

Chapter 5:
Meadowlarks and Magpies

In the sunny summer mornings, brown-bodied, yellow-throated meadowlarks call to their mates in a series of mellifluous notes rippling down the scale.

The black and white magpies called out their raucous caw, caw, caw—piercing the air with their raspy, sinister noise.

To me, the meadowlarks were a sign that it was going to be a sunny, happy day and good things might happen.

On the other hand, the magpies were a sign to me of bad things: dark thoughts, unhappiness, and dying.

However, these were the good old days; it was like being in heaven—most times.

My World

My world in the 1930s was four square miles or so in and around Stewart Lennox Addition. The area's residents included Granny, Uncle Kirk, Aunt Co, and about a half-dozen other kinfolk.

Up along the highway were Lean's Grocery and the mechanic's garage. A slaughterhouse, later turned into a Royal Crown Cola bottling plant, was at the bottom of the hill on the highway to Klamath Falls.

The juniper woods, lava rocks, swimming hole, cornfield, Klamath River, and Weyerhaeuser lumber mill were downhill to the south.

The mountain—some people called it a hill—was a quarter of a mile from our house. I named it "Jack's Mountain" and claimed it as my own. Short yellow grass, a few scattered Indian paintbrushes, clumps of small junipers, and lava rock outcroppings dotted the mountain's slopes.

Fairhaven Elementary School was on the other side of the mountain—less than a mile as the crow flies or a couple of miles by road. This made up the main part of my world.

In my first winter and spring in Oregon, I learned to read. Granny got secondhand newspapers at Lean's and from relatives and neighbors for me to learn to read.

Eventually, with Granny's help and what I learned in the first grade, I became fascinated with reading and tried to read everything that had writing on it.

In the first grade, I brought books home from school when I could and read them from front to back. I looked forward to school every day—just to read.

Granny was a saint. She read from her Bible every day. She would never miss Baptist Church on Sundays and often would go in the evenings during the week. If she could not get a ride, she would walk to church, walking back after dark.

Granny become a widow at an early age and raised two daughters and a son by herself before she took on the responsibility of raising my brother and me—and, later on, two girl cousins. She was a God-fearing, churchgoing, Jesus-loving woman who never tasted a drop of alcohol nor smoked a puff of tobacco. She was opposed to gambling, playing cards, and "belly rubbing" (dancing).

She got me started reading the Bible and helped me with the parts that I did not understand. I started reading the Old Testament about God creating the earth and heaven and stars and stuff, but I got all hung up with the Book of Genesis and set it aside until I was older. It took a long time, but eventually I read the New Testament from Matthew's gospel through the revelation of Jesus Christ.

Mrs. Walker, my Sunday schoolteacher, gave me my own Bible, a prize for reading the New Testament. That Bible is on a shelf in my office.

Perry and I had arrived in late November and missed the start of school. Granny signed us up for school, although we were starting a couple of months late. Fairhaven had classes for first grade through the eighth grade, a gymnasium, a woodworking shop, and a sloping, rock-strewn playground with swings and teeter-totters.

First Day at Fairhaven School

I started first grade in early December 1933. Granny woke me up early.

"Get up sleepyhead—today is your first day at Fairhaven School," she said.

I was excited and started to dress quickly.

"Hold your horses there, boy," she said as I started to pull on my dirty pants and shirt. "Get right out of those clothes. You have to brush your teeth and take a spit bath before you dress yourself—even if you did have a washtub bath on Saturday night."

I did as she told me, washed, dressed, and got ready to go. Granny had a clean pair of pants and shirt for me, and I found my shoes under my bed.

I ate a quick breakfast of oatmeal and a glass of milk. The milk, made from a white powder mixed with cold water, tasted good. President Roosevelt gave Granny the paper bags of powdered milk and oatmeal and some other things. Perry and I walked up to Lean's every month to pick up the powdered milk, as well as paper bags of buckwheat flour, corn flour, and dried beans.

Sometimes we got a pound of sugar or a pound of lard. Later, we got cellophane-wrapped margarine that had a bubble of orange dye inside that you squeezed open to turn the margarine into yellow butter. However, it tasted more like lard than butter.

I had two tiny framed pictures hung on the wall above my bed: one was President Roosevelt, who gave us food every month, and the other was Jesus, who died on the cross. Both were gods, and sometimes I wondered which one was the highest.

When I finished dressing, Granny said, "Shake a leg, Jerry. You're going to be late for your first day of school."

I ran out the door and headed up to the narrow highway to the school bus stop. I did not look back, but if I had, I would have seen Granny waving in front of our house.

Mrs. Dietrich, the first-grade teacher, greeted each student by name at the classroom door. She assigned me a desk from a chart and showed me which desk I was to use.

I looked around expectantly at the other kids; they stared back at me dismissively. Most of them had started school together two months earlier and had friends or made new friends among their classmates. They had been together from the start of school, and I was starting from scratch. I did not know anyone—not a single kid.

Mrs. Dietrich was nice looking, tallish, and slim. Her hair was as yellow as corn silk, and she had a stern, but kindly, face. Her wire-rimmed glasses matched her hair.

I went to the back of the room and dawdled in the walk-in clothes closet that ran the width of the back of the classroom. I inspected some debris on the floor that the janitor had not removed and examined each item. There was a left-foot, high-top, scuffed-up tennis shoe, scattered scraps of paper with crayon pictures, and other miscellaneous items. Overshoes and galoshes were neatly arranged in rows, and coats hung on hooks on the back wall.

I had been there for a short time when Mrs. Dietrich called my name. I was in my own world—a place I often visit when things do not feel right around me.

Mrs. Dietrich came to the front of the closet, but I did not see her. She reached down, pulled me up to my feet, and said sternly, "When I call you, Jerry Jack Watson, come right away! You have held up the start of the whole class. Hold out your hands—both of them."

I showed her the palms of my hands to show that I had nothing to hide, but apparently, I had missed the point.

"Knuckles up," she demanded.

I turned my hands over, and she whacked my knuckles several times with the edge of a wooden ruler. I winced at the blows, but did not pull my hands away or let out a whimper.

"Now go get in your seat and pay attention the next time I call you!"

All of the girls were giggling and had their hands over their mouths to hide their smiles. The boys snickered and guffawed until Mrs. Dietrich gave them the eye, and the room fell silent.

As I slipped quietly into my desk seat, I thought, *Don't always believe everyone who has a kind face is what they seem to be.*

My first day at Fairhaven was not a resounding success. I had looked forward eagerly to going to school, but actually being there was a different story. My knuckles would feel the whack of the ruler many more times before I got away from Mrs. Dietrich's class, her wooden ruler, and her absolute rule. I really wanted Mrs. Dietrich to like me, and I think she did like me—a little bit.

I did pretty well in first grade, winning the book-reading contest by reading and reporting on twenty-one books—the entire first-grade library.

Miss Dietrich was pleased and said, "Jerry, keep on reading like you have started, and you will get somewhere in your life."

I thought that was all right, but I really wanted her to like me—and maybe lay off the ruler on my knuckles a little. She even whacked me on the knuckles once when I sat at my desk reading a book, not bothering anybody—just because she was teaching spelling to the rest of the class at that particular time.

Uncle Kirk

Kirk Coffman was the first of our relatives to go to Oregon. Uncle Kirk was a caring person who put the needs of others ahead of his own. We found over time that he did not have a drop of pretense or self-importance in his being. He was a real man's man, but also was kind and gentle. He was like a surrogate father to both Perry and me.

He built his house with his own hands. In addition, he built a better road for his neighbors and himself. He hauled discarded creosote tar, rocks, and gravel from the Southern Pacific powerhouse in his truck each day for months to make the road passable during the rainy, snowy winter.

When he came home from work with a load, he shoveled the creosote and broken bricks along the rutted dirt road until it became a winter passage for his neighbors and him—no more bogging down or being stuck in the mud and deep ruts.

Perry and I were excited to find out that our uncle worked on the Southern Pacific Railroad, the same railroad we had taken. He maintained and kept the pumps and compressors running and operated the train's steam engine in and out of the roundhouse, where the locomotive rode onto a giant wheel in the floor called a turntable.

The turntable operation was something like making a U-turn in a car and heading in the other direction. He let me ride in the engineer's cab while he drove the locomotive onto the turntable. It rotated with the steam locomotive on it and headed in the opposite direction. It was neat! I bet none of the other kids had a chance to ride on a steam locomotive on a giant turntable.

Whenever anyone in the family had a problem or emergency, they would send someone for Uncle Kirk. He was the kind of person who always responded to everyone's emergencies. More than once each winter, the water pipes under Granny's house froze during the night, and he would come to her house with his blowtorch to thaw out the pipes.

Tripe Tripping

Uncle Kirk asked if I would like to bring tripe from the slaughterhouse to feed his hunting dogs.

I asked, "How am I going to get the tripe up the steep highway from the slaughterhouse?" I had seen the pile of tripe in the dog kennel and it looked heavy, but I was willing to do any work that I could handle.

Uncle Kirk said, "Boots, come with me. I want to show you something."

I followed him to Spasm II, and he showed me what he had in the back—a Radio Flyer wagon! I was speechless.

Uncle Kirk said, "It's yours, Boots! Now you can haul tripe for me. I will pay you two bits a load. What do you say?"

"Wow," I said. "Thanks, Uncle Kirk, I have always wanted a red wagon, and the Radio Flyer is the best. You don't have to pay me nothing for hauling tripe. I'll do it for free."

"Don't get carried away, Boots. You are going to earn every penny of the two bits a load."

I was ecstatic—not only did I have a brand-new Radio Flyer wagon, but also a job for real money.

Tripe is the stomach tissue of a cow; it is grayish and wrinkly, with green particles of the stomach contents adhering to the creases and folds. Someone said that people in France and other countries eat tripe and consider it a delicacy. Are they nuts? I don't even see how the dogs eat it, but I guess dogs will eat about anything you give them.

I found out that hauling tripe was not as easy as I thought and Uncle Kirk was right—I earned every penny I got. Going down to the slaughterhouse was easy. I just pulled my empty wagon up to the highway to a steep slope, swung the pull handle around to steer, got in the wagon, and zoomed down the highway to the slaughterhouse, hoping no car would run over me. Coming back up the hill with a load of tripe was something else, but two bits were two bits.

Sometimes when I was halfway back up the hill, I turned the wagon around, flipped the pulling handle up to steer with, and rode down the hill on top of the pile of tripe. This was a losing proposition, however, and I eventually had to defer my instant gratification or I would never get the tripe up the hill.

When I delivered the tripe to Uncle Kirk's, I put it in a washtub by the chicken-wire dog pen. Only Uncle Kirk fed the tan and black Labrador retrievers and the mottled German shorthaired hounds. I think he wanted to make sure the dogs knew the hand that fed them so they would obey him in the hunting field.

Uncle Kirk, besides working for the railroad, was a hunter. He owned and trained hunting dogs, mostly German shorthaired hounds that tracked and treed the hunted animal and the Labradors, which swam out and retrieved the shot ducks and geese. He hunted bear, mountain lion, bobcat, deer, antelope, opossum, rabbits, pheasants, ducks, geese, and most any other animal that walked or flew.

His relatives were the beneficiaries of his hunting, and nothing went to waste. He shared the meat from animals and fowl from his hunting with those relatives who were on hard times and needed food to feed their children as well as themselves. They were happy to have Kirk's meat to feed their families.

Kirk said, "Kids need protein to grow up strong."

I wondered what that was, but I believed him and ate venison, bear, ducks, geese, and any other meat whenever I got the chance.

Uncle Kirk raised a couple of hogs every year, and he butchered and gave away most of the meat to relatives. He built a large outdoor wood-burning stove to boil the water for scalding and scraping the hog's hair from its hide, and made a scaffold with a block and tackle mounted at the top to raise and hang the enormous hog for butchering.

A single shot to the brain from his heavy, long-barreled .45 Colt Peacemaker revolver killed it instantly.

Kirk said, "The shot was so quick and powerful that the animal did not feel a thing."

I thought, *If I were shot in the head, would I feel it?*

Once, Perry and I searched in Uncle Kirk's house when he was not home, and when Great Grandma was not looking, we found his big Colt revolver wrapped in a bandanna in the bottom of his trunk.

It was loaded, and we decided to take it into the woods, shoot it, and return it to the trunk. We were going to shoot only one shot and remove the discharged cartridge from the cylinder so that he would not notice that we had borrowed his gun, and the plan worked.

Perry and I argued who was going to get to fire the shot. He won because he was bigger than I was—and he had the gun. When he fired the revolver, it sounded like a cannon, echoing through the trees. A flock of magpies in a tree flew away, flapping their wings and squawking furiously.

On my first Christmas in Oregon, I got a mackinaw coat, which kept me warm through the winter. On my second Christmas, I got a Daisy BB gun—the best present I had ever gotten—and I shot up everything in sight.

I sometimes swiped Van Dyke cigars from Uncle Kirk to smoke in the woods by our house or at the pond by the sawmill. I promised myself that someday, when I could, I would buy him a whole box of Van Dyke cigars to make up for what I had swiped. But later, when I could have, I did not and I regretted it. He died in a crash on the highway.

Gypsy

Uncle Kirk got a dog from a friend and gave it to me; she was a six-month-old German shepherd-Airedale mix. The German shepherd breed was dominant; it had sharp black ears, a pointed black nose, a bushy tail, and a larger and longer body.

I named her Gypsy and called her Gyp. She went almost everywhere with me: the mountain, the juniper woods, Klamath River, and the swimming hole. She was very protective of me and growled and bared her teeth at anyone appearing aggressive toward me. She stood her ground until I called her to stay. I used this advantage with some of the older boys who were aggressive toward me. When I said, "You better get away from me, or I am going to sic my dog on you," they backed off.

Gyp was such a good dog that I did not even need a leash. All I had to do was call her, and she would come to me from wherever she was.

One day after I had Gypsy for less than a year, I came home from school and called her, but she did not come to me. I wondered what was wrong.

I asked Granny where Gypsy was. Granny, with a sad frown on her face, told me that a man had come to the house and told her that Gypsy was dead. The dog had run right in front of his car on the highway, and he could not avoid hitting her. He had gotten out of his car to see if the dog were injured or dead and found that she was barely alive, but so badly injured that he went to his car and got a hammer and put her out of her misery.

I ran out the front door, tears streaming down my cheeks, to get my wagon and go up to the highway to get Gypsy and bring her home.

She was alongside the highway near the mailboxes, with one eye open and seeping blood from the hammer blow that had smashed her brain. The impact had burst her stomach, and blood oozed onto the ground.

I rubbed the wetness from my cheeks, placed her carefully in my wagon, and took her down our road to the big tree near our house. Granny was on the front porch looking in my direction, wiping her hands on her apron.

I walked over and asked her if I could use the pick and shovel that Uncle Kirk had been using for something or other. Granny said, "Of course, Jerry. I am so sad that Gypsy is dead. She was a nice dog and was never any trouble for me."

I took the pick and shovel and dug a grave in the rocky ground. Granny brought me a cloth to wrap Gypsy with, and I laid her in the bottom of the hole. I sprinkled dirt on her until she was covered and then shoveled the rest of the dirt into the grave and made a mound of earth on the top.

I nailed two wooden lathes together to make a cross, pounded it into the softened earth, and said good-bye to Gypsy, **Forever.**

Granny's Farm

Mom arrived in Oregon about a year after Perry and I did. She brought Perry and me things and visited when she could, while working at the largest hotel in Klamath Falls. Since she did not have a car and the three miles each way was too far to walk every day, she rented a room at the Rex Arms Hotel in Klamath Falls.

The Willard Hotel had a large dining room and a large banquet room. Mom was a waitress and served both rooms, according to the hotel's needs. The waitresses served the meals from large aluminum trays carried overhead on one arm, which took a considerable amount of balance and strength.

Estallee was a strong woman, well suited to the demands of the job, but suffered from the weight of the heavy trays on her joints and ligaments. She never complained or missed work—it was not in her upbringing or nature—but she paid the price in constant pain in her joints and suffered acute arthritis in her retirement and old age.

Ethelene Is Gone

Ethelene dropped off our cousins, Maqulene and Billie Jean, at Granny's house. Later, Ethelene completely disappeared, perhaps following Estallee's path to freedom.

Ethelene was a fine woman and treated her daughters, as well as Perry and me, with kindness, love, and attention. I knew her for only a few short years.

She vanished from sight, and nobody knew how—or where—she was. Eventually, most of the family concluded that she must have come to a bad end and died. Ethelene was a young, vibrant woman, and her dying of an illness was not believable.

As our grandaunts Co and Eve said, "She must have come to no good." I thought so too.

When our girl cousins, Billie Jean and Maqulene Blaine, came to live with us, Mom knew that we could not all live in Granny's small house and she found a nearby house and rented it for us. The house was bigger and had a large yard for growing vegetables.

Granny's garden was just a small plot of ground, but it was Granny's farm. Folks told her it was almost a quarter of an acre.

She said, "It's not very big, but it's ours to use; and when it's used properly, with care and hard work, it will help provide for all five of us. The dirt is good, and we can grow most anything we want. You kids can be a lot of help." She added, "This here dirt is a lot better to grow things in than the dirt on Grandpa's farm in Oklahoma. I can tell you that by a long sight. And the dirt doesn't blow away neither in the dust storms because, thank God, we do not have them here."

Livestock on Granny's farm consisted of rabbits and chickens. We did not have a cow. We made our milk from powder that we got from President Roosevelt, and it was good enough.

Granny raised a few rabbits before we came to live with her and decided that, with four more mouths to feed, she needed to raise more livestock. The big buck and doe rabbits that she picked out for breeding produced more baby rabbits than you could shake a stick at, and we got more rabbit hutches for them.

A neighbor gave her some baby chicks and sold her a young rooster for two bits. The rooster had a red comb on top of his head, a red-feathered cape around his neck, and a large fan of black tail feathers. He turned out, when he got bigger, to be really noisy and crowed every morning before the sun came up. He chased the hens around the yard for most of the day—when he was not pecking on scraps of broken glass or something else.

We let the big old cock-a-doodle-do rooster stay anywhere he wanted to—as long as it wasn't in the house.

"Nature takes its course as it always does," Granny said. Soon we had rabbit hutches full of rabbits and a chicken coop full of chickens.

Granny Goes to Market

Whenever Granny needed money for shoes or clothes for us—or sewing supplies and other items that were hard to do without—she slaughtered some rabbits to sell at the Piggly Wiggly.

She picked out a rabbit from its hutch and hung it by its hind feet into baling-wire loops that hung from a two-by-four board nailed to two trees. She killed the rabbit with a blow behind its ears from a short wooden club or with the side of her hand. Both methods killed the rabbit instantly—most of the time.

She cut off the rabbit's head with her butcher knife, slit the belly open, and removed the entrails, saving the liver, heart, and lungs. She slit the skin around the legs and stripped the skin off the carcass.

When she had all the rabbits she needed, she rinsed them in a pan of water, dried them off with a towel, and put them in a clean cotton sack. She went into the house to prepare for her walk to town. She washed her face and hands and put on her town dress. The long cotton dress had short sleeves and had two pockets in front. She did not carry a purse; the purse was only for church.

She picked up the sack of rabbits, walked up the dirt road to the highway, and walked three miles to the Piggly Wiggly. The round trip took two and a half hours.

When she arrived at the Piggly Wiggly, the meat counterman asked, "How are you today, Mrs. Stover?"

"I am middling well, but my feet are a little sore."

"I am sure sorry to hear that. What have you got for me today?"

She set the sack of rabbits on the counter and said, "I have got five real nice frying rabbits."

He put a piece of butcher paper on the counter, removed the rabbits from the sack, and placed them on the paper. He picked up each carcass and examined it carefully.

"My, Mrs. Stover, you have some real fine rabbits here, and you have done a first-rate job of skinning and dressing them, but of course you always do. Many of my customers are tired of chicken and eat rabbit when they can. These rabbits will make a tasty meal for them."

"How much can I get for them?"

He thought for a while and said, "I am sorry to say that prices for rabbits are going down, but these are nice rabbits. I can offer you two bits a pound for them. What do you say, Mrs. Stover?"

Her brow wrinkled as she thought. She felt that something was just not right, but she said, "All right, if that's the best you can do. I'm not going to haul those rabbits all the way back home after carrying them all this way."

He weighed the rabbits on a metal scale that hung from three chains over the counter. "That is fifteen pounds exactly." "Let's see now," he said as he did some figuring on a piece of paper. His eyes squinted as he said, "That will be three dollars and six bits. Is that right, Mrs. Stover?"

She counted the amount in her head and said, "Seems correct to me."

He sifted through the cashbox under the counter and saw that he had several silver dollars and two half dollars. The rest was small change: quarters, nickels, dimes, and pennies.

He counted out three dollars and seventy-five cents in coins and put them on top of the counter. Granny picked them up and put them in her pocket.

She saw a sign saying "Cold Soda Pop: 5 cents." She was thirsty from the walk to town, but she was not about to spend any of the rabbit money on soda pop. She hardly ever drank it anyway.

She said, "I would be much obliged if I could have a drink of water."

"You most certainly may, Mrs. Stover. It would be my pleasure!"

He filled a glass of water from a tap and handed it to her. "There you are, Mrs. Stover. Is there anything else I can do for you today?"

"No, thank you," she replied coolly, recognizing his tone as a slight.

She took the water, walked outside in front of the store, and sat down on a bench to rest for a little bit. She sipped the water slowly, savoring the cool drink. She had known the man for several years and always considered him to be honest, polite, and friendly to her, but something was wrong! *Why are rabbit prices going down when more people are buying them? Why are his customers a little tired of chicken and eating more rabbit?*

She sensed that his forced politeness was overdone and did not sound sincere.

He is cheating me, and he knows that I know! It is the Lord's will. I will just have to let him get his comeuppance in the hereafter.

She picked up the empty rabbit sack and started walking home.

Although tired from her trip, Granny was fixing supper in the kitchen when we arrived home from playing with our friends and were ready for supper. We were hungry.

Granny said, "You girls set the table, and Perry and Jerry bring in some more firewood—it's bath night."

When the food was ready and the table was set, we washed our hands and faces and sat down to eat. We bowed our heads as Granny said, "Dear God, who art in heaven, we give thanks to you who in your mercy has bestowed many blessings upon us. Bless the poor and the hungry and the sick and bless the food we are about to eat. In the name of Jesus. Amen."

We all said "Amen" together and started passing the food around the table. Mackie brought the bowl of chicken and dumplings hot off the stove, and Billie brought the collard greens, some hot biscuits from the oven, and margarine.

At dinner, Granny told us kids about her trip to town. She said that sometimes you have to take what you can get and leave the person to get his comeuppance in the hereafter.

We finished with a Saturday night treat: rhubarb pie, made from rhubarb grown in Granny's garden. Granny had baked the delicious pie the day before.

Busting Leo

Leo Snyder was a year older than I was and twenty or more pounds heavier. For some reason, he had a grudge against me and would just as soon pound on me as look at me. He hated my guts and always tried to catch me to beat me up when I got off the school bus. I always ran like heck to get away from him. I could either get beaten up or run like heck.

One day, he was chasing me, and I made it to Granny's house in record time—yards in front of Leo.

Granny, seeing what was happening, came out of her garden, where she was collecting some carrots for supper, and yelled to Leo, "What is going on? Why are you chasing Jerry like that?"

Leo stood speechless under Granny's interrogation.

Granny said, "You get away from this house this instant— and I mean it, or I'll have the law on you."

There was no law in Stewart Lennox; the closest law was three miles away, and nobody had a telephone. However, there were our male relatives in Stewart Lennox, and Leo knew that if it came to that, he could be in bigger trouble. Leo turned around and left.

Granny said, "Jerry, remember what I have told you about bullies. Bullies are cowards underneath, and if you do not fight back, they will never stop chasing you; sometimes you just have to take a beating to hold your ground."

After this episode, Leo Snyder still tried to catch me and beat me up when I got off the bus. I once pulled my pocketknife on him on the bus and was sent to the principal. Mr. Hough gave me three solid whacks on my backside with the large oak paddle he kept in his closet. It hurt, but it did not change my mind about defending myself when I had to. I just decided to do it more carefully.

I always tried to get a seat close to the driver, where I could avoid Leo by getting out the door fast and hitting the ground running. Sometimes, to avoid him, I did not even ride the bus home—I ran over the mountain to get home. I was stuck up front, three seats back from the driver, and Leo was behind me, making comments about me being a scrawny jerk and that he was going to get me.

When the door opened at my stop, I hopped down the stairs, hit the ground running, and scooped up a fist-sized rock from the ground. Leo was only a few yards behind me. I suddenly turned, wound up, and slammed him with the rock with all my throwing power. The rock hit him solidly in the chest, and he stopped cold in his tracks, bending over and wheezing like a tired-out mule.

I yelled at the top of my voice, "That's just a sample of what you will get the next time you chase me. Next time, I will kill you!" I vowed never to run from anyone again, but I did several times before I learned to defend myself.

After this confrontation, it was no longer necessary for me to sit in the front seat to escape Leo, and I took any open seat on the bus. I did not have any serious trouble with Leo again. In fact, we became a little bit friendly and even ended up deer hunting together with one of his older brothers.

Nobody even got shot.

Pears, Home Brew, Hops, and Octopuses

Sometimes our grandaunts, Aunt Co and Aunt Eve, took us to Medford, on the other side of the Green Spring Mountain, to pick up leftover pears at the packing plant. The Bartlett pears were delicious. Our aunts bottled the pears when they get home and stored them for the winter.

Once, we went to the Oregon Coast to pick hops from bushes in a hop orchard and put the hops in a large cloth bag that we dragged behind us. The hops looked like small green pods, and each one weighed about as much as a bumblebee. I picked seventy-five pounds and skipped lunch and, at two cents a pound, made a buck and a half for my day's work.

When we finished picking hops, Perry and I went to the seashore to look for giant octopuses hiding in the rocks in the shallow ocean water. We never found an octopus, but we were sure that they must be there.

Above the noise of the crashing surf, we heard Aunt Co and Aunt Eve yelling and calling for us to come back to the campsite. When we returned to camp, our aunts were quiet. Aunt Co finally told us to get a fire started because she was going to start cooking supper.

We got firewood, and I started a fire.

"Jerry, watch the way you handle those matches. I don't want you to burn down these woods!" Aunt Eve said nervously.

I was very careful with the matches and fire. I dug a deep pit and stacked a ring of rocks around it. We carried water in a bucket from a faucet in the campground. Our aunts cooked the trout that a fisherman had given them for supper and boiled some potatoes they had brought with them.

We ate our supper and washed the dishes. The sun had set, and we arranged ourselves around the campfire.

As we looked at the red coals in the fire, yellow-orange flames licked up through the firewood, and pink and silver sparks drifted upward like fireflies against the dark sky. Aunt Co said solemnly, "I want to talk to you boys about what happened today."

We both listened closely because we had never seen her so serious.

"Aunt Eve and I were terrified today when you did not return to camp. We were worrying ourselves to death that something had happened to you boys. We called and called, worrying more each minute, until you finally came into camp. We thought that maybe you had drowned. We wondered how we were ever going to tell Granny that you boys had drowned in the ocean."

Looking us in the eyes, she said, "If you boys were us, how would you feel if you had to tell Granny that Perry and Jerry drowned in the ocean?"

Perry and I, startled by Aunt Co's statement, looked at each other for an instant, and Perry said, "That would be awful—we won't ever do that again."

I said, "No, we won't—never."

Our aunts nodded their heads approvingly and smiled at us. We thought that they were the best aunts in the world!

We had a swell time overall—except for our aunts worrying about us. We had been worried that they might think that we had gotten snarled up with a giant octopus, but as it turned out, they were only worried that we had drowned.

We returned home a couple of days later. It was very late, and we ate a cold supper and fell into our beds to sleep. It was raining cats and dogs, and the roof leaked while we slept.

In my light sleep, I heard the pitter-patter of raindrops on the tarpaper roof echoing in the night and fading away, replaced by the heavy drumbeat of hard rain.

I enjoyed listening to rain on the roof and the water leaking into the pots and pans on the floor. It soothed and comforted me, but it was soon time to empty the pots and pans.

Granny was using the coal-oil lantern to light her way to the outdoor privy, so I lit a candle and saw that the receptacles were overflowing. I made several trips, emptied them outside into the stormy night, and returned them to their places.

Back under the covers with the satisfying sound of rain drumming in my ears, I smiled and fell fast asleep.

The Outsider—Prince of the Hallway

Miss Botens was my fifth-grade teacher at Fairhaven. I liked her a lot and had a crush on her younger sister, Effie, who was a grade behind me.

Miss Botens was a good teacher, but was very strict about all the kids paying attention. She did not permit any of her students to daydream in her class or do anything else when she was teaching.

"Pay close attention all the time," she said. "Paying attention is the only way you can learn."

In class, we occasionally practiced charcoal sketching. Unfortunately, one day Miss Botens was teaching about the Civil War, and I was sketching a charcoal portrait of Forrest Mann, a classmate who had his desk near mine. When Miss Botens looked my way and saw what I was doing, she walked over and stared over my shoulder at the sketch in process.

I wasn't aware that she was there, but when the room went dead quiet, I looked up. I mistakenly thought that she was going to compliment me on what a good sketch I had made.

Instead, she agitatedly said, "Come with me, Jerry."

I followed her out into the hallway.

Pointing to a niche with a half wall protecting the downstairs stairway leading to the basement classrooms, she said, "You are going to sit right here until you learn to pay attention in my class."

I sat there most of the rest of the day. I graduated to a longer stay on a step-by-step process to where the hall seemed like my new classroom. Once or twice a day, she would come out to where I was sitting to give me a class book and lesson.

"Read chapters two and three, and you will learn about the Applegates, the Oregon Trail, and how Oregon became a state." Or she would cite other stories and lessons that I should learn.

As she left to return to her class, who were probably throwing spit wads all over the place, she turned and said, "If you had paid attention in class, you would already know about your state's history."

When she was back in the classroom and the door was shut behind her, I set aside the book and lesson she had left for me and reached into my pocket for a small rubber ball. I had cut the white cover off a golf ball that Perry had brought back from the golf course, where he caddied golfers.

Inside the golf ball was a reddish, hard rubber ball about the diameter of a walnut. The ball had a good bounce to it and rolled smoothly on the hallway floor.

I practiced shooting the ball down the long hallway to the far wall and back. As my skill increased, I was able to use the corners at the end of the hallway to rebound shots off the far corners and return the ball to where I was sitting. I saw a ricochet shooting one time when Perry took me to the Boys Club in Klamath Falls. Four boys were playing pool, ricocheting the balls all over the place—sometimes even into one of the six pockets of the table.

Miss Botens said, "Another day in the hall for you, Mr. Jerry Jack Watson."

She had snuck up on me from behind, saw what I was up to while I was engrossed in making my shots, and when I heard her approach, I slipped the ball into my pocket when she was not looking.

After several days, I finally became bored at ricocheting the rubber ball and dove into the schoolwork that Miss Botens brought out in the hall for me to do. Miss Botens, seeing my changed attitude, returned me to the classroom, and I spent my full time learning. I graduated the fourth grade, and surprisingly my grades were good.

I thought a graduation ceremony in the hallway might be in order.

One day, I visited Jackie Miller at his dad's RC Cola bottling plant at the bottom of the hill, and I was walking back up the hill on the highway. I saw something shiny in the gravel by the road and the stub of a cigar lying nearby. I picked up both items and reached into my pocket for a wooden match that I always carried. I lit up the cigar stub, sucked the smoke in, blew it out, and coughed.

When I looked at the other item, a broken piece of belt buckle, I was startled at what I saw. I knew the owner of this broken buckle: Forrest Mann. A week after I made the charcoal portrait of him, a car killed him on his bicycle on this very spot.

We were friends, and he liked the portrait that I had drawn. I felt very sorry that a car on the highway killed him.

In Love

I was in the fifth grade, and Effie Botens was in the fourth.

One day, I had an experience that embarrassed and shamed me. I wrote a love letter to Effie. I said that she was very pretty, and when we grew up, I was going to marry her. I put the letter in my back pocket and hoped that I could find a way to give it to her in private. However, that was not to be.

We were in the gymnasium for physical education, where we passed the basketball around, dribbled the ball, and tried to shoot baskets. Both boys and girls were in the gym for classes at the same time; the boys were generally on one end, and the girls on the other—although when we were chasing balls, we were all over the court. We did not wear gym clothes, just our usual school clothes, and we usually played in our stocking feet, although a few who had tennis shoes wore them.

While running after a ball in the girl's end, my love note worked its way out of my back pocket and fell to the gymnasium floor without my noticing.

I was shooting baskets with the other boys and was trying hard to make a basket when we heard high-pitched giggling at the girls' end. All of us boys stopped playing basketball, wondering what the giggling was all about.

The girls were prancing around and trying to read the note. Eventually they got together in a huddle, and one girl read the note to the other girls. Shrieks of laughter and giggles filled the gymnasium.

The boys swarmed to the girls' end to find out what was happening, and soon everyone in the gym knew the whole story.

I wished I were dead! I wanted to make myself invisible, but had no such luck.

I vowed to never again write a love note. Never!

The Gold Buyer

One afternoon, a man came down the dirt road to our house.

I said, "Look, somebody is coming. I think he's a doctor."

"Naw," Perry said. "He ain't no doctor. Look at his shoes. Doctors don't go around in dirty brown shoes."

The man was dressed in a shabby suit and a dirty tie. He carried a satchel, but he did not look like any doctor we had ever seen.

It turns out that he was a gold buyer. We went and got Granny, and the man greeted her, "Howdy, Ma'am. It's a nice day, isn't it?"

Granny asked, "What is your business with me?"

"Have you got any gold jewelry to sell? Lots of people are selling their gold. I've already bought several rings from some of your neighbors."

Granny was fingering her wedding ring on her left hand, turning it one way and back. She said, "How much are you paying?"

"I always pay top dollar—depends on the weight and fineness of the gold. If you like, I'll weigh and grade that ring you got." He had been closely watching Granny nervously twirling her gold wedding ring.

Granny pulled her thin, worn wedding band from her finger and said, "You pay top price?"

"Sure do," he said.

"Well, how much is this worth?" She handed him the ring.

My brother and I were listening intently to the conversation. *Would Granny actually sell her wedding ring?* We suspected that the Piggly Wiggly man had told her that they did not need any frying rabbits for a spell and she would not have any money to buy us any necessities.

The gold buyer opened his bag and took out a small brown bottle and a scale smaller than the one we saw in the post office in Klamath Falls. He weighed the ring on the scale, unscrewed the cap on the bottle, and, holding the ring between his fingers, squeezed a drop of the liquid from an eyedropper onto the inside of the ring. The liquid foamed and changed color.

"Hmm," he said as he handed the ring back. "Maybe I can't give you as much as I thought."

"Why not?"

"Well, it's just not fine enough gold for a top price, and it weighs less than I expected."

"Well, how much can you give me?"

"Three dollars," he said.

She was silent for a long time, and then she said, "Just take it." She thrust her wedding band into the man's hand.

He paid Granny three silver dollars from his pocket and smiled as he turned to go. "Nice doing business with you, ma'am."

Granny turned her face to hide a tear in her eye.

"Granny, what's wrong?"

She clutched the three silver dollars in her right hand, looked down at her empty ring finger of her left hand, and with a faraway look, said, "Your grandfather Joseph, who you never knew because he died before you were born, gave me that ring on our wedding day. It was the only thing I had to remember him by."

Brushing the tear away from her eye, she said, "You boys go on and play now—everything is all right."

As we walked away to play, we wondered about the sad things that happen to older people.

I Ain't No Rat

When I was twelve, Perry and several of his friends found a car out in the high brush about two miles from our house. The blue 1935 Chevrolet was covered with dust and almost hidden by sagebrush. The car looked to be in good condition, and we assumed that someone had stolen it and dumped it in a remote area where no one would discover it.

The next afternoon, I tagged along behind Perry and his three friends to visit our car. They did not want me to come along, but I did anyway.

When we arrived, one of the boys threw a rock through the windshield, and an immediate hail of rocks started. Everyone, including me, was smashing everything on the car. We bashed in windows, headlights, taillights, and every door and fender. The car looked almost like a train had hit it when we finally quit.

It was frenzy, like a prehistoric band of hunters attacking a vicious animal to kill it for its meat and skin. However, this obviously was not the reason. Something else was going on here that we could not—or did not—want to fathom. We had a rage inside us that wanted out.

The sun dipped below the horizon, and it started to get dark. We were still excited as we walked home, slipping by the houses, which now had lights on inside.

Halfway between Stewart Lennox and the Klamath River, a wildcat lived in the rocks. Perry and I had seen it a few weeks before.

Marty said, "Let's build a fire—it's starting to get cold."

Perry produced some matches, and we started looking for wood, which wasn't easy in the dark. We got the fire started, the flickering flames casting patterns on the rocky wildcat's lair, and sat around talking and snickering about what we had done to the car and watching to see if we could see the wildcat's glowing yellow eyes in the dark.

Leo said, "I wonder how the owner will feel when he sees the car—if he ever does?"

No one answered, and a sudden despondency came over us. Gloom and guilt sank in as we thought about what we had done.

We considered going home, but were reluctant to go. We lingered, sitting around the fire, quietly watching the flames curling up through the wood, the smoke drifting slowly away with our thoughts.

Suddenly, bright, blinding lights came on us from every direction, and a loud voice said, "Put your hands in the air and don't move. This is the state police! We are coming in now, so for your own safety, keep your hands above your heads and stay where you are—do not move!"

Marty said, "Jesus, what the heck is going on?"

Perry whispered, "Shut up. Do you want to get us shot? You know why they are here."

We sat quietly with our hands in the air as five uniformed state troopers came into the light of the fire, each pointing a rifle or pistol in our direction.

"Where are your guns?" one of the officers demanded.

We said, "We don't have any guns."

The trooper in charge said, "We want to know what you are doing here and where you have been. We want to know what you know about a car out on the flat on the other side of the highway."

Perry said, "We don't know nothing about no car. We have been hiking around for fun down by the river and decided to check out the wildcat that lives in these rocks. We couldn't find the wildcat, so we made a fire and sat around, like on a camping trip."

Each of us nodded our heads and repeated the same story in our turn.

At that, the head trooper said, "You boys are coming with us to the station."

We walked in a group up to the highway, surrounded by the troopers, who used their flashlights to light the way. They squeezed us into three police cars and drove off to Klamath Falls.

At headquarters, they put us in separate small rooms. Four of the five officers took turns questioning us.

"Where were you today—all day?"

"Why did you steal the car?"

"Why did you smash up the car?"

"How did you find the car?"

"What were you going to do with the car?"

"Do your folks know that you are out stealing cars?"

"If you lie to us, you will be in big trouble."

"How would you like to go to jail?"

"If you do not tell us the truth, you are going to jail."

And on and on …

Often, when they questioned me, they would say that so-and-so said this or so-and-so said that, trying to get me to agree, but I repeated the same story. They continued to tell me that all the others were going to jail and he was going to lock all of us up, including me, if I did not talk. I was worried. *What would Granny think?*

Apparently, we all had told about the same story and denied even seeing the car, which frustrated the officers, and it showed on their scowling faces. They seemed determined to break one of us—even if it took all night. They probably thought that I, being the youngest, would be the easiest to break down.

Two of the cops began to concentrate on me. The slim one had changed into tan civilian pants and a white woolen sweater and spoke softly in a friendly manner.

The heavyset cop wore his full uniform—belt, cap, gun, boots, and all. He said in a gruff voice, "Your name is Jerry, right?"

"Yes, that's my name."

"Look, kid, if you don't start telling the truth, we are going to have to start really sweating you until you do." He dropped his voice to a menacing snarl and continued, "*We have our ways to make you talk.*"

He sounded like a cop in a movie.

"Jail tonight and reform school tomorrow."

However, I didn't spill any beans. I knew all about the cop's tricks from watching Jimmy Cagney gangster movies at the Rex Theater, and I didn't tell them anything. *I ain't no rat.*

The questioning went on for about an hour. Eventually, the head trooper brought us all into one room and said, "We have talked to you enough, but we still think you are all lying. You can go home now; however, remember that if any of you had anything to do with stealing the car or smashing it up and we find out, you will go to jail!"

They dropped Perry and me off close to our house. Perry convinced the trooper driving the patrol car to drop us off by the highway. Perry said, "We have some bad ruts in our road, and you might break an oil pan."

The officer, not wanting to end up in godforsaken Stewart Lennox at the end of his shift in the middle of the night with a busted oil pan, agreed.

It was already ten o'clock at night, and we would have some explaining to do—every boy to his own story. It was important that Granny did not see us riding up to the front door in a police car.

Perry fibbed to Granny that we went to a movie in town and we did not realize it was so late. Granny worried so much about us that she did not pay much attention to our excuse. She was just glad we were not dead or injured in a ditch out in the dark from a hit-and-run car or logging truck.

We heard nothing more from the Oregon State Police about the car, but the incident left a lasting impression in my mind.

The night had been scary, and I never wanted to repeat it. I felt uncomfortable from then on with the police and their devious methods and hard, superior attitudes. I was guilty as heck and admit that I should have learned not to tag along with the older boys, but I did not and I would face other bad situations in the future tagging along behind them.

Aunt Co's Log-Cabin Roadhouse

Granny's sister, Cora, decided to build a log-cabin roadhouse. Roadhouses were popular with travelers, who would stop in to have a beer or a glass of liquor—or two—and a bite to eat for breakfast, lunch, or dinner. Aunt Co had been thinking about and planning to do this for a long time.

One day, she started telling everyone, "I have decided to build a log-cabin roadhouse." She had a strong personality, and no one questioned her. Aunt Co found a vacant parcel of land at the highest part of Stewart Lennox Addition along the highway, close to Uncle Kirk's house. After negotiating with the owner of the land, she told her husband, Ernie, "I've got my land, and I'm going to build the log cabin!"

That evening, she gathered Ernie, Dean Gillock, her cousin Kirk, and Frank Clayton. "We are going to build the log cabin, and I need all the help I can get. I would like for each of you to talk to the rest of the kinfolk and see who is willing to help. Ask them to come see me if they have any questions. I am going to be busy with the plans and preparations, but I want them to come and see me."

A number of the kinfolk came to Co's house to talk and find out what she had in mind.

She said, "I cannot pay cash, but everybody who works will get free meals. I will cook the meals myself. I will also make sure there is enough food so those who need to can take some food home for their kids and spouses—even if there is only sandwiches when I do not have time to cook a meal."

We all knew that Aunt Co was a good cook. Everyone in the family went to her house for most Thanksgivings—and sometimes for Christmas.

When all the kin got together to celebrate, Uncle Ernie put all the table leaves—and extra leaves that he had made—in the dining table and expanded the table through the living room with sawhorses and boards.

Even with this long table, sometimes we had two servings: one for the grown-ups and a second table for the kids. We did not mind much because Uncle Ernie, when Aunt Co was not watching, would sneak us snacks before the meal began.

Sometimes Uncle Ernie, in a conspiratorial way, would sneak me down to the basement, where he hid his whiskey bottle. He reached up in the floor joists over his head and produced a three-quarter-full pint bottle of whiskey.

We would each have a snort or two from the bottle, and I would follow him back up the stairs. My face flushed and I was a little dizzy, but I felt good. I was no stranger to alcohol, and it was not my first drink. Whenever I could, I sneaked drinks of whatever alcohol was available.

All of the kinfolk who could get there came to Aunt Co's and Uncle Ernie's for these occasions, including our great-grandmother.

Everyone pitched in and brought what food they could. They sacrificed their meager funds to make these holidays very special. The grown-ups and the children always had a grand time just having their stomachs full and being together.

They brought assorted salads, desserts, hot dishes, casseroles, bowls of mashed potatoes, sweet potatoes, cooked okra, string beans, cakes, and pies. My personal favorite pie was mincemeat.

Mom and Aunt Co made their own mincemeat. They chopped venison tenderloin into cubes and cooked it together with lemon and orange juice and some peelings from the rinds, apples, currants, molasses, brown sugar, six or eight different spices, citron, cinnamon, cloves, nutmeg, allspice, pepper, salt, and the key to the whole concoction: brandy. If somebody didn't have a given spice, the cook just removed it from the recipe.

They poured the hot mixture into mason jars, sterilized the jars in pans of boiling water, and set them on the back porch for a couple of months. Then the mincemeat was ready to go into mincemeat pie.

The other high point of the meal was Aunt Co's turkey, browned to a dark bronze, with delicious stuffing, thick brown gravy, and mashed potatoes. Sometimes, as a special treat, she would add several tasty roast ducks or geese if someone had had good luck hunting.

After the meal, I was so gorged with food that I laid my skinny bones down on the floor with my stomach on the basement furnace hot-air vent to placate my groaning belly.

The womenfolk were happy to work with Aunt Co in her kitchen and gossip about who was doing what, bragging about their children, telling stories about their neighbors, and comparing the inadequacies of their husbands.

Work started on the log cabin. It was a Saturday, and Kirk was off work and came. Ernie, Dean, Bill, R. A., and other volunteers also showed up. All the men brought their tools and were ready to go to work.

Aunt Co used the savings that she and Uncle Ernie had to buy the logs, lumber, cement, windows, doors, plumbing pipe and fixtures, roofing, and other assorted building materials.

Uncle Kirk said, "I can pick up the stones in the fields around here and bring them in my pickup after work each day. You can build the foundation out of rocks and mortar; it will save a lot of cement."

Aunt Co said, "Lordy, Kirk. You are always Johnny-on-the-spot when a body needs something. That cement is real expensive."

Once the building began, other relatives and friends pitched in and helped according to their abilities and available time. Some worked in the evenings, and some on their day off—and some, who were out of work, worked most every day. Aunt Co worked twelve-hour days, helping place and cement the stones for the foundation, and helped on many of the other jobs, but her main job was supervising the work crew and cooking food for the workers and their families. She cooked and made good on her promise to feed everybody.

She was scurrying around every which way. Sometimes she was barking orders, and sometimes she was putting mercurochrome on a scratch or commiserating with someone who had hit his hammer in the wrong place and was jumping up and down with a banged-up finger. Nobody fell off the roof, broke an arm or leg, smashed in their head with a falling log, or sawed any fingers off. Overall, everyone fared pretty well in the injury department.

Uncle Kirk, in addition to hauling stones, installed the piping; while Uncle Ernie framed the structure, with help from Bill and some of the older boys. When the framing was complete, he laid the floor and installed the doors and windows. Dean Gillock, a part-time brick mason, knew how to build masonry and set the bricks for the large fireplace and chimneys.

Uncle Ernie took Aunt Co to Klamath Falls, scoured the used-furniture stores, and rustled up a stove, an icebox, an assortment of pots and pans for cooking, silverware and dishes, some tables and chairs, and other necessary items. They had to borrow a truck and make several trips to get all the stuff back to the log cabin.

There was a lot more work to do, but it was eventually done and the log cabin was finished. Amazingly, they completed the two-story building in a little over six months. It had a kitchen, a bar, and seating areas, with tables and chairs in the center of the room and built-in booths alongside the windows, a dance floor on the first floor with a large fireplace, two apartment rooms on the second floor, and two outdoor privies in back.

The first customers were the people who had pitched in to build the roadhouse. Aunt Co and Aunt Eve and some of the other women cooked and served food to everyone who had helped—and a few who had not. Aunt Co did not mind—everyone was welcome. Aunt Co and her helpers had to cook and serve food the next day too because some of the relatives had missed the first day of festivities.

Eventually, she was very tired and went home. She felt good about everyone's accomplishments. Everyone had been generous with his or her time and hard work in completing the building. As she fell into her bed, she said to herself, "Building a log cabin is sure hard work, but it was worth it!"

Little did I know that years later, my first wife, Jean, and I would have a wedding party given us by our relatives, and we would dance to "The Wedding Waltz" in Co's log-cabin ballroom, followed by everyone dancing the polka and schottische. Afterward, we withstood a traditional "shivaree," where I pushed Jean in a wheelbarrow with tin cans tied to it down Main Street, with everyone participating noisily in the fun. Jean and I were as happy as young kids—which we were—at seventeen and twenty years old.

The Li'l Old Whorehouse

Aunt Co and Uncle Ernie had their own home in Stewart Lennox. They were going to move into the rooms at the Log Cabin and sell their house if they needed to, but decided to stay in their home and rent out the rooms to boarders to bring in some cash. After she made this decision, she put out a sign along the highway, but no one came looking for a room for the next several weeks.

Co told Ernie, "I have about decided that no one is going to rent those rooms. We can probably just forget about it." By this time, her business was picking up, and she was having enough customers to make a small profit. She felt that the business would improve even more with a little more time.

A few days later, two young women drove their sleek 1930 Model A coupe into the driveway, parked, and came in.

"Hello," the yellow-haired one said. "We would be interested in your rooms for rent. We saw your sign on the road. If they are not taken yet, we would like very much to see them."

The other woman, whose hair was a reddish color, said, "This is a real nice place. How long have you been open?"

Aunt Co said, "Thank you. I'm pleased you like it. We have been open almost a month now. The rooms are available; would you like to see them now?"

The young women looked at each other for an instant and replied almost simultaneously, "Yes." The redheaded woman added, "We would appreciate that."

Co led the way up the stairs to the two rooms.

She said, "They are large rooms, as you can see. There is also plenty of room in the closets for you to store all your things. The rooms are light in the daytime from the two windows in each room. The rooms are also wired for electricity, and the lights can be turned on and off with this switch over here by the door. You just rotate the switch around to the right to turn them on or off. We put two beds in the room, but I will take one out if you like.

"There is a double privy behind the cabin, with his-and-hers privacy. There is always a supply of 'Monkey Ward' catalogues, so you do not have to bring your own unless you prefer. To get to the privy, just go downstairs and walk out the back door. It is to your left. You can eat in the cafe downstairs if you want. That would be extra—twenty cents for breakfast, the same for lunch, and twenty-five cents for supper. Each room will be twenty dollars a month. If you want to double up in one room, it will be thirty dollars for both of you."

While the women thought over Co's terms, she looked them over with a critical eye and asked, "Exactly what is it you girls do for a living?"

They laughed and said, "We are writers."

"What kind of writers?"

"We are freelance writers," the redhead said. "We write mainly for magazines. We are lucky to be able to write our stories anywhere we happen to be. We are able to travel anywhere we want."

Co finally said, "Well, I have never had any association with writers—especially lady writers—but you are welcome to take the rooms so long as you keep the rent up on time."

The two women looked at each other for an instant, and the yellow-haired woman said, "We'll take one of the rooms."

The next day, they began moving into their room and busily started to make their place homier. They drove to town and returned with curtains, small rugs, lamps, pictures, and some other miscellaneous items.

About a month later, Perry, when nobody was around, sneaked into their room and found some Kodak pictures. The photographs were of the two female boarders cavorting naked and having sex with different men.

Later, it got out that the Log Cabin was a whorehouse. When Granny found out about the rumor, she was distressed and angry. She went to Uncle Kirk and told him that he had to do something about the situation.

Uncle Kirk took on the sensitive problem. First, he talked to the relatives who had heard the rumor and found out about the naked photographs that Perry had found.

He then went to see Aunt Co and said, "Co, there is a rumor going around that you are running a whorehouse."

Alarmed and indignant, Aunt Co said testily, "What do you mean, Kirk? I am not doing any such thing! How can you say that? Who is saying so?"

Kirk replied, "The rumor is going around with the relatives, and photographs have been found of your boarders running around naked, posing with naked men, and performing sexual acts."

"What pictures? Who is showing them?"

Kirk said, "I talked to a couple of boys who saw the photos and they admitted that they had seen them, but they were reluctant to tell me who showed the photos to them. They promised not to tell, and they did not want to break their word. If it absolutely comes to it, I will go to the parents of the boys and get the truth."

Aunt Co indignantly said, "That does it! I am going to go see those whores right now and settle this."

Although they initially denied the allegation that they were whores, the two women relented when Aunt Co said that there were Kodak pictures of the two of them with men in compromising sexual positions.

She told them, "Pack up your stuff and get out!"

They did.

Over the next several weeks, there was a straggle of men coming to the Log Cabin asking for one or both women, but the women were gone—with no forwarding address.

A Knuckle Sandwich and a Shotgun Suicide

Perry and I moved to Klamath Falls to live with our mother
for the first time since we had been in the children's home in
Colorado Springs seven years earlier. We lived in the Frazer
Courts in Mills Addition. I enrolled in the seventh grade at a
new school, Mills Elementary. Perry enrolled as a freshman at
Klamath Union High School.

Mom had a boyfriend, who lived across the alley. His name
was Carl Jarrett. His dad owned a used furniture store, and he
and his two brothers skinned muskrats and mounted the hides
on boards in the back room of the store. They also loaded
and unloaded used furniture and heavy parts from junked
automobiles that they bought and sold. They were stacked
behind the store in the alley.

Carl was a nice guy to Perry and me.

One day when I was walking home from Mills School, two kids a
grade ahead of me at school told me, "We're going to kick your
butt and rub your face in the ground."

I usually used my quick feet to protect myself in these
situations. I had to be fast on my feet because sometimes I was
somewhat of a cheeky smart-ass and did not know my place. I
got into all sorts of trouble from it.

My brother said, "Don't let anyone bully you or beat on you.
If somebody does, tell him that your big brother will beat the
crap out of him and any of his friends who want to join in."

One day, instead of racing off when I was threatened, I
decided to threaten them with my big brother. They told me
that they did not give a shit about my older brother and said
they were not afraid of him.

Perry did exactly what he said he would: he caught the two
older boys on their way home from school a few days later and
gave them some knuckle sandwiches until they said uncle; then
he let them get up off of the ground. He beat up those kids with

just his fists, and they took off running—probably all the way home to their mommas.

I did not have any more trouble with them. If they tried anything with me again, they had a good idea of what a knuckle sandwich would taste like.

Perry could hit hard with his fists—I should know since I got hit with them every now and then when we got into an argument. He started boxing at Mills School and was never beaten. He even turned pro for a short time and fought a huge Indian from the Chiloquin Klamath Indian Reservation. He won, but that was much later.

There was a suicide in the house across the street from our house. Several people were bunched up on the sidewalk, trying to see what was happening. Three policemen were there: one outside and two inside the house.

My friend Jim and I didn't know the name of the man who lived there, but we sometimes saw him outside doing chores or trying to make his brown plants turn green with a little garden hose. He never spoke to us—even when he saw us across the street playing and sneaking looks his way.

"Something isn't right with that old man," I said to Jim.

"You can say that again," Jim replied. "He gives me the creeps."

Jim said, "I wonder why his house is always dark? His lights are always off, and the curtains are always closed. And no one ever comes to see him—not that I ever saw."

"Search me," I said. "Maybe he's loony or something."

Jim got restless and took off for home, but I stayed, wanting to know what had happened. I stood across the street to see if I could see inside.

The police allowed nobody in the house. After a while, the dwindling number of people who had been standing around ogling at the house left, and I was the lone spectator.

I casually walked over to the side of the house away from where the three cops were congregated by the patrol car, smoking and talking and not looking my way. I sneaked up to the side window. The cops had opened the inside curtain to get some light in when they were investigating the scene, and I could see inside.

I put my face up close to the window, and I could see into the shadowy room. A man was slumped on the floor in the middle of a barely furnished room, gaping blood all over where his face should have been. A wooden chair was overturned beside a double-barreled shotgun. A spray of splattered blood and gore, like a bat's wings, climbed the wall behind, and flecks of blood clung to the ceiling above.

The next day, Jim, whose father was a cop, told him about the suicide. The man had shot himself in the face with a shotgun. Jim passed the information to me at lunch period. I did not tell him that I had looked in the window and saw the whole thing because his dad might get me in trouble.

Later, I wondered how hard it really was to do what he did. I have to admit that from time to time, the same action had occurred to me.

Chocolate Cherries and Pain

I caught up to my brother and some of his friends one Saturday morning.

"Go on home," one of them snarled. "We don't want no kid follering us around."

Perry, probably because the older boys said that I couldn't come, said, "He can come if he wants to—so long as I say so."

One of the boys had swiped a box of cherry chocolates at Walgreens. He led the way to a vacant garage behind a vacant house, and we went inside. After eating the chocolate cherries, they started talking about girls and their "cherries."

I thought at first that they were talking about chocolates, but I soon grasped what they were referring to. I heard a lot of words that I hadn't heard before: *poontang, knocked-up, nooky,* and *horny,* among others. The oldest and biggest boy, whose name was Sam, stood up and said, "Let's have a masturbation contest—the first one that comes, wins."

93

I wasn't really too sure what he meant and said so. One of the older boys told me, "It's playing with yourself—jerking off, dummy."

"So what does that have to do with anything?" I asked.

Perry said, "Go on home, Jerry. Nobody wants a kid around here anyway."

I stayed.

All of the boys except me stood facing each other in a circle and were kidding about different words and their meanings. They had their weenies out of their pants and were playing with them and stroking them up and down.

They were joking about words and arguing the difference between the words *coldcocked* and *cornholed*.

One of the older boys said, "*Coldcocked* means you're knocked out and you're unconscious. *Cornholed* is when a guy puts his thing in your backside and you're conscious." Everyone but me guffawed.

A painful memory of what my brother had done to me spun through my mind. I felt as if my blood had stopped flowing in my veins; my heart skipped a beat, and my body went cold and stiff. I could not speak and gasped for breath. I ran!

I ran out of the garage and across streets without looking, hoping a car would hit me to end my pain, but there were not any cars around. I had to get away, or they would see the dirty secret on my face or in my eyes.

That night I twisted and turned—and did not sleep.

In the morning, I dreaded going to school. They would all know what had happened to me—what I had let my brother do to me. He should not have done what he did—even if I let him because he said he would give me one of the rifles that he and his friends had swiped.

He was the big brother and was supposed to take care of me, but instead, he took advantage of my weakness to have a lousy, stolen rifle, which I never got anyway.

I was surprised as the school day ended and no one said anything. I vowed to bury the secret forever and never think about it again as long as I lived. I knew that if I dwelled on it, it would become a festering sore, so I tried my best to forget.

I loved my brother—but I never forgot.

Granny's Gone

Mom liked Carl Jarrett very much, and we thought they were in love and would get married. Instead, they broke up after a while, and Perry stayed with Mom in Klamath Falls because he had started high school. I moved back to Granny's house and started the eighth grade in the fall at Fairhaven.

One day when school let out, I decided not to ride the school bus home and ran over the mountain to Granny's house.

The mountain called to me, and I could not resist its beckoning. Ignoring the school bus pulling away from the school, with friends and adversaries cutting up, acting silly, and frolicking inside the bus, I set my sight upward to the mountain and started a slow lope toward the peak. It was a clear, cold winter day, and there were patches of snow scattered around on the mountain's slopes.

Arriving at the highest point on the mountain, I sat down, retrieved my jackknife, and started to whittle on a dead branch that I had picked up on my run. I surveyed the panorama below like a scout on the frontier. I was in no hurry to get home and enjoyed the view from the mountain.

After a while, I looked down at our house in the distance and sensed that something was amiss. A feeling of foreboding flowed over my body like an unwelcome second skin. I saw the reason for my concern: a car that I could barely make out was pulling away from Granny's house, followed by a second car. This was a very unusual occurrence at our home. There was hardly ever a car there—let alone two cars.

I jumped to my feet and ran down the hill as fast as I could. When I got to Granny's house, nobody was home—not Mackie or Billie, and Granny was gone too. This startled me; Granny was always there when we came home from school.

After a few minutes, I ran to Mr. Tweet's house next door, the only other house on our short dirt street. Nobody answered,

95

though I pounded furiously on his door. I ran up to Uncle Kirk's house, but I knew that he probably would not be home from work yet—and no one was there.

Puzzled, I returned to Granny's house, sat down on the front step, and waited. My imagination swirled, and my apprehension grew. I guessed by the sun's position that an hour or so had passed.

Eventually, Uncle Kirk drove up with Mackie and Billie, but Granny was not with them.

Uncle Kirk opened his car door, stepped out, and said in a somber but soothing voice, "Boots, your granny is in the county nursing home—she is very sick. It is a good thing that Mackie and Billie came home when they did and ran to Co's to tell her about Granny being sick. Co got the ambulance out here to take Edna to the hospital and then called me. I am going to take all of you to Aunt Co's to stay for a while."

A week later, we learned that Granny had a cancer in her liver—even though she had never had a drink of liquor in her life. I did not know what cancer was—I thought it was just one of the illnesses that older people get sometimes.

Aunt Co and Aunt Eve shared caring for us kids at their homes while Granny was in the nursing home, and soon things started to get more normal. Although we missed Granny, we figured that she would be home as soon as the doctor fixed whatever was wrong with her.

Before Granny went to the nursing home, she had been acting differently—not the way she always had. Something wasn't right. She told us that we needed more room in the small bedroom since we were all getting grown up.

She said, "I am going to move my bed out of the bedroom up to the attic and sleep there. That will give you kids more room."

The next day, she climbed a ladder and moved her bedding and a quilt up into the attic. The rafters were just above her head, and she could not walk upright. She had to walk in a crouch or crawl to move around to get to her bed. Although she had a candle, which provided some light, it was more like a dark cave than a bedroom.

Her behavior had begun to puzzle us. She seemed to want to be by herself, away somewhere, like the story of the old dying Indian squaw who left camp to stay in the cold, snowy woods until her death. However, being kids, we did not think too much about what she was doing. We did check to make sure she was in the house at night.

Granny did not drink coffee or tea—just hot water in the morning that she heated in a kettle and cold water or powdered milk the rest of the time. She had been eating sliced raw onions on cornbread or biscuits, spread with margarine, and not much else.

She said, "Raw onions are good for you, and they make you healthy."

However, we found out later that onions do not cure cancer. Nobody told me that Granny was dying.

One day, Mom told Perry and me, "Granny wants you boys to visit her and for Jerry to bring his guitar. She wants to hear Jerry play."

Before Granny got sick, she had paid a dollar for steel guitar lessons for me once each week for three weeks. I took the lessons on a Hawaiian steel guitar and used a small steel bar to play notes or chords while strumming the strings with metal picks attached to my fingertips.

A few days after Granny asked to see us, Mom drove Perry and me and my steel guitar (which really wasn't mine; it was the music teacher's) to the nursing home. It was the only time that we were at the nursing home, but Mom visited Granny there almost every day between her shifts at the Willard Hotel.

Granny was alone on a narrow metal cot. The room was dark, with no windows. Odors of uneaten food, chemicals, and sweaty bodies mixed with the sweet smell of flowers from Granny's garden—a bouquet that Mom had placed in a glass jar on the table beside her bed.

Mom knelt by the side of Granny's low bed and gently woke her up. Mom said, "Perry and Jerry are here to see you, Mom."

Granny, her pain barely suppressed, answered in a small, tired voice, "Did Jerry bring his guitar? I want to hear him play. Is Perry here too?"

Perry said, "Yes, I am right here, Granny, and Jerry is here too—and he has his guitar. The teacher let him bring it to play for you."

Granny looked much older. Her saintly eyes were dulled to a grayish brown. Her healthy, sun-darkened skin was sallow and had a yellowish tinge. Beads of sweat clung to the surface of her skin. Her hair, normally combed back neatly with a bun tied in the back, spread in disarray across the pillow.

Mom started to brush her hair, but Granny feebly waved the hairbrush away and said, "Jerry, are you going to play for me on your guitar?"

"Yes, Granny—if you want me to."

It was as warm as an oven, and I could feel the sweat starting to run down into my collar. I sat down and played the only three songs I knew as well as I could, but I could not play very well yet.

When I finished, Granny looked at me with a little smile and said softly, "Jerry, you need to practice more."

Mom and Perry both laughed nervously. I wasn't angry with them for laughing, nor was I unhappy with Granny's comment because it had brought a small smile to her face. She had not smiled once before I played my guitar.

Granny died a week later, on February 20, 1941, at fifty-seven years old.

I was thirteen years old. Granny was like a surrogate mother to us kids. I was in a state of denial—my mind frozen. I could not weep or grieve her loss; my heart was crying, but my eyes were dry.

I cannot remember her funeral or internment. Although I was there in body, my spirit was somewhere else. It was as if she had never died and been buried and would be calling us in for supper as usual when evening arrived.

I could not stop thinking about Granny. Sometimes, when I was alone, I remembered how caring and patient she had been with us. She cared for us in every way she could, with little regard for her own needs—even when, unknown to us, she was suffering from cancer.

I hated God for letting Granny suffer and die. *Why did he do it?* My question went unanswered.

She fed us, bathed us, and always made sure we had clean clothes for school and church. She gave us encouragement when we needed it and discipline when we earned it. She taught us how to raise and tend rabbits and chickens—our main sources of protein. Granny taught us about Jesus and encouraged us to go to Sunday school and church and read the Bible.

She asked nothing in return except a little help around the house and garden, help with the chickens and rabbits, and for Perry and me to hang our bedding on the clothesline outside to dry when we accidentally wet our beds.

Granny had a remedy for most all ills. If you had a sore throat, you gargled warm salt water and wore a Vicks VapoRub-coated wool rag around your neck—even to school. If your stomach were hurting and growling, you got a dose of Milk of Magnesia. If you couldn't go potty, you got an enema on the cold kitchen linoleum. Granny would hold an enema bag in the air and put a tube into your backside.

When it was cold, Granny taught us to sew. Perry and I were interested in her pedal-operated Singer sewing machine and learned to sew—and even replace a bobbin or needle. In her "notions basket," she kept needles for the sewing machine, regular sewing needles, an assortment of spools of thread of different colors, ribbons, and a variety of buttons that she had cut from old worn-out clothes.

She taught us to crochet rugs from strips of cloth torn from discarded clothing. She taught us how to carve a crochet needle from a wooden stick, polishing the hook carved in the end to prevent snagging the cloth.

Granny told us that knitting was harder than crocheting. She told us that she would show us how to knit sometime if we wanted to, but we never got around to it.

Our small rugs were colorfully patterned from the variety of cloth remnants we used. We were proud of our accomplishment. Granny was very complimentary of our work. It made us happy to see her smile.

We would never see her smile again.

I could hear the magpies' raucous caw, caw, caw—a sign to me of bad things, dark thoughts, unhappiness, and dying.

Chapter 6:
Vignettes of Growing Up

fter Granny died, we four kids were separated and sent in different ways. Mackie and Billie Jean Blaine went to live with Aunt Eve in Altamont Addition, and later in Portland. I lived with Aunt Co and Uncle Ernie so I could finish the eighth grade at Fairhaven.

After I finished grade school, I moved to Klamath Falls to live with my mother. Her rented house was a few blocks from Klamath Union High School, where I enrolled as a freshman in the fall of 1942.

In high school, I enjoyed mechanical drawing and wood shop and spent time sparring in the boxing room. Uncle Ernie got me interested in carpentry when he showed me his carpentry tools and told me that I could have them when he was gone, but I never got them.

English bored me. Trigonometry was intriguing, but tedious. Geometry was interesting, but algebra did not appeal to me and I missed one or two algebra sessions every week. (When I went to college, I had to make it up and got the only D in all my college classes. In my senior year of college, however, I made the honor roll.)

My English teacher was not very good at inspiring the students—especially me. She wiped out my composition of a true story about a multiton boulder crashing down onto a fire crew, including me. I thought the composition was reasonably good, but I got a D and received no explanation from the teacher on how to improve the work. To heck with writing! I vowed that I would never write another composition if I could help it!

I saw a used single-speed bike in the shop for fifteen dollars and gave the bicycle shop owner five dollars to hold it for me. It took two weeks to pay off the bike so I could ride it to my work at the bowling alley.

My paper route required that I get up at five thirty to meet at the paperboy shack and roll papers. After I finished rolling my papers, I rode my bike to the opposite side of town and delivered them. I usually finished before eight to make my first class.

My best friend, Calvin Worley, and I worked nights and some weekends at the bowling alley. My usual night's work was from 6:45 p.m. to 12:15, and I earned $2.37.

Who would have thought a boy named Jerry who set pins at the local bowling alley and earned $2.37 for a night's work would become chairman/CEO/president and build a multimillion-dollar company?

Molatores Bar and Grill

Taking a break from setting pins, I got a job at Molatores Bar and Grill and worked in the afternoons and evenings after school as a soda jerk. The work was easy—all I had to do was pour cokes and make milkshakes, ice cream cones, chocolate sundaes, and banana splits—and wash the dishes and keep the place clean. Some of my school friends came in and tried to get freebies, but I said, "What—and get me fired? No way, Jose!"

Molatores was the oldest and most popular bar and grill in Klamath Falls. It had a large bar, where liquor and beer were served, a restaurant, a pool hall with six pool tables, and the soda fountain. The boss paid me a quarter an hour for my work, and I got free supper.

One night I said, "George, how about one of your delicious hot beef sandwiches with lots of mashed potatoes and gravy?"

The cook's answer was always the same. "Sorry, kid, we are all out of roast beef and mashed potatoes and gravy."

The first time he told me that, I felt downcast since I had not had any lunch, and I was starving. I had been looking forward to a delicious hot beef sandwich with layers of sliced beef, mounds of mashed potatoes, slices of white bread, covered with hot brown gravy.

When he saw my look, he slapped a hot beef sandwich smothered in gravy on a platter, set it on the order counter, and said, "Well, what do you know? We have one left." He smiled broadly as he wiped his hands on his apron.

We got along pretty well, but he continued to play tricks on me. We became friends in the short time I worked at Molatores. Slipping him an occasional chocolate sundae did not hurt any— at least I never went home hungry, and he got his sundaes.

Mom Won't Come Home

I was working on a model airplane, a small replica of the Navy F4F Hellcat fighter. Mom got off her shift at the Willard Hotel at eight o'clock and should have been home over an hour and a half earlier. It was almost ten o'clock, and I needed to go to bed.

I was worried about her and did not want to go to bed until she came home, so I decided to go find her. I thought she was probably at Molatores, which she frequented sometimes. She normally just sat at the bar talking to people around her and sipped on a glass of beer.

I put on my clothes and walked nine blocks to Main Street, turned right, and four blocks later I was standing in front of Molatores. I had a hollow feeling in my stomach. *How will I ever get her to come home?* This was not the first time I had to get her out of a bar.

I saw her smoking a cigarette on a barstool and talking to a man. Her nearly empty glass of beer sat flat on the bar in front of her. I figured that she was just sipping it. It was a bad sign. I knew from experience that if her beer were flat, she was just sipping it to extend her stay because she was enjoying herself.

Crowding up to the bar between Mom and the man she was talking to, I slid her beer glass closer in front of her and said,

"Mom, it's time to go home. Please finish your beer, and I will walk home with you."

"Jerry, I'll be going in a little while. I will just have one more beer." She sipped from the nearly empty glass and motioned with her hand to the bartender for another beer. "Go home, Jerry. You have school tomorrow morning. I can get a ride when I am ready to go home."

The man sitting next to her was behind me now since I had crowded between him and Mom. He stuck his head between us and said, "Go on home, kid! Your mother will be all right. I will see that she gets home."

I ignored the man, blocked him off with my shoulder, and pleaded with Mom to come home, while she sipped slowly on her beer. Finally, after another half hour of pleading with her, I left alone and walked home.

I could not sleep, and I went into the living room, where I could see the street and our small yard and driveway in front. I waited for a car to drive up with Mom. Nodding off, I awoke when car lights flashed in front of the house.

Mom got out of the car and stood unsteadily, saying goodbye to someone and making her way to the front door. I hurried back to my bedroom and heard her bedroom door close. It was almost midnight. I went to bed with a feeling of relief, but I was sure that it would not be the last time I waited for her to come home from a bar.

After the house was quiet, I crept into the kitchen. I knew where Mom hid the bottle of sloe gin. Perry and I occasionally took a sip of the gin and replaced it with a little water. I pulled up a chair, reached up to the top shelf, took down the bottle, and had several swallows. It burned all the way down my throat and made my eyes water and my stomach turn. Then, although dizzy, I took another big gulp.

As I unsteadily crawled back into bed, I wondered if, when I grew up, someone would have to try to drag me home from a bar. *Was I to be just like my mother?*

I arose at six thirty the next morning, after six hours sleep, and the day began: school in the morning and jerking sodas at Molatores in the evening.

In the Woods

Large logging trucks roared up and down roads and highways in and around Klamath Falls, carrying huge loads of Douglas fir and ponderosa pine logs, three to six feet in diameter and twenty feet or more in length. These logging trucks were symbolic of the large logging and lumber industry, which was a substantial part of the Klamath County economy, along with ranching and farming, when I was growing up.

I was fascinated with the huge trucks and their skillful, but sometimes foolhardy, drivers. Most everyone living in the area had seen or heard of a logging truck crash, often dumping the load of massive logs onto the highway or street and sometimes injuring or killing the driver.

There were many logging operations in the mountainous forests of Klamath County, and I wanted to get a job as a logging truck driver. I had just gotten my driver's license at the age of fifteen, but was unable to get a job driving a logging truck because I had to be sixteen to get a truck driver permit and had to have some experience driving trucks, which I obviously did not have.

Instead of driving a logging truck, I got a job as a choker helper in a logging operation. It was wartime, and available workers were difficult to find. A choker setter attaches a steel cable connector to felled logs once the branches are stripped from the trunk. The trunks are then loaded onto trucks and transported to the sawmill, where the logs are sawed into lumber.

The hiring boss told me to report to the rigger slinger at the logging office, and I did.

He said, "So, you are going to be a choker. Is that right, son?"

I replied, "I sure am—if someone shows me how to do the job."

He said, "Okay, look down to where I am pointing."

He pointed toward the logging area downhill from where we were standing. "See there, down yonder—the man in the red shirt? His name is Shultz, but everybody calls him 'Red.' He's the choker boss who is going to show you the ropes. Go on now and get to work. And one more thing—pay close attention to him and do exactly as he says."

I muttered, "Thanks," and loped off down the hill to meet Red and start work.

When I got to Red, I told him, "My name is Watson, and I am ready to start work."

Red seemed old to me—he must have been all of thirty years old. His thick hair was flaming red, matching his nickname.

He spat a wad of chewing tobacco onto a nearby log, barely missing a small lizard warming itself in the sun, and replied, "Good, son. We can use the help—we are behind schedule. What moniker do you go by?"

I said, "My name is Jerry."

"Do you know anything about logging or chokes, Jerry?"

I replied honestly, "No, but I have walked logs on the Weyerhaeuser sawmill pond for fun and worked the green chain and tailed off the multiple trim saws. I don't know a lot about logging or chokes, but I am a pretty fast learner."

I was beginning to like the man's manner from the way he listened attentively to me before he spoke.

He said, "Okay, kid. I will teach you on one condition, and that is that you will never get yourself in the bite of the line—no matter what! If you get caught in the bite of the line, you can get cut right in half, or you can get your legs cut off right out from under you. A taut steel cable can be a deadly weapon."

This statement should have alarmed me, but it only made me more inquisitive. I said, "Okay, but what the heck is the bite of the line?"

"The line is the woven steel cable that you put around the log and connect the cable to the log using this choker."

He held up a woven steel wire cable with steel fittings on the ends, showed it to me, and said, "The cable is attached to a bulldozer—or dozer as we call it—and the choke is attached to a logged tree." He went on to explain that if the cable were not in a perfectly straight line between the choker on the log and the bulldozer, which it never was, the cable would snap taut when the bulldozer started to pull the log.

"That cable can move sidewise at a hundred miles an hour and slice anything in its way like a hot knife through warm butter." He had my attention.

"Wow! Have you ever seen anybody get caught that way?"

He went quiet for a moment and seemed to age before my eyes. He blinked and said, "Yes—my younger brother. He's dead—three years."

His simple statement held me in awe. His calm demeanor in speaking about his brother's death was astonishing. I was embarrassed about my dumb question, and I felt sorry for having asked it.

He never mentioned it again, but I never forgot it.

I found out that setting chokes was no picnic. The logs, like giant jackstraws, strewn around the ravines and sloping hillsides were a formidable challenge.

I climbed over and burrowed under the logs to fasten the choke around the girth of the log like a collar at the right place to allow the bulldozer to pull the log out of the piles of trimmed, felled trees. I was very aware to get out of the bite of the line when the cable was set and before I signaled the bulldozer to pull out the log.

The dozer skidded the logs to the landing, loaded them on logging trucks, transported them to the sawmill pond, and dumped them with giant splashes into the log pond, where they remained until they were needed.

When the sawyer who ran the big circular saw needed more logs, they were retrieved from the pond by a log walker. The log walker moved the logs with a long wooden pole with a pivoting, hooked metal arm and spike at one end, called a cant hook. Most of the loggers called it by a more vulgar name. The log walker manipulated the logs to the log chain with peaveys, which pulled the logs from the pond and into the sawmill, where they were sawed into rough lumber.

As it turned out, my choker job lasted only four and a half weeks. The logging company decided to let half the crew go, including me, and moved their operation to another site.

To this day, I have never forgotten the bite of the line symbolism and have used it to good purpose in my life many times. Sometimes I did not heed its warning, and I suffered the consequences.

I have since paraphrased this cautionary phrase to, "Don't stick your head in where you can't get your ass out!"

Planks, Wool, Mountain Oysters, and the Smell of Burning Flesh

Cal Worley's dad had worked on the Gary Ranch, a huge cattle ranch and seed-grass farm not far from the Lake of the Woods. Cal sometimes worked on the ranch in the summer. Cal and I drove out to the ranch, about twenty-some miles from Klamath Falls, to see if I could get work. The foreman brought us into the office, and "Old Man Gary" interviewed me himself.

His small office had stacks of papers on his desk and a large window overlooking the vast, verdant fields of seed grass, crisscrossed with irrigation canals and ditches and widely scattered herds of grazing cattle and sheep.

He recognized Cal immediately and said, "Well, hello, Cal. I have not seen you in a while. How is your mother?"

Cal answered that his mother was fine. He then told Mr. Gary that I was a good friend and a hard worker. I was lucky; it was a busy time for the ranch, and he needed additional hands. He hired me on the spot. Old Man Gary, of course, rehired Cal.

Cal showed me the bunkhouse and the dining room, which had finished serving supper, but where we would eat breakfast. Cal asked the cook if we could get something to eat.

"Sorry, kid, the dining room is closed. Go ahead and settle in for the night; the chuck-wagon triangle will sound at six, breakfast at six thirty. I will have sandwiches in the morning for you to take with you for lunch."

Cal said, "A truck will pick us up at seven and take us out to the job."

We slept in the bunkhouse with the other hands, woke up to the metallic clanging of the chuck-wagon triangle, washed up, and headed to the dining room.

My eyes went wide as I sat down at the large table seating some fifteen or so, mainly old-timers, and saw the awesome array of food.

Plates of sunny-side up and overeasy fried eggs, stacks of pancakes, piles of crisp thick bacon, large bowls of oatmeal, mounds of thick, brown biscuits, plates of golden butter, and pots of black coffee covered the table! We dug in as the others were already doing and packed in enough food to last us a couple of days.

I was starving for real food. It was the best meal I had eaten in a long time. I found out, however, on the first day of work, that I needed every ounce of energy the food provided to get through the day.

Cal and I rode in the back of a pickup truck to a series of large irrigated fields. The driver told us to report to the tractor driver, who was sitting on his idling tractor by an irrigation canal. The tractor driver was a wiry fellow with arm muscles like steel cables, and he got right to the point.

"Okay, boys. I am going to tell you first of all that if you screw up and get me crippled or maimed, I'm going to personally wring your goddamn necks!"

We glanced at his muscular forearms and biceps, believed him, and nodded our heads.

Cal had not worked on this particular job before. He said, "We've got it. Don't worry; we will do it right—just tell us what you want done."

He ignored Cal's platitudes and continued, "Your job is to set these planks across the irrigation ditch so I can cross over this ditch without stopping every time I finish dusting a row. I have a lot of fields to cover and not much time. I will show you how to do it."

He picked up the shovel, measured the distance between the tractor's wheels, and mentally made a note of it. "This is how far you set the planks apart so my wheels are on the planks—not in the damn irrigation canal."

He took the shovel and cut two slots into the canal bank a little larger than the width of the planks, waded across the irrigation ditch up to his waist, and cut two identical slots in the opposite canal bank. He came back, grabbed a plank, and dragged it into the slots on both sides of the ditch, repeating the same procedure for the second plank. He climbed onto the tractor and drove over the planks to the other side of the canal, turned around, returned, and stepped off the tractor.

"Got it?"

"Yeah," we both replied.

He got on his tractor and started down the side of the canal. He hollered, "I will begin on the long side of the field. It will give you enough time to get used to setting the planks. As I get closer to the short side of the field, my trips will be shorter, and you are going to have to bust your asses to keep up."

Cal and I were as ready as we were ever going to be and followed the tractor to the long side of the field. We finished setting the planks while the tractor driver poured fertilizer from bags into the hopper on the tractor. He finished loading the fertilizer and drove the tractor over the planks, heading for the far end of the field and fertilizing the plants as he went. When he reached the opposite end, he returned and fertilized the opposite side. Cal and I had hurriedly set the planks for the next row, and we waited a couple of minutes for him to return.

As he repeated the process, the tractor drew closer to the short side of the field, and the time interval became shorter and required Cal and me to set planks without a pause. We were exhausted and did not know if we could keep up the pace. Remembering the driver's admonition, we kept setting planks continuously.

The driver approached the canal at a fast speed and literally bounced over the planks, scaring the hell out of us every time, remembering his admonition to wring our necks if we got him injured.

At the end of the day, we were dog-tired and could barely drag ourselves into the back of the pickup truck for the ride back. At the bunkhouse, we immediately jumped into the communal shower to try to remove the nettle dust from our bodies.

Nettle dust originated from decades of nettles, a plant with bulbs full of tiny, stinging stickers, decomposing in the soil. The natural itching powder never left our skin the whole time we worked on the ranch. A wrangler told us that urticaria is the medical term for this condition. He found out the name of the ailment when he first started working on the ranch and had to see a doctor for a severe rash. Called by any name, it was a constant irritant to us—on and off the job.

After we finished setting the planks, our next job was dealing with sheep and calves. At sheepshearing time, the ranch hands, with the help of sheepdogs, herded the sheep into a corral. It was attached to the shearing shed by a narrow wooden chute with low wooden walls on each side. The chute was open on the top, and there was enough room in the chute for a single line of sheep.

The trick was to get the individual sheep into the chute and get them to move along into the shearing shed. Cal and I got the job of moving the sheep into and out of the shearing shed, where the sheepshearers sheared the thick, oily wool from the sheep, leaving them standing in their birthday suits, wondering what had happened.

We found out that sheep are the most stubborn, stupid animals on God's green earth. Moving sheep down the chute was the most difficult part; the sheep would not budge. No matter how hard we pushed and pulled, they would not budge. They went as stiff as a piano leg and wouldn't move.

We finally found a method that worked reasonably well. One of us got in front and pulled the sheep by the ears, while the other sat on top of the chute behind the sheep and pushed with

111

both feet until the sheep moved and the front guy hopped on the top of the chute to let the sheep go by.

Lanolin covered our arms and hands and made our skin as soft as a baby's bottom. It was aggravating work moving sheep, but it was a lot easier than setting planks.

After a few days, the shearing was done, and the foreman assigned us to the calf roundup, which we found to be considerably more instructive, if not more demanding. I showed up not knowing what to expect, but Cal had already worked calf roundups.

The ranch wranglers cut the calves out from the herd, drove them into a corral, and brought them out one at a time. Their horns were just beginning to protrude from their skulls. Cal and I had to catch the calves by hand, throw them to the ground, and hold them down while the ranch hands performed a number of procedures on the calf.

Throwing a calf on his back is an art I had to learn. Sometimes I ended up on the calf's back while the calf tried to buck me off. To succeed, you needed to grab the calf's legs on the underside of its body, pull them out from under him, and sit on the calf while the ranch hands did their jobs.

Using a hollow, short, pipe-like tool, sharpened around the lip, the ranch hands loosened the calf's stubby horns from the skull by screwing the sharpened pipe over the horns and removing them by pulling them out or breaking them off from the skull.

They plunged a long needle into the calf's rump, emptied it, and inoculated the calf from disease.

We spread the calf's hind legs, and one of the ranch hands took a pocketknife, slit open the calf's scrotum, severed the testicles, and tossed them into a bucket. The calf testicles, "Rocky Mountain oysters," were sent to the kitchen as a special treat for the work crew—unless Old Man Gary intercepted them for his own dinner table.

The hands branded the calves with a two-foot-long branding iron. The ranch's brand identified the owner of the animal. The brander heated the iron in the campfire and pressed the red-hot iron firmly against a hindquarter of the calf, holding it until the brand burned into the calf's hide. Pungent smoke rose and settled in our nostrils as the calf, kicking and shrieking, tried to get away.

When the roundup was finished, the foreman assigned us back on the plank-setting job. One day, the driver quit a little early and told us to wait for the truck, which would be there in a half hour. We waited around for a while and got bored, so we started cutting up and horsing around. Cal and I were doing running somersaults on a grassy area—one of us crouching down on all fours while the other took a run and somersaulted over him, trying to land on his feet but usually landing on our butts in the grass.

Old Man Gary drove up just as I was doing a somersault. He jumped out of his pickup truck, ran over to me, shoved his finger in my face, and said, "You're fired. I hired you to work—not to play. Come up to my office, and I will pay you off."

Cal and I rode in the back of Mr. Gary's truck to his office.

While Cal waited outside, Old Man Gary said, "Sit down, and I will get your pay and you can get off my ranch."

I sat in the chair while he went to his safe to get the money. Internally, I digested the unfairness that he had just perpetrated by not finding out that we were done for the day and were waiting for the truck to pick us up, but I kept my mouth shut.

Cal stuck his head in the door, getting Old Man Gary's attention. "What do you want?"

Cal replied, "You can let me go, too. I was doing the same things as Jerry and—"

Old Man Gary cut him off and said, "Cal, your dad worked here for several years before he drowned. He was a good man, and I will not fire his son or let him quit for no good reason."

Mr. Gary finished his speech, frowned at me, and counted out the money for our wages. It was the end of the week and was payday. He put the bills and change in two stacks on his desk in front of me. I picked them up, handed Cal his pay, and stuffed mine in my pocket. Cal and I silently moved to leave as Old Man Gary's eyes followed us with a bemused expression.

"Damned kids," he murmured.

This was my first unjustified firing, but not my last.

Cal and I had enjoyed being together on the ranch, and the hard work we shared, but we looked forward to going back to Klamath Falls, Cal for the weekend and me for an undetermined length of time. We collected our clothes from the bunkhouse and, not bothering to change into them, hitched a ride with one of the ranch hands to Klamath Falls.

Cal would return to work at the ranch on Monday, and I would be trying to find another job. It was no use crying in your beer.

Pelican City

On August 30, 1941, Mom married a man she had been going out with for some time. His name was Earl Muskopf. We moved to Pelican City—three miles north of Klamath Falls. Pelican City was a small Saw Mill Company town, and the supervisory and management employees rented company houses from the company.

Muskopf worked as the first shift supervisor of the sawmill. His father was the sawmill superintendent. Earl and his parents both lived in separate company houses on company property, which were located a hundred yards across the road from the sawmill.

Earl Muskopf was of Russian descent. His thin hair was slicked down on his head, and he had a strong build. He was authoritarian by nature, which would be the basis for disagreements, harassment, and violence with Mom, Perry, and me during their marriage.

He was a stingy bastard and a pilferer of electricity. He put together a jumper cable to divert the incoming electricity around the house's electric meter, circumventing the meter and getting free electricity, which he hooked up each night and removed each morning.

Mom worked hard making nutritious meals each night with meat, potatoes, a vegetable, a salad on a salad plate, and often dessert. She took special pains to set the table correctly with a clean tablecloth, napkins, and table knives, forks, and spoons in their proper places and salad on the left of the dinner plate. It was a lot of extra work for her, but she wanted all of us to enjoy a nice meal in an appetizing environment, in addition to practicing the rules of etiquette that she had taught us.

Mom organized our dinnertime chores. I chopped the wood and stacked it on the back porch for the kitchen stove, and Perry washed, dried, and put away the dishes. Earl hung around the kitchen scowling and complaining.

Muskopf continually bitched at Mom. "You're wasting money on those goddamn boys of yours—treating them like kings and picking the last dime out of my pocket to feed them."

What he said was not true. Mom was still working part-time as a waitress and helping with the household expenses. Perry and I had jobs before or after school and sometimes on weekends to pay for our personal expenses. It did not make any sense that his last dime was anywhere other than in his own damned pocket—and if he had his way, it would stay there.

The House on Link River

I had just completed my first year at Klamath Union High School. It was a little past midnight, and I was bicycling my way home to Pelican City on a borrowed bike since someone had stolen my bike. It was Saturday morning, and I had been setting pins at the bowling alley since early Friday afternoon.

The full moon was a silver sphere surrounded by a halo formed from the moist air rising over the lake. Patches of thin clouds drifted slowly by, briefly shrouding the moonlight.

A mysterious force drew me to a two-story house that faced Klamath Lake to the north and Link River to the south. Cal Worley and I often rode our bicycles together and had ridden past this house several times in daylight. It was apparent to me that the house was empty of any human habitation.

Even though it was dark and late, I decided to take a short detour to look around the house—and maybe explore it. I have an inquisitive, adventurous nature that my Aunt Co had commented on more than once.

My inquisitive nature was responding to the pull of the house as if it had its own power separate from my conscious mind. The night was as still as if there were no living soul on earth; the birds were sleeping, and the moon was frozen in the night sky.

As I quietly placed my bike down by the house, the pull of the house was stronger than the gravitational force holding my feet to the ground. With an incipient fear in my gut, I moved toward a side door. My intent was not to steal anything, but merely to explore.

Oddly enough, the door was unlocked. I opened it a crack and stuck my head inside, nodding my head as if bobbing for an apple in a tub of water. It was dark inside, and I squeezed my eyes tightly shut until I could see fireworks inside my eyelids. When I opened my eyes and looked straight ahead, my peripheral vision began viewing my left and right sides. A few more seconds passed, and gradually I could see all around the shadowy hallway.

Rays of faint moonlight filtered through a window in a room with an open door down the hallway. The dim light provided a foggy view of a hallway leading to a stairway. I silently proceeded down the hallway and climbed the stairs, nervous about who— or worse, what—I might see. Something scuttled away in the dark—a rat? A startled bird? Or was it a bat?

The upstairs hallway had several doors along each side. The left side of the hallway faced the water, which was reflecting the moon at the front of the house, and the right side looked out on the dark, shadowy hill behind the house. One door near the end of the hall was partially opened, with moonlight flowing weakly into the hallway.

I grasped the doorknob of the door to my left. It was as cold as a corpse's hand, and I started to shiver with dread. Steeling my nerve, I turned the knob slowly and listened for any sign of human occupancy, but there was nothing. I slowly opened the door and stepped into an empty room lit only by thin streaks of moonlight.

As I stood in the middle of the room, strange things began to happen. Although it was a relatively warm spring morning, the temperature seemed to drop by the second. I felt a chill in my bones and became alarmed.

A layer of clouds passed in the sky, obscuring the moonlight, and the room went shadowy dark. I sensed a presence in the room; a nauseating odor filled my nostrils. I swung my body around and looked over my shoulder, but there was nothing there. I turned around and started to panic; the hair on the back of my head stood at attention.

I fled blindly out of the room, running down the stairs three at a time, almost stumbling and falling out the door. Jumping on my bike, I jammed the pedal to the metal, sped away, and arrived home ten minutes later.

I found out later that an old man who lived alone in the house had shot himself in the temple with a shotgun, splattering blood and shreds of his brain across the room.

On December 7, 1941, "A day of infamy," the Japanese bombed Pearl Harbor with devastating effect, and the United States declared war on Japan.

Perry joined the marine corps in November 1942, leaving me to protect Mom from Muskopf. There had been a number of squabbles, pushing matches, threats, slaps, and punches since they married—and things were escalating.

One evening, Mom and Earl came home from a bar, and I heard loud voices coming from their bedroom. Only a bathroom separated my bedroom from theirs.

When I heard a thump and Mom's scream, I ran to their door. It was unlocked, and I slammed it open. Mom was crying naked on the floor; the side of her face was red from an apparent slap or punch. Earl was naked by his side of the bed; the mass of hair on his chest and body reminded me of a gorilla.

Muskopf roared, "Get the hell out of here!"

I stood my ground, expecting to take a beating, and said in as firm a voice as I could muster, "I am not going anywhere as long as you are threatening my mother. If I have to, I will go get Uncle Kirk's shotgun, come back here, and shoot you in the ass!" I meant it with all of my heart and resolve. I think Muskopf believed it too.

Earl pulled on his pants and shirt as Mom was getting up and pulling on a housecoat. "I'm leaving. I am going to stay with Dad and Mom until we get this straightened out!" Earl picked up his shoes and socks, cinched his belt, and went next door to his parents' house.

Mom and Earl separated, and Earl filed for an annulment because Mom had only divorced Homer recently and not enough time had passed before her marriage to Earl. After the annulment on June 16, 1941, Mom bought a house in Klamath Falls, and she and I moved there.

Lake of the Woods

In the summer of 1943, I turned sixteen. One day, I ended up at the Lake of the Woods Resort. The resort was in a wilderness area in the Rogue River Mountains, thirty-six graveled miles west of Klamath Falls and forty-five miles south of Crater Lake. Time had limped along that summer like a cripple on a crutch.

Two fellows and I had been cruising around Klamath Falls with nothing to do and were in Moore Park talking about cars and girls. I had been thinking about driving up to the Lake of the Woods to spend some time and decided to go right away.

I told them of my decision and said, "If you guys want to go up to the lake and fool around there, get in. If you don't want to go, I will drop you off back in K Falls—it makes no difference to me."

I opened the passenger door of my 1930 Chevrolet and waited to hear their decision. They got up and lackadaisically got in the car.

I did not know Bill and Don very well; we had just sort of bumped into each other at the bowling alley a couple of weeks earlier and started talking. Don was the short, heavyset, slow-witted one and outweighed me by more than thirty pounds. Bill was thin and appeared to be smarter than Don was—or at least I thought so. We started out driving along the lower end of Klamath Lake and onto the gravel road to the Lake of the Woods.

We did not quite make it to the lake—at least not on the first shot.

I noticed that we were running on empty. The gas gauge needle was dead flat in the empty zone.

Why the heck did I not check the gas before I left? Damn!

The Chevy started sputtering and lurching and finally stopped. The last drop of gasoline had been consumed in the car's four cylinders. Unfortunately, we were dead in the road and were like roadkill ready for the picking by some carnivorous creature.

Fortunately, we were on a flat straight stretch of road, rather than on one of the hills or curves. A car speeding around a blind curve or over a hill could easily smash the car and us if we were in it. The afternoon sun would not set for four hours or so. None of us had a watch, so I estimated the time by the sun's position. Uncle Kirk taught me how to tell the time from the sun when we were hunting together, and it came in handy for times like this.

We were about seven miles from the lake, and there had not been any cars on the road for some time—perhaps because it was the middle of the week.

"Let's get out and start walking," I said. "It looks like we are going to have to hike to the lake."

Bill and Don started whining and bitching, and Bill said, "Let's wait here with the car—somebody will come."

Don said, "It's too far to walk. I'm going to stay right here. I'm not walking anywhere."

I replied agitatedly, "Well, you guys can stay here if you want, but I am heading out for the lake. I do not need any help to get the gas—I can get it myself. You guys just sit here on your asses and wait until I get back."

I retrieved my empty gas can from the back of the car and started striding briskly in the direction of the lake.

A couple of minutes later, I heard a holler, paused for a second, and looked back to see the two of them running to catch up to me. Don was yelling, "Hey, Jer. Slow down—we can't keep up."

I kept them fifty yards or so behind me, even though they kept yelling for me to slow down. I didn't want them around me—they were lazy slackers without any gumption.

Why did I ever agree to these two jackasses riding around with me? I should have come alone.

I slowed down and yelled, "Hurry up."

They slowly caught up, and we started walking together.

The traffic had been thin, and the only vehicles were loaded up. There was no room for three more passengers—or they just did not like the looks of three young men out in the middle of nowhere. I should have thought about that and left Bill and Don at the car. I probably would have had less trouble hitching a ride if I were alone, but I did not mind walking. In fact, I like to walk—and to run. I had been running all my life.

We made it by shank's mare to the resort in a little over two hours. The Lake of the Woods Resort consisted of a large log-cabin lodge with two dramatic fireplaces made of stone, guest rooms upstairs, two bars, and a restaurant. There was a boat dock with boats for rent, a general store with a gas pump outside, and a number of small guest cabins spread over an acre of forest.

Tall pine and fir trees and some smaller cedars surrounded the beautiful lake. It was always a satisfying and tranquil experience to come here, especially when there were few people around.

The woods were quiet—except for the wind's soft murmur in the tops of the tall trees, the clatter of jays, and the occasional woodpecker. Squirrels streaked across the pinecones and spiraled up the trunks of trees in their ritual chases. Stark white cumulous clouds floated lazily in a pale blue sky.

I went to the store to get my gas, leaving Don and Bill outside. Gas was twenty-four cents a gallon at the resort, but only twenty-one cents in Klamath Falls. I supposed that the difference was probably the cost of bringing the gas up the mountain.

It was wartime; gasoline rationing was in effect, and the Office of Price Administration made the rules and issued ration coupons for gas.

I got a three-gallon ration coupon every week for my car. It helped a lot when I was driving out to the ranches and farms trying to get work—or just fooling around.

I gave the disheveled man my last silver dollar and the three-gallon ration coupon. I said, "I ran out of gas down the road a few miles. I will just take one gallon now and pay for all three gallons. I'll come back and pick up the other two gallons later today."

He said, "That comes to seventy-two cents." He placed a quarter and three pennies change on the counter. He hocked his throat, spit a stream of phlegm into a can behind the counter, and added, "You better get back here today. I only hold those damn ration coupons for the day I get them."

His speech did not make much sense, but I was coming back for the other two gallons today and had paid for them, so there was no problem.

No cars came by, and we did not get lucky and hitch a ride at the resort. The walk back took another two and a half hours. Finally reaching my car, I poured most of the gas into the tank, saving some gas to prime the carburetor to start the engine. Sliding behind the steering wheel, I told Bill to remove the air filter and pour a small dribble of gas into the carburetor while I cranked the starter.

The Chevy fired up with only a few turns of the starter.

I looked up and jumped out of the car—the side of my car was on fire! The bastards, probably out of spite, had splashed the remaining gas on the side of my car, tossed a match, and lit it afire—all in fun, of course. I frantically threw handfuls of dirt from the road onto the fire and put it out.

I shouted, "You stinking low-down jerks nearly burned my car up. Are you guys nuts? I should boot both your asses out right now and leave your mangy butts right here on this road. Maybe you'd learn a little respect for a person's property!"

Somebody's going to get hurt, I thought. *I may have gone too far with these idiots—there are two of them and one of me. The odds are not favorable, and maybe I should just jump in my car, bug out, and leave them behind.*

Bill said, "Jer, we was just kidding around and being rambunctious. We didn't mean any harm. The fire just scorched the paint a little. We'll help you fix it when we get back. Don't leave us stranded here on this godforsaken road; it's going to get dark pretty soon."

Don leaned against the passenger door, as if he suspected what I was considering, and added, "We'll make her good as new, for sure—you can depend on that."

I thought I saw a shadow of a snicker on his face, but he immediately erased it.

After fuming a while, I decided to control my rage and gave them an unearned break.

I reluctantly replied, "Okay, get in, but if you give me any more crap, I'll darn well leave you on the road, and you can fend for yourselves." They were silent during the drive to the lake—like two mute jaybirds sitting on a telephone wire.

I parked my car by the gasoline pump and took my gas can to the general store, leaving them outside while I went to get the rest of the gas. The store was empty except for the same man behind the counter, but now he was a red-eyed drunk and mean-spirited.

"You ain't gitten no gas without you give me a gas ration stamp," he snarled.

I replied as calmly as I could muster, "I already gave you the three-gallon gas ration stamp earlier today and only took one gallon of the three gallons I had coming. I also gave you a dollar to pay for the three gallons of gas, and you gave me a quarter and three pennies in change. I stood right here on this very spot and told you that I would come back today for my other two gallons. What's wrong with you?"

I knew all right what was wrong with him. He had gone from drunk to stinking drunk in a few hours. His bloodshot eyes glared at me, and spittle ran down the side of his mouth as he spat out the next words. "You summabitch kid, you git outta my store, or I'll shore make you wish you had of!"

I stood my ground, since I had no choice. No gas meant not getting back to K Falls. I continued to state my case in a more heated way. "I have two dad-gummed gallons of gas coming, and you know darn well that—"

Out of the corner of my left eye, I saw a blur flashing toward my head. Everything happened lightning fast. The heavy end of a pool cue stick was traveling at a dizzying speed toward my left temple. It seemed to be in slow motion, like in a film. The angry, drunken man behind the counter was wielding a twenty-ounce pool cue, sawed off to a three-foot-long club that he had kept hidden under the counter.

In a fraction of an instant, I ducked my head to avoid the blow as the club collided above my left ear. Blood gushed from my lacerated scalp and ran down my white T-shirt. My right fist instinctively started a looping roundhouse swing to the face of my attacker. My clenched fist hit his jaw, left of the point of his chin, and sent him stumbling backward, tripping over a chair, landing on the floor, and banging his head against the back wall.

Lucky punch! I thought.

"Shit!" I exclaimed as I realized the severity of what had happened. The asshole was slumped against the back wall, but I could see that he was breathing. I walked behind the bar, picked up the pool cue club, and tossed it into the pine needles in front of the store.

My gas can was sitting beside the counter, and I carried it outside to the gasoline pump. I grasped the long lever on the side of the tall gas tank and pushed and pulled it back and forth to pump the gasoline up into the glass cylinder on top of the tank. I stopped pumping when the gas reached the two-gallon mark. Using the hose attached to the gas pump, I drained two gallons of gasoline into my gas can. After putting the gas in my car, I gruffly said to my passengers, "Get in the car if you're going. I'm leaving now!"

The mass of blood on my head and face drained down, soaking my T-shirt, and I was feeling woozy. I packed mud onto the gash in my scalp, and it stopped most of the bleeding.

Don and Bill wanted to know what had happened. I said, "Forget it—we're getting out of here." I accelerated the Chevy out of the resort, dust kicking up in a billowing cloud.

Bill said nervously, "Jer, you are not in such good shape. You can't drive down the mountain like that. You'll kill us all! Let me drive. Please!"

Adrenaline raced through my veins. I was still pissed at them for setting fire to my car.

Although having some empathy with Bill's apprehensions about me driving, I said, "I'm driving down the mountain, and I don't give a damn whether you two walk or ride. Get out now if you want to."

I lurched to a halt and gave them a couple of seconds to get out. When they did not, I sped off toward Klamath Falls, gravel from my tires splashing the sides of the road.

I drove with my left hand because my right hand was starting to swell and ache. When I needed to shift gears, Bill shifted the gearshift while I worked the clutch with my foot. It was awkward, but it worked.

It was getting dark, and I had to slow down to avoid hitting a deer or a stalled car on the road or running off the road on a curve and down the steep embankment into the rocks and trees below.

Luckily, the moon was out, but when the clouds floated in front of the moon, there was partial darkness, and the dim light from the Chevy's headlights barely lit the road ahead. My eyesight blurred off and on.

Approaching a curve, Bill screamed, "Look out, Jer. We're going over the side!"

The car's front wheel struck the berm, and we were close to going over the side.

I yanked the steering wheel sharply to the left and hit the accelerator hard. The rear wheels skidded sideways toward the drop-off; the rear right wheel churned into the berm, throwing off a thick spray of earth, and the car climbed back onto the road.

Although I was sixteen, I had been driving for more than a year and had practiced handling a car in rain or snow.

"Whew, that was a close one," I said and got no reply.

Bill and Don were as silent as two muzzled mice.

Maybe they should check their britches, I thought. *They probably crapped in them when the car's back wheel went over the side of the road.*

I felt better and said, "Okay, no problem, we'll be in K Falls in a half hour."

We were making good time, considering the circumstances. I pulled into Mom's driveway and told Bill and Don to find their own damn way home! I was not used to cussing much, but this had not been one of my best days.

Mom was aghast at the sight before her. In an alarmed voice, she asked, "What happened to you, Jerry? Lie down right now and let me see your head. Do not worry about getting the couch dirty. I can wash it. How in the world did this happen?"

I told her, in my most nonchalant, heroic manner, "Nothing much, Mom—a flying pool stick just collided with my head."

I did not mention my swelling right hand because I did not want to worry her anymore than she already was.

Dr. Head showed up a little while later. He looked carefully at my head and said. "Son, you have a nasty laceration there and a possible concussion. You need stitches to close this laceration. I do not have any Novocain in my bag—I guess I forgot to refill it when I left the office in a hurry to get here. I am going to have to do this the hard way."

I said, "That's okay—it won't make much difference. What is a concussion?"

He replied, "A concussion is a jarring injury to the brain, which can result in a disturbance to the cerebral function."

His laugh was soft and friendly as he said, "All right, young man, let's get to it."

After dousing my scalp with alcohol, he started stitching. I felt the curved stitching needle go through my scalp and heard the sound like the noise made by tearing or punching holes in canvas.

This is not going to be fun, I thought.

It was twice as bad as I had imagined, and I gritted my teeth and clenched my fists while I tried somewhat unsuccessfully to act calm and nonchalant.

After nine stitches, the wound was closed.

Dr. Head said, "Boy, it is all done. You will be as good as new in a week or so, but stay off your feet for the next few days. Come to my office in a week, and I will take the stitches out. It is very important that if you start getting any dizzy spells to call me right away! You should also try to sleep with your head raised a bit on a pillow for a few days."

He looked at my hand and manipulated it as I sucked my breath in with every movement.

He said, "Nothing broken in your hand. What did you hit with it—a telephone pole?" He laughed as if he had told a funny joke. "Put your hand in some cold water for a while, with ice, if you have some. You have a sprained hand; do not use your hand much for a few days or until it feels better. I have never seen such a brave boy," he said to Mom on his way out the door. "You can be proud of him, Mrs. Watson."

Little did he know! I would have yelled my head off and howled to the sky if Mom had not been there. Our family had never taken much to anybody in the family carrying on, complaining, or otherwise making a fool of themselves.

A night of tossing and turning finally ended at sunrise. My head was throbbing as if a concrete drill were working on my skull, and my hand was sore as heck. Carefully, I swung my feet down to the floor and placed them on the crocheted rug that Granny had made by hand before she died. Every time I looked at one of her rugs, I felt close to her.

After sitting for a while, I got up and walked across the room.

Mom came in and asked, "Jerry, are you sure you are all right? How is your head?"

She looked worried, but I knew that she needed to get herself ready for work.

"I'm just fine; don't fuss over me. Just a little bump on the head is all."

"All right, but remember that the doctor said to stay off your feet for a while." She left to get ready for the first of her two split shifts.

The second morning after I returned from the lake, I felt reasonably good—the dull throbbing of my head had diminished. The swelling in my hand had gone down, and I could use it.

I started thinking about going up to the lake and getting things straightened out with the guy who had clubbed me.

I found Mom in the kitchen having coffee before she had to leave for work.

"I think I will go up to the lake this morning. I have to get some things straightened out."

In one of the few times she ever raised her voice to me, she said, "No! You are not going up there because you will just get yourself in trouble! Remember what Granny always said, 'Leave sleeping dogs lay.' You're not in any condition to go anywhere."

I had never seen Mom so agitated. She was shaking, her hands trembled, and she wrapped her arms around her shoulders, like there was a chill in the air.

That was not to be the last of it.

I spent some more time thinking about going to the lake in spite of what she had said.

What was I going to do if I went there and found the drunken bastard? Hit the guy up aside his head with a pool cue? Smash him in the face again with my fist? The thoughts made me grin.

I was more angry than hurt. I thought of my brother and his buddies facing serious injury and suffering or death in the war against the Japs in the jungles of the Pacific Islands. My injury was a mere scratch compared with what was happening to the marines fighting for their lives.

My anger was for my attacker, and I wanted to get even. I think that he was probably only stunned from hitting his head against the wall. He probably was okay and was bragging about how he showed that damned kid who was trying to rob him.

Finally, I made my decision. I was going to the lake to settle things for once and for all!

Mom left for work, and I was promptly on my way—after checking to make darn sure that I had enough gas this time.

When I reached the lake, I went directly to the general store to look for the man who had clubbed me.

There were no customers in the store. The man I was looking for was behind the counter, but he looked different. He was clear-eyed, neatly dressed, and clean-shaven. His hair was combed in place, and he had a purplish welt on his chin.

When he saw me enter the store, his face broke out into a broad smile. "I am sure glad you showed up here, son. I was hopin' that you would come by."

Puzzled, I stared at him and said nothing. I was so surprised by his metamorphosis that I did not know what to say. He seemed like an entirely different man from the one that I remembered.

"I am really pleased that you came back here, boy. One of the people at the lodge was telling people about seeing you with a bloody head and blood running down onto your shirt, and I heard about what I had done to you. I have felt terrible bad about what happened, and I thought I would never git a chance to tell you that I am real sorry for what I done. I was worried sick when I thought about the crack on the head that I gave you and wondered how you was."

I continued to stare at him in disbelief.

"Son, I've got to confess I drink too much, and when I drink too much, I get mean and ugly and sometimes crazy as a cockeyed jaybird. I've got no friends anymore because they gave up on me, same as my wife did five years ago. My own kids won't talk to me 'cause of the beatings I gave them when I got drunk—that was before they got big enough to fight me back."

He looked me in the eye and said, "How is your head? I sure hope it's all right."

"Fair to middling, I guess. I expect I will live."

"That's good—I'm glad to hear it. I don't expect you are very fond of me after gitten' hit on the head and all, but I am truly sorry. I would be much obliged if we could shake hands and let bygones be bygones. I am going to beat this 'devil rum' and be a sober man—even if it kills me."

I thought for a short time about what he said, took a deep breath, let it out slowly, and finally stuck out my hand. He grasped my damaged hand like a lifeline and beamed as we shook hands.

Massaging my bad hand, I said, "I appreciate you telling me how you feel about what happened. I came up here today to settle things with you—one way or another—but I do not bear a grudge against you anymore."

"I understand. Was me. I'd hope to feel the same way."

"Good-bye. And good luck on the booze."

As I turned to go, he said, "Son?"

I turned my head to hear what he was going to say.

"You got one hell of a punch, kid!"

It brought a small grin to my face. I gave a farewell wave over my shoulder and headed for the door.

I never mentioned my visit to the lake to Mom. Let sleeping dogs lay, as Granny always liked to say.

On my trip back home, I thought about the old, sorry-ass drunk and his desire to repent and give up the curse of alcohol that had wrecked not only his own life, but also the lives of his innocent wife and children—and no doubt others as well.

I had been drinking alcohol since I was ten years old, whenever I could get it: beer, wine, or liquor.

Am I going to end up an angry, crazy, abusive drunk, like this sorry old man at the Lake of the Woods?

US Navy

The young men who landed on the beaches of Normandy seemed like our older brothers on the gray, overcast morning of June 6, 1944. I saw the faces of the American soldiers in England preparing for the invasion of Europe on the *Movietone News* at the Tower Theater in Klamath Falls. Some of the men were only a couple of years older than I was.

In June 1944, I finished my junior year of high school and turned seventeen on July 29. I tried to keep up with the war as best I could, but there were events that no one—or nearly no one—knew about.

Japan, in a sneak attack, bombed Pearl Harbor on December 7, 1941, and began attacks on the Philippines the same day. President Franklin Roosevelt declared war on Japan. With Japan in a war against the United States, Germany declared war on the United States, and President Roosevelt reciprocated and declared war on Germany and Italy, Germany's ally.

Perry was in the middle of the war in the Pacific. He fought the Japanese in Bougainville, Peleliu, and other places as the war continued. I hoped that Mom would receive another V-mail letter from him so we would know where he had been. We knew that he could not tell us where he was while he was still in action.

I decided to join the Navy. Cal Worley and another close friend, Bob Kennedy, and I, and several others, including Lloyd Chidester, and an older guy, George Greenwood, whom we did not know, wanted to sign up for the US Navy Pilot School.

We had to wait for acceptance. In September, I began my senior year at Klamath Union High School, not expecting to finish the term. As it turned out, I did not finish the second semester and did not graduate high school. Instead, I enlisted in the US Naval Reserve for the duration of the war.

In December, we finally received our orders to report to Seattle for mental and physical exams for acceptance into naval pilot training. After my second trip on a train, I spent three days, mainly waiting to complete our physical exams, which we finally did.

All of us but one failed the physical exams for one reason or another, but it looked to us like they had too many candidates for pilot training and were using every pretext to flunk us—all but the college boy. We left dejected and disappointed, our hopes dashed.

I wanted with all my being to be a Navy pilot; however, because I had not yet finished my senior year in high school and had no college, that dream was not to be.

We left Seattle, stayed over in Portland, and showed up at the Portland Navy Recruiting Office the next morning. On January 26, 1945, we enlisted in the US Naval Reserve. I still wanted to fly, so I applied for air crewman and hoped to go to Naval Air Gunnery School and have a chance at an aerial machine-gunner position.

We caught the train the next morning and returned to Klamath Falls.

Thirty days later, we received orders to report to boot camp at the Naval Training Station in San Diego. We were excited about our future in the Navy and boarded the Southern Pacific train the next Monday for the trip. Mom and Beth, a girl I knew, were at the railroad station to see us off, along with some other parents and friends.

Our heads were sticking out of the train's windows, and we were happily waving good-bye, but you would have thought that we were on our way to a firing squad, the way the women and girls carried on. They were blubbering, sniffling, and red-eyed, with tears running down their cheeks—except for Mom. She was dead quiet, a wan smile on her face, slowly waving a white lace hanky in farewell.

I figured that my leaving for boot camp reminded her that Perry was still in harm's way in the middle of the Pacific and might not make it home at all. Now that there were two of us to worry about, another framed blue star would go in her window for all to see her pride in having both her sons in the military. She hoped that neither—and certainly not both—of the blue stars would turn to gold.

Jack Watson

On the first day at boot camp, we scurried through a gauntlet of shots in both arms by flanks of corpsmen on either side, using us for dartboards for their long, mean-looking hypodermic needles as we passed by in lockstep. We got our mouths and teeth inspected, did the bend-over, and underwent the grit-our-teeth procedure and the turn-your-head-and-cough drill, while the doctor gently supported our testicles in his cold, gloved hand.

We quickly learned to roll, wrap, tie, and store all of our worldly possessions in a seabag and carried it on our shoulder when we moved from place to place. We marched to our barrack, which would be our home for the next nine weeks.

We looked like a gaggle of geese trying out for marching drill and spent hours marching back and forth in attempted formations and close-order drills, stumbling over the other boots until we were physically exhausted.

The drill instructor called out the cadence and the drill. "Stand at ease. Attention. Forward march. Your left, your left, your left right left. Right face, left face, about face." After a while, it became: "Stan' at ease. Ten-shun, for'd harch', yer lef, yer lef, yer lef rye lef. Rat faze, lef faze, abot faze." We picked up the lingo of the DI's guttural utterances, and after a while, they started to sound normal.

Several of us from K Falls began messing up in formation, trying to trip each other while marching, which was very disruptive to the DI, and he applied appropriate corporal punishment on the spot.

He yelled at the perpetrator, "Get out here and hit the deck! Give me twenty-five," and the sorry-assed boot flopped to the ground on his hands and toes and did twenty-five push-ups. The rest of the company marched away grinning as the boot finished his push-ups and ran to catch up with the formation.

After evening chow, we showered, cleaned up the barracks, organized and stored our gear, lined up for inspection, and finally were allowed to climb into our bunks. We called them racks or sacks, or fart sacks.

132

A bugle playing "Taps" piped into the barrack's loudspeakers announced lights out at 21:30 hours. The boots in their sacks were yelling back and forth to each other to let off steam. Many of the boots were from Louisiana; a few were from other states, and the remaining five or six of us were from Oregon.

The Louisianans had a favorite word that I had not heard before, and they used it about three or four times in every sentence that they hollered out in the darkness. Mutha f--ka this! And mutha f--ka that! And on and on! I wished that they would stop their bullshit hollering back and forth; I wanted to get some shut-eye.

The drill instructor swung his office-sleeping room door open at the end of the hall, and the door hit the wall with a resounding crash. He switched on the lights and yelled to the startled recruits trying to form a line and make an effort to stand at attention, "You keep your mouths shut. Reveille is at 05:30 hours, and if any of you don't know what time that is, just sleep in in the morning and enjoy yourselves in the brig, while the rest of us go about learning to be sailors."

As he started to leave the room, he swung around, faced all of us, and said loudly so that every boot in the barracks heard his words loud and clear, "The next time I hear the words mutha f--ka, the guilty party will do push-ups until he drops on his face and an extra two hours marching on the gridiron. If you don't tell me who the guilty party is, all of you will be out there all night if necessary. Is that clear?"

All of the boots gave a loud, "Yes, sir!"

The following day, we took our physical strength and stamina tests, rope climbs, running, pull-ups, push-ups, and other exercises, including sit-ups. We did the sit-ups on our backs, knees up and hands clasped behind our neck, with a fellow boot holding our feet while we did full body sit-ups, elbows touching opposite knees in each sequence. My performance on most of the tests was pretty good, but I was determined to do my very best on sit-ups. I did over two hundred sit-ups, which turned out to be a record for our platoon.

The next day on the gridiron, my stomach muscles were contracted into a tight fist. I could not straighten up and had to march bent over at a forty-five-degree angle like a large pretzel. I could not straighten up—even a little—without excruciating effort.

The drill instructor pulled me out of formation and snarled, "Watson! Get with the drill; straighten up and fly right—you are marching like an old man. Now give me twenty-five." He meant twenty-five push-ups, the usual penalty for marching offenses. I tried to assume the push-up position on the ground, but my stomach muscles prevented me from straightening my body for the proper stance.

"What in the hell is wrong with you, Watson?" Then he remembered the sit-ups I had done and yelled, "Get up and get the hell back in formation!"

Of all the adversaries I have had, the worst adversary was myself. What was wrong with me? Doing all those sit-ups and paying dearly for them today—what was the point? I guess I just wanted to prove what I could do.

There were two Watsons in our platoon: an old guy and me. He must have been twenty-three or twenty-four, while I was only seventeen. He was a college graduate and felt and acted as if he were privileged and deserved to be treated as a superior person—even though he was a boot just like the rest of us.

The other Watson placed below me in the battery of intelligence tests that we had to take so that the Navy could decide what jobs we might be best suited to perform. I was fortunate to place near the top of the list, while his name was half a dozen names lower. He made a point of repeatedly informing me that he was smarter and had a college degree and I was a dumbass kid who probably cheated to get my score on the intelligence tests.

This did not sit well with me, but I ignored him. I did not want to start any trouble, particularly after having had the military rules of conduct and the consequences of misconduct read aloud to us.

The drill instructor posted a list of ratings on the bulletin board that showed the openings for the various specialties available to our company. Many of the jobs required some specialized training, such as aviation machinist mate, aviation electrician, aviation ordnance, and a few others. The best job on the list, some thought, including me, was aviation ordnance, but there were only three slots open, and I was lucky to get one of them. I was determined to get a job that would put me close to aircraft, with the possibility of going to aerial gunner school.

The other Watson failed the cut and was given a less desirable slot. I do not remember what it was, but I knew he was pissed. The next day, he caught up with me on a break and said, "You are a jerk, Watson. People get thrown down ladders for your kind of bullshit."

We were alone, and I replied, "What's your problem?"

He said, "You stole my position in aviation ordnance, and I am going to get even. One of these days, you are going to fall down a ladder or stairway—an accident, of course."

I was seething, but I turned around and went on my way. That night, I tossed and turned in my sack, thinking about the encounter. It made me angry, and I made up my mind to fight if his shit kept on. I remembered the code of military conduct and possible consequences, especially Leavenworth. I had never thrown the first punch in a fight, except in the boxing ring, but thought this may have to be the exception.

A couple of days later, returning early from noon chow to the empty barrack, I ascended the stairs to the second floor. Nearing the top, I looked up and saw the other Watson standing at the top of the stairs—with hands on his hips and a scowl on his face—blocking my way. He apparently had been waiting for me, and I knew what was coming.

I vividly remembered his threat.

My first instinct was to turn around, go back down the stairs, and avoid a confrontation and the serious problems a fight could cause. Instead, a surge of adrenaline suffused my head like a blowtorch on bare skin, and I lunged to the top of the stairs. We were about four feet apart—almost fighting distance.

He moved back several feet, his hands off his hips and in front of him, slightly above his waist, but not yet in a fighting stance. His eyes were wide, and although he was thirty pounds heavier and a couple of inches taller than I was, he looked startled and flustered at my unexpected, belligerent move toward him.

I started moving slowly around him to get my back away from the stairs; that would give me a maneuvering advantage to throw a sucker punch to his jaw if it came to that. Neither of us said a word for a long, drawn-out minute.

Regaining his composure, he said, "Who do you think you are—stealing my slot in aviation ordnance?"

My inner rage was building. I wanted to punch this sonofabitch right here, right now, but I said nothing; my eyes stared into his. I was reluctant to start the fight since I knew that one of us could be seriously hurt or even killed by knocking the other down the stairs, where he could strike his head on the hard floor surface and incur a fatal concussion or a broken neck.

One way or another, no matter the consequences, once it started, I knew that I would be in deep shit. I usually am slow to anger, but I can be irrational when angered and stupid enough not to back down.

Becoming more confident from my silence, he said, "You know something? People are always falling down ladders in the navy—accidents happen. Maybe you are going to fall down this one—or maybe I will throw you down!"

A rage exploded in my head, but I said slowly, "You are not throwing anybody down any ladder! Back off. Now! *Or I am going to rip your goddamned face off and shove it down your f_ _ king throat.*" I continued to glare at him, letting my words sink into his stupid head. I was enraged and almost out of control!

He looked startled, as if I had just slapped him on the face, and then he went quiet, perhaps thinking over his alternatives. After a few moments of shifting his eyes around as if looking for assistance, without a word, he turned his eyes, then his feet, and finally his body, and carefully moved to the ladder, giving me as much berth as the space allowed, and went down the stairs and out of the barrack.

I stood alone contemplating what had just transpired, the adrenaline rush slowly abating. I felt like a spectator to a slow-motion accident scene in a nightmare. The vehicle in the narrowly averted accident had bars on its windows and a sign painted on the side: "Leavenworth Prison."

I started to calm down and chuckled as I thought, *Going to rip your goddamned face off? Shove it down your f_ _king throat? Where did you come up with that shit, Watson? You are going to get your skinny butt kicked hard one of these days.*

There was no liberty (permission to leave the base) for the first three weeks of boot camp, and then we got liberty every weekend if we did not have duty or were confined to barracks for some transgression. We drank beer, walked the boardwalk, and visited the burlesque shows. My favorite show was an act by a virtually nude, beautiful redhead doing the grinds to the song "I'm Beginning to See the Light." Some of us, including me, went back to see her several times when we had liberty.

We also saw a new attraction, "Candy Colt and her Twin .45's." She was a platinum blonde and danced almost nude, with plastic propellers stuck on her huge boobs that her bodily gyrations caused to spin. For some inexplicable reason, I cannot remember the background music.

One night, when we got an overnight liberty, Cal, Bob, another guy from K Falls, and I had our picture taken in front of the Owl Bar. We got plastered and spent the night sleeping on the beach. I still have the picture of us at the Owl Bar. One could title it: "Youth and Its Goofiness."

Over the next eight weeks, we marched, ran, navigated obstacle courses in the mud, climbed towers, shot on the firing range, learned how to survive in the ocean by turning our trousers into floatation devices, and endured a simulated assault on a barbed-wired beach from landing boats, with nonlethal firing over our heads and explosive charges detonating around us. Pretty exciting, but I am not sure it would be a first choice for my day job.

We also entered into simulated ship fires and doused the flames with high-pressure water hoses that thrashed around like pythons trying to get loose from the fire crew's grip.

The instructor showed us how to don our gas masks properly, and we walked single file through a room full of tear gas. To give us a real demonstration, the instructor commanded us to remove our gas masks and walk to the exit. As we straggled out of the tear-gassed room, tears ran down our faces, and we gasped for fresh air.

April 12, 1945—President Roosevelt Is Dead

Several of my buddies and I were in the mess hall drinking coffee from thick ceramic mugs. The loudspeaker started squawking, "Now hear this."

We all dropped our conversations and listened. "President Franklin Delano Roosevelt died today of a cerebral hemorrhage at his home in Warm Springs, Georgia. Vice President Harry S. Truman is now the president of the United States."

The loudspeaker repeated the message, and then there was the mournful sound of a bugle playing "Taps." We stood at attention until the bugle finished. We looked at each other with the same question on our faces: Who is Harry Truman? We were soon to find out. It turned out he was a decisive leader—just what America needed to win the war.

At the end of our training, we got a ten-day leave, and I went to Klamath Falls and spent some time with Beth, the girl who lived there. She was a nice girl, but it was nothing serious. We heard President Truman's speech to the nation at her house, and we were impressed with Truman as a tough, plainspoken man.

Homer Reappears

Homer found Mom and me at Aunt Co's house while I was visiting during my leave. I was sitting on a couch on the far side of the room when Mom opened the door. She was very surprised, but let him in. He was wearing dark slacks and a white shirt without a tie and was slim and tallish. His graying hair was cut short, his teeth yellowed, and his face a weathered bronze.

Mom was very distant with him, but she was polite. I shook his hand and left the talking to Mom and Aunt Co. Homer told them of his going back down to Mexico and Central America since his trips there in 1938, but did not give them a reason for his trips. He just said that it was something for the government.

Before he left, he told me that he was going to be in town for a while and maybe we could talk a little. He was working as a fry cook at the Tip Top Café at the top of the highway going north out of town. I had mixed feelings about seeing my father after almost eight years, but after thinking about it, decided to see him anyway.

I dropped in at the café the next morning, and he fried a hamburger for me. There were several other patrons, so he didn't have a chance to talk much. Before I left, we agreed to meet at Molatores the next day for a couple of beers and a game of pool.

As I left, I had mixed feelings between a feeling of betrayal of Mom and being friendly toward Homer and wanting to know more about him. I was leaning toward Mom.

We met at Molatores the next day and had a couple beers as he ran the pool table. As he took aim at the last ball on the table, the eight ball, I suddenly became incensed. All the pain of his abandonment, the years of wondering, and the pent-up anger over his rejection was overwhelming. I told him, "You sonofabitch, you left Mom to take care of Perry and me when we were just kids and ran off like a coward. *You are a goddamned sonofabitch, and I never want to see you again!*"

He slowly looked up from the pool table and replied softly, "Jerry, things are not always as they seem. There are always two stories to tell, and you have not heard mine."

I was becoming more agitated and replied, "I don't give a damn what your story is. I do not want to see you or hear from you again, you sonofabitch."

These words would come back to haunt me later when I really did want to know about him and his life and whether he loved me and wanted me to be successful, instead of the emptiness of not knowing.

I turned on my heel and headed for the door, slapping the cue stick down on a pool table as I passed by. Out of the corner of my eye, I could see him standing there, an immobile statue holding a cue stick, his eyes looking in my direction ... into the future.

I never saw him again.

Later, I tried to find Homer, but had no luck.

The day after I returned to Naval Training Station, we lined up and got our orders to depart to our previously assigned ships or bases. Cal's orders were to Tokyo, and my orders were Aviation Ordnance School—the Naval Air Technical Training Center in Norman, Oklahoma.

The next morning about thirty of us loaded our seabags and were bused to the railroad station and loaded onto a train, which reminded me of my train trip from Colorado Springs to Oregon, a lifetime ago.

The 1,300-mile trip from San Diego to Norman took three and a half days, including the stopover in Albuquerque.

Arriving in Oklahoma City in the evening, we loaded ourselves and our seabags onto the "Toonerville Trolley." The trolley took us on a fifteen-mile ride to the training center. We got used to the trolley and used it to get to "Okie City" when we had weekend liberty.

In the next weeks, our heads were crammed with information and knowledge that would equip us to perform our aviation ordnance duties to help win the war.

We began our indoctrination in both the classroom and hands-on sessions and gained a familiarity with the workings, maintenance, and malfunctions of a wide range of weapons and ordnance.

I was happy to meet Rollie Berry, the brother of Bill Berry, whom I chummed around with in Klamath Falls. He was in another aviation school on the base. Rollie and I became fast friends and later went to Oregon State College together. While there, we hoed strawberries on weekends in the large strawberry fields outside of Corvallis. We laughed at the dual interpretation of strawberry hoers versus strawberry whores. We also flew together when we obtained our pilot licenses, boxed each other in the ring, and later on socialized as couples after each of us had married.

Unfortunately, an incident in Oklahoma City during one of our liberties was not conducive to strengthening our relationship, but he showed a resiliency and good humor that sustained and strengthened our friendship.

Four of us were on a thirty-six-hour liberty and checked into the Cadillac Hotel in Okie City. We were drinking beer, getting drunk, and dropping things out of the second-story window, including empty beer bottles and a large pitcher of water.

Rollie was taking a bath. The three of us got plastered and decided to pull a prank on Rollie. We snatched him out of the bathtub naked and pushed him out the door bare-assed naked into the hotel hallway and locked the door. We stood unsteadily inside the door on chairs to look into the hallway through the small transom window above the door to see what happened. Rollie was pounding on the door and yelling for us to open the door. But we didn't.

We heard the elevator come to our floor and the door start to open. Rollie heard it too and scurried to one of the recessed doorways across the hallway, trying to make himself invisible by backing into a doorway, flattening himself against the door, and trying to hide his genitalia with his hands. A man in a suit and tie and an expensively dressed woman exited the elevator and started walking down the hallway in Rollie's direction.

We were guzzling beer, laughing uproariously, and elbowing each other to shush. The couple walked by Rollie, who was standing in the doorway, petrified, with his eyes tightly closed, his back pressed solidly against the door's woodwork.

The couple glanced casually in his direction, sized up the situation, and continued on down the hall. Their attitude was as if a naked man plastered to a recessed door were a usual sight—at least for the Cadillac Hotel.

We now had a problem on our hands. Rollie was pretty pissed. How would we get him back into the room with a truce? Circumstances provided the opportunity. The elevator stopped again at our floor, and we rushed out and pulled Rollie into the room, profusely expressing our apologies. He was so relieved to be back in the room that he grudgingly murmured an acceptance of our apologies. Rollie was a great guy!

I spent my final two weeks in Airborne Radar School, where we learned the functions of radar and its use aboard ship and on aircraft. Radar had some distinct advantages—for one, it could see in the dark.

The End of World War II

A sailor was raffling off a bottle of Jack Daniel's in the barracks. Everybody gathered around watching or participating in the raffle. Suddenly, the loudspeaker abruptly announced, "Now hear this! Now hear this. The United States, on August 6, 1945, dropped an atomic bomb—the most powerful bomb in the world—on Hiroshima, Japan! Stand by—more information to follow."

There was a momentary silence as we looked at each other, digesting the news, and then broke out in a roar of cheers. The war was over! By God, we won! The sailor who was raffling off the bottle of Jack Daniel's removed the cap and passed the bottle of whiskey around for everyone to have a celebratory gulp. When the bottle was empty, he reached into his bag and passed a second bottle around.

However, the war was not over.

Three days later, a second Japanese city, Nagasaki, was obliterated by a second atomic bomb. We got news that the bombs dropped on Hiroshima and Nagasaki, Japan, were unlike any bomb ever made. The bomb dropped on Hiroshima had a power equivalent to 20,000 tons of TNT. Each bomb was thousands of times more powerful than any other bomb in existence!

All of us wondered when the war would be over. The Japanese knew that we could obliterate every city in their country. Why were they waiting? Were they nuts?

About three and a half weeks later, on September 2, 1945, the Japanese surrendered to General MacArthur and the Allies on board the USS *Missouri*. The Germans had already signed two surrenders, one to America and one to Russia.

World War II was officially over.

The Emperor Hirohito addressed the people of Japan for the first time, announcing Japan's surrender over the radio, saying they should "bear the unbearable and endure the unendurable."

Sure, I thought. *What about the Bataan Death March, the rape of Nanking, Pearl Harbor, and the thousands of atrocities perpetuated in whatever country the Japanese conquered and occupied—as well as the ghastly medical experiments on American and Allied prisoners of war?*

Thirty-five years later, as president and CEO of Grove Valve and Regulator, I visited Hiroshima as a guest of our Japanese Grove Valve licensee. After the tour of the Hiroshima site, my host asked me to sign a visitor book. My first thought was to write, "You should never have bombed Pearl Harbor," but considering the tension that this would cause with an important business associate, I didn't. However, I now wish that I had.

Sand Point

We received our orders to report to various aviation installations. My orders called for me to report to Sand Point Naval Air Station, outside of Seattle. Rollie's assignment was to Aerial Gunnery School in Jacksonville. The lucky guy ended up at North Island Naval Air Station near San Diego.

I traveled to Seattle on the train with several aviation-rated sailors and took a military bus to the air station.

Arriving at the gates, we showed our papers to the marine guard, who gave each of us the number of the barrack where we would bunk, along with directions. The Ordnance Office at the Sand Point Naval Air Station is in a Quonset hut called the "Ordnance Shack," where the paperwork for the inventory scheduling and ordering and personnel functions was performed. It sat diagonally across the street from the Admiral's Headquarters, a large, two-story brick building.

Since the war was over, there was not much ordnance work to do around the base. I drove an ordnance truck with a boom on the back and moved munitions around to various warehouses away from the populated area of the base, but this did not last long.

For some unknown reason, maybe just to spend their time, of which they had plenty, or just for fun, the two petty officers who supervised our company seemed to hate my guts—probably because I didn't kowtow to them. They always found ways to put me on a shit detail, cleaning urinals and toilets or doing scullery duty in the mess hall. They came up to my bunk at night, found something out of place—or at least not where they wanted it to be—and gave me additional work to do or cancelled my liberty. Pricks!

I did not mind the shit work; work is work as far as I am concerned, and I completed every job no matter how insignificant or demeaning. I would not let them get my goat and cause me to do something rash that would put me in the brig for five years.

However, I felt deep in my bones that there would eventually be a showdown with the asshole petty officers. I believed that they were looking for a showdown with their malevolent attitude toward me—probably because they could not break my spirit.

I spent what free time I had in the gymnasium on the speed bag to improve my hand-and-eye speed and doing heavy punching on the large punching bag, practicing hard shots to get myself in shape for a showdown with the petty officers. I knew that it was going to come to a head, and I was preparing myself to meet whatever was going to happen.

One afternoon, the petty officers confronted me in front of the ordnance shack. After some derogatory words, one of the petty officers grabbed me from behind, entrapping my arms to my sides, where I could not move them, while the other petty officer positioned himself in front of me to take a swing at me.

I threw my head back hard and smashed the nose of the petty officer behind me. As he released his hold, I swung a hard left hook at the other petty officer, catching him solidly on the jaw. He stumbled backward and plopped down to the pavement on his ass.

I stood my ground, glancing up to the admiral's offices to see if there were any witnesses. I thought I saw a woman looking at the scene from one of the windows, but I could have been mistaken.

The petty officer who had been behind me pressed a handkerchief to his nose to stanch the flow of blood dripping down on his shirtfront, while the other petty officer squatted down on his haunches with his head propped up with his arms on his knees.

A cold chill ran up my spine as I thought, *It looks like I am going to spend the next five years in a cell in the brig in Leavenworth Penitentiary and get a dishonorable discharge!*

Instead, a couple of weeks later, I received orders to report to the Bremerton Naval Base for discharge. I rode the ferry to Bremerton, went through all the discharge procedures, and was honorably discharged from the Naval Reserve on May 21, 1946.

I wondered whether the petty officers had orchestrated my discharge to save their asses from a court-martial. The woman looking out of the second-story window may have seen the entire thing.

A Jar of Money

The day after I received my "Ruptured Duck" discharge certificate, I arrived home. The ferry ride from Seattle to Bremerton and back was the only time I was on a ship while in the Navy. Some blue-water sailor!

Mom and I discussed what I wanted to do with my life. I told her that I really wanted to go to college. This was surprising to her since the last and only family member to graduate from college was my great-great-grandfather on my mother's side, who was a Union veterinarian in the Civil War.

I said, "I found out in the Navy that education is the way to get ahead. Most of the petty officers I had over me were no smarter than I was, but they had the authority to make me jump through hoops on their command—and they got their jobs because they were more educated than me."

I told her that I had borrowed the *Mechanical Engineer's Handbook, Fourth Edition* and studied most of the 2,274 pages of small print at night in the barrack.

"The book was fascinating and covered such things as logarithms and slide rules, hydraulics and measuring flow, how to make steel and other metals and their metallurgy, and tons of other stuff, and I've decided that I want to become an engineer."

Mom said, "Jerry, your grandmother and I always told you kids that you could be anything you want to be—if you set your mind to it, put in the effort, and stick with it."

"Well, I believe it now," I replied, "and I am going to show everybody that I can make it—no matter what."

Mom asked, "Then what is stopping you from going to college?"

I answered, "I have decided that I want to go to Oregon State College at Corvallis, but before I go up there to enroll, I need to work a few months to get myself set up financially, until I can get help from the GI Bill. The GI Bill will pay for my tuition, books, and school supplies—plus some money to live on for a while. I just have to get there and get settled on my own until the GI Bill checks start coming."

Mom said, "Jerry, go sit down on the rug in the living room. I want to show you something."

I went into the living room and sat. She returned with a large glass jar with a screw top and set it in front of me.

She said, "Jerry, the Navy has been sending me a check each month for family support—that you signed up for and they took out of your pay—and I have been saving it in this jar. I cashed each month's fifteen-dollar check and put the money in the jar. When I had to use some money from the jar for an emergency, I replaced most of it from my tips. I am sorry, but I had to use a little of the money."

"Mom, you did not have to give me the money—the money was for you."

"Nothing is worthwhile unless you earn it yourself. This is your money—not mine. You are the one who earned it."

She unscrewed the top of the jar and emptied the bills and change into a pile on the rug. We counted it together: over a hundred and fifty dollars in bills and coins!

I was speechless, but elated over this unexpected windfall.

I said excitedly, "Now I can start college! Thanks, Mom. This is great. I really appreciate it."

She nodded with a bright smile. "You earned it; I just saved it for you. And now you will put it to good use!"

Oregon State College

My school load and sideline work at OSC was almost overwhelming: seventeen credit hours of courses as well as working several jobs, "flunkying" in the cafeteria, serving food, washing dishes, and carrying out garbage.

In the early mornings, I swept and mopped floors in the classrooms, and I cleaned toilets and urinals. In the evenings, I drove a taxicab until midnight, studying under the dash light between the scarce twenty-five-cent fares.

However, I successfully completed my first year at Oregon State College and also won the 1947 Oregon State Middleweight Boxing Championship.

"Gee, I Have Never Seen a Dead Man Before"

While I was attending OSC, I spent the summers working in Klamath Falls and later in Corvallis after Jean and I married.

Once, I got a job in Klamath Falls over the summer as a laborer on the construction crew of a National Guard armory. My job was to move broken concrete slabs dumped over the armory wall by a man on a backhoe and to level the slabs to pour the concrete foundation.

There were several of us on the crew. Each time before the backhoe driver dumped a load of broken concrete slabs over the wall, he got off the backhoe, came inside the area in which we were working, made sure that we were aware that he was going to dump another load, and told us to keep clear of the area for our safety.

One day, I was bending over with a steel pry bar to move a broken slab into place when suddenly a load of broken concrete slabs came down on top of me. The backhoe driver, without notice to us, had dumped the load over the wall where I was working. Everything went black. Fortunately, all of the slabs had fallen in a pyramid, protecting my body. Only one slab struck my head, but it was enough.

I gradually became aware of two workers frantically moving the broken slabs away from my body. The backhoe driver was telling me that he was sorry; he was not thinking when he dumped the load over the wall.

A high school boy in the crew was straddling on top of me. He peered down at me and said to a friend, *"Gee, I have never seen a dead man before!"*

I heard him—and felt him sitting on me—opened my eyes, and said, "Get the f--k off me and get me the hell out from under here!"

I spent ten days in the hospital recuperating. I had a concussion, and it took eleven stitches to close my scalp wound. The nurse would not allow me to get up or go to the bathroom. Instead, she provided a bedpan for me.

Nevertheless, after a few days, I shuffled to the bathroom anyway when she was not around. I hate bedpans.

One day, I asked Liz, who worked at the same gas station as I did, if she would like to go swimming with a couple of friends. When she said yes, I was surprised and elated.

I drove Liz, Bob, and Cal out to the Lost River. It had a nice swimming place with flowing clear water. Liz wore a brief—for the times—two-piece bathing suit, and we swam in our shorts, which we always did, not having any swimming suits.

She was like a goddess with her shining blonde hair, her sexy figure, and her beautiful face. We had to stay submerged some of the time to hide the bulges in our shorts.

We had a fun afternoon swimming, eating sandwiches, and catching the sun's rays, and eventually returned to K Falls.

My second year at OSC went very well. I was going to classes and working before and after classes, as I had also done in my first year. No Delta Phis or fraternity parties; I lived in a men's dorm and ate my meals in the back room of the cafeteria, as did most of the other cafeteria workers.

My grades improved, and I enjoyed all of my classes—especially the hands-on metallurgy, metalworking, foundry, machine shop, and other industrial administration and industrial engineering courses.

Iceman

When I returned to K Falls the next summer, I got a job as a deliveryman for the Klamath Ice and Bottling Company. My job was to load several three-hundred-pound blocks of ice into the back of the truck and deliver ice in twenty-five and fifty-pound blocks to a regular route of customers.

Each three-hundred-pound slab of ice was scored to allow the iceman to easily split it apart with an ice pick to separate the large, three-hundred-pound block into smaller hundred-pound, fifty-pound, and twenty-five-pound chunks. The ice company supplied me with a truck and a pair of metal tongs and a leather protector, which I strapped over one shoulder and tied at the waist and used to carry a fifty-pound block of ice on my shoulder.

The job turned out to be full of surprises!

A front or side door was usually left open for the iceman. After a perfunctory knock on the door, the iceman entered, put

149

the block of ice in the icebox, picked up the money from the top of the icebox, and left.

One day when I was delivering ice to a house, my bladder was full, and I needed desperately to go to the bathroom. No one was there so I stepped into a small bathroom off the large kitchen. When I came out, a very attractive, sexy young woman was making a sandwich at the kitchen counter—completely naked!

Surprisingly, when she noticed me, she was not alarmed at my presence. She said, "Would you like a sandwich?"

I fumbled around for an answer, trying unsuccessfully not to look at her naked body, and replied, "No, thank you. I am sorry for barging in on you. I really had to use the bathroom, and seeing no one, I thought it would be all right. I did not mean to disturb anyone."

She said, "You are not disturbing me. Why don't you come over here, and I will make you a sandwich. You are hungry—aren't you?"

This was too much for me to handle; she fascinated me. I could hardly keep my eyes off her beautiful naked body. All sorts of sexual thoughts swept through my mind, but I was uncomfortable in making any move toward her.

I reluctantly said, "Thanks, but I have to get back on my ice route; people are waiting for their ice."

As I headed to the door, I turned my head for one more look, and she smiled a come-hither smile. I proceeded out the door and down the steps to my ice truck, thinking, *Damn it, damn it, damn it! What's with you, Watson? Are you nuts?*

The memory of the encounter and the possible missed opportunity stayed in my mind for several weeks when I brought ice to her house, but the episode never repeated itself. Darn.

That was not the only encounter I was to have.

Another day, I brought ice to a new customer. The house was small and had only three rooms and a bathroom. I put a block of ice in the small icebox and turned around when I heard my name spoken. It was Liz, and she looked more beautiful and sexy than ever in her transparent slip with nothing underneath.

I could see the contours of her naked body—her breasts and nipples and the faint shadow of the triangle between her legs.

"Hello, Jerry. Nice seeing you again! Please sit down and have a cup of coffee with me."

I mechanically sat down at the small kitchen table. She was standing behind me while she talked. The heat of her body on my back sent shivers down my spine.

She poured two cups of coffee, brushing her breasts against my shoulder, and asked, "Cream and sugar?"

I answered hoarsely, "Sure—thanks."

Leaning over my shoulder again with her breasts pressing tightly against me, she poured some cream and a couple of teaspoons of sugar into our cups and stirred them.

"Why don't you stay for a little while, Jerry?"

My mind filled with lust and apprehension, but apprehension won against my desires and I reluctantly told her, "I have to get back on my ice route."

After a few minutes, I got up to leave. She faced me and put her arms around my neck, pulled me into her arms, and kissed me warmly on my lips. With her tongue in my mouth and her warm breasts and nipples pressed against my chest, her body heat enveloped my entire being.

I had never, ever been kissed that way before, and her wet kiss, warm body, and beauty mesmerized me. She whispered in my ear, "Come back again when you can stay longer. Won't you, Jerry?"

I mumbled affirmatively and left, kicking myself all the way back to my truck.

I returned to the house over the next two weeks, but she was not there. I found out later that she had joined the Women's Army Corps.

I kicked myself again!

I remained a virgin until I married Jean Shadduck. I guess I feared what women could do to a guy ever since Effie Botens

151

shared my love letter with her friends on the basketball court at Fairhaven School.

In high school, Vanice Vernice Vaupel rejected me because I didn't wear a ring, wristwatch, or jewelry—or even a wallet. When Evelyn and I were smooching in the backseat of my Ford, she always dodged the question because she was having her period—about six times a month.

There were several other rejections, including Helen, who lived down the street from me. She said that she liked me, but would not let me kiss her. So what was the point?

Jean Shadduck

Jean Shadduck ("Jig") was an Irish girl, who lived with her sister in a rented house in Klamath Falls. Jig worked at the Woolworth Dime Store, but we met in 1947 at the Tip Top Café.

I finally got her attention by throwing wadded paper-balls in her direction, and we talked and liked each other immediately. After we had known each other for a short time, I asked her to marry me. She was not ready for marriage and told me so, but I did not give up. After a month of asking and pleading, she finally agreed to marry me. We were two dumb kids pretending to be adults. Cal drove Jig, her sister Betty, and me to Reno. Jean and I married on August 16, 1947. The preacher's wife and Betty witnessed our marriage.

After the quick ceremony, we looked for somewhere to stay overnight. The only place we found within our price range was in a rundown motel that had two rooms connected together. Betty threw a fit and did not want to stay overnight. Although it was late and Klamath Falls was hours away, we started out for home.

Betty and Jean crowded into the front seat with Cal to keep warm. The only heater in the car was in the front. I rode in back and froze my butt off. My wedding night was a real bummer. Riding in a freezing backseat alone for hours was not exactly what I had envisioned.

I moved into the rented house in Klamath Falls where Jean and her sister lived and brought my car down from Corvallis to work on in my spare time.

High Rigger's Helper

That summer, I got a job with a group of vagabond sawmill painters as a high rigger's helper. On my first day, I was almost pulled off the peak of the roof of the sawmill.

I was trying to manipulate the long ropes of the painter's bosun chair into a steel hook on the peak of the roof, while lying facedown at the edge of the eighty-foot-high pinnacle of the slippery, corrugated, blazing metal roof.

The weight of the rope around my wrist and the swaying chair was pulling me off the roof, inch by inch. I was able to grasp my hunting knife in a sheath on my belt and cut the rope, releasing the rope and the chair, and stopped my slide toward the edge of the roof.

When I queasily got down from the rooftop, the boss told me to use a fire hose and spray down the outside walls of the building to prepare them for painting. And that was it.

While I was spraying down the walls, the heavy stream of water from the hose went through the large open windows that exposed the 440-volt lines of the large traveling crane and could have caused a high-voltage electrical shock and possibly electrocuted a person holding the metal nozzle of the hose.

The boss, noting the danger, told me to shut off the water hose and climb up to the overhead crane and close all the windows. Inside the sawmill, I climbed on top of the overhead crane with thirty-inch iron wheels to close the sliding windows. I could have lost a leg—or my life.

Fortunately, I saw the pinch point between the crane's iron wheels and a huge timber joist. At the last second, seeing the danger out of the corner of my eye, I swung my leg away from the pinch point. My leg could have been pulled out of its socket and ripped off under the crane's wheels, and my damaged body could have fallen sixty feet to the floor.

I should have known better than to almost get caught in the bite of the line.

Three times in one day was enough for me. A cat has nine lives, but a person only one. I decided to quit while I was ahead!

The crew took me out to a bar to party, and we drank up my day's salary. I staggered home to my new wife—broke, worn-out, and dizzily drunk, but still alive!

In June 1950, I graduated from Oregon State College with a bachelor's degree in industrial administration. I made the honor roll and won the middleweight boxing championship.

Mom and her new husband, Jim Hevern, drove up to Corvallis to join Jean and me and our baby son, Roland Eugene, at the graduation ceremony.

Chapter 7:
Starting Up the Corporate Ladder

Boeing Airplane Company

The week after graduation, I was to report to work as a time-study man in the industrial engineering department at the Boeing Marginal Way Plant in Seattle. We were busy preparing for the drive to Seattle to find a place to live and get settled.

Roland was almost a year old, and Jean was pregnant with another child. We packed all our worldly possessions on a small, one-wheel trailer hitched to the back bumper of the car and piled blankets in the backseat for Roland.

I stopped by the office of Professor Milton Sheely to say good-bye. Milt was an unusual person, whom I admired and respected during my four years under his professorship. He was a brilliant instructor and a devoted motivator. I considered him my mentor and a good friend.

Milt was an avid fisherman and fished whenever he could get away. He was particularly enamored with fishing in the ocean.

Milt casually asked me if I was financially set to go to Seattle. I told him truthfully that I had been able to save some money to rent an apartment with a few dollars extra, but as for living expenses, we would have to pull in our belts. We would make do somehow.

I had seventy-five dollars saved for the trip. He pulled out his checkbook and wrote out a check to me for $125. He put the check in my hand and said, "That should get you started."

I looked at the check in disbelief and said, "I can't accept this, Milt. We will make it all right."

"Nonsense," he replied. "I know you will pay me back."

My annual starting wage at Boeing was $1,595 per year or $132.90 per month. Not much by today's standards, but it was a good beginning white-collar salary in 1950. We found a low-priced apartment and moved into the modest Kitsap Court Apartments.

When I advanced to supervisor of labor standards and methods analysis and had paid Milt back, I also had the opportunity to nominate Milt for a visiting professorship for the summer.

As it turned out, Milt was selected and was able to fish the waters of Elliott Bay and other prime saltwater salmon fishing spots in Puget Sound every weekend—or any weekday that he had free—for the entire summer. He was as happy as a clam, and I was delighted for him. He said to me later that it was the best fishing that he had had in years, and he thanked me profusely.

I replied, "You were a lifesaver for me. I am not sure what I would have done without your help. I will never forget it."

The Best Airplanes in the World!

On my first day at Boeing, I was introduced to the industrial engineering department and assigned to a time-study crew in the final assembly section.

The Boeing facility was huge, with many acres of factory space for manufacturing several airplane models and office space for the engineering and administration of the business. There were subassemblies of shiny, aluminum sections of bodies, wings, and fuselages—and the final assembly of complete airplanes. It was magnificent!

The component manufacturing departments had sheet metal cutting, punching, shaping, and forming. The shops had large forming presses and spot welding of component parts. There was a large machine shop, with huge Keller profile milling machines, a variety of types of smaller mills, drills, lathes, and many other machine tools and specialized operations, covering thousands of square feet.

The company had previously designed and produced the famous B-17 Flying Fortress, an icon that helped win World War II, but its mission was completed and it was out of production. The company was assembling the last B-50 propeller-driven bombers and was starting production on the swept-wing B-47 bomber powered by four jet engines under the wings. It was developing a new commercial passenger plane, the Dash-80, which was to become the first jet-powered 707 commercial aircraft. However, the largest R&D program was the giant, swept-back wing, eight-jet B-52 Stratofortress, with long-range capability to drop atomic bombs on targets around the world. It was the first prototype constructed in a top-security area.

On April 15, 1952, the first B-52 took off on its maiden flight. I, and fifty thousand others, watched Tex Johnson take off and soar into the air for a two-hour flight. It was an amazing sight.

Industrial Engineer and Supervisor

Of the fifteen men in my time-study group, all but me were shop foremen who would learn the assembly methods and then be assigned as assembly foremen. Our job was to time every operation in the assembly process, identify the sequence of jobs, and assure that every part or subassembly was riveted or bolted to the correct location in the airplane—and in the proper sequence, to avoid rework.

After a few months, my boss promoted me, and I supervised time-study men in the machine shop, using stopwatches that detailed time recordings of every element of the work the operators did.

I advanced from time-study supervisor to methods analyst to labor standards supervisor in a relatively short time.

Working and being at Boeing was a joy. There were great managers, compatible coworkers, sometimes-hilarious associates, and interesting work. I looked forward every day to going to work. I was promoted to supervisor of methods and special assignments. Something different or new happened frequently, and I never knew what special project I might work on next.

Like a kid in a candy store, I enjoyed walking through the various production shops and marveled at the machinery, tooling, and the intricate operations and complex parts and assemblies that went into the finished airplanes. I absorbed as much information as I could. It was interesting and proved valuable to my work in the future.

Bud Farnsworth was the manager of industrial engineers, ensuring labor standards were met. He was older and more sophisticated and was a good manager. He had a New Year's Eve party and invited us all to attend. He had a very nice home: spiral staircase, paintings, and a basement recreation room with a well-stocked bar, a dance floor, and a record player.

This was a new environment for most of us, including Jean and me. As the evening went on, some of us fellows who were more boisterous were mixing drinks at the bar from whatever bottles were at hand and were getting drunk, rowdy, and noisy.

The wife of my direct supervisor came up to me and asked me if I would like to dance. I agreed, and we proceeded to the dance floor. A tango was playing loudly on the record player. My partner was no lightweight, and when I bent her over backward, she dropped from my arms and fell to the dance floor, breaking her leg.

I apologized to her profusely as the ambulance team carried her out on a stretcher to take her to the hospital.

David James was born in Seattle, Washington, on August 12, 1950. He was named after Jean's brother, James. David was a little rascal from the start and continued to be a cutup and daredevil in his youth.

The American Institute of Industrial Engineers selected Seattle as the city for their regional conference and asked our industrial engineering manager if he could provide an auditorium and four speakers from industry. They had several speakers lined up, presidents and vice presidents from various industries, but needed four more for manufacturing.

He asked me if I would take on the task of finding the additional speakers. Of course, I said I would. I called several presidents in the manufacturing industry and eventually filled three of the speaker spots and offered to and gave a personal presentation myself. One of the presidents who offered to give a presentation was Wade Williams, an entrepreneur who owned his own manufacturing business.

The conference was a great success, and I was particularly impressed with Wade Williams. Jean and I eventually gave his name to a new son, Allan Wade Watson.

In 1951, I cast my first vote for the president of the United States. I was elated when Dwight Eisenhower won the presidency.

Hunting in Washington

Washington was a hunter's paradise for deer and elk. I hunted whenever I could, usually alone, but a couple of times with one or two other people. I preferred to hunt alone and take care of myself.

I hunted elk on the Olympic Peninsula in the Hoh River country. A hunting trip on the back of a motorcycle to the Snoqualmie Falls area ended up with the driver, me, and a deer on the back and two rifles strung around my neck. The motorcycle slid and crashed into an iron gate, but luckily the driver and I were unhurt.

I enjoyed hunting alone in the Cascade Mountains in snow over my knees and sometimes almost up to my waist. I'd go ten days without seeing another person or a buck deer. It was peaceful and dead quiet, which I enjoyed very much. After my supper, cooked over a campfire, I settled in my tent, slipped into my sleeping bag, read until I was ready to go to sleep, and turned off the Coleman lantern.

I had a number of hunting trips to the rolling hills and forests of the Okanogan area, where there were deer aplenty.

I sprained my ankle jumping over windfalls on a downhill slope and got back to my car over a mile and a half away using a tree branch for a crutch. On driving down the mountain, I ran over a sharp rock in the road and ruptured a hole in my oil pan, forty miles from the highway and Trout Lodge, but was able to carve a small plug and hammer it into the hole in the oil pan to stop the loss of oil.

Eventually getting to civilization, I slept in a ditch on the side of the road in my sleeping bag. The next morning, I got a wrecker to take my car and get it repaired, caught a ride with some hunters, and spent the day hunting.

However, the eeriest hunting trip I ever had was in a wilderness near the high Icicle Mountains of the Cascade Range.

I drove alone up the steep mountain to a large pond and set up camp in a spot I had never been to before. I brought along a watertight, zippered body bag from an army surplus store (used to transport a dead body to the morgue for temporary storage). I put my sleeping bag into it to protect me from rain or snow, as well as to keep me warm in the cold mountains.

The sun set and shadows began to fall on the large pond. Over the pond, lifeless trees stood upright in the dark water.

Several small, fluffy birds were roosting on the limbs of a tree a few yards from me. I aimed my rifle at a bird and shot it for no reason. Its body burst in a spray of feathers and down.

Later, a half-moon caused eerie shadows on the moonlight-drenched water of the pond.

I looked out on the pond and saw what looked like ghostly figures standing in the water, silently watching me.

I crawled into my sleeping bag, which I had placed inside the body bag, and slept a restless sleep, shivering and dreaming about the innocent dead bird and the ghostly figures.

All of a sudden, I awoke and, half-asleep, sensed the presence of someone or something in the bag with me.

In a panic, I threw off the body bag, broke camp, and drove down the steep mountain road in the darkness, hoping to find a less formidable place to camp. In retrospect, the body bag was not the problem. The problem was my own conscience and the innocent bird I shot. The figures in the water were a metaphor for my Uncle Kirk, who would turn over in his grave had he known what I had done.

I vowed to never repeat it.

We bought a home in South Seattle, and I painted the outside barn-red. On April 12, 1954, in Seattle, Washington, Teresa Ann was born. She was cute and lively, but her vision was not very good. When she was very young, we had her eyes examined and found that she needed treatment to reduce her eyes' tendency to cross.

The doctor recommended glasses and eye patches. Jean also alternated an eye patch from eye to eye each day, and it helped. However, when I looked at her, tears came to my eyes. It was so sad to see a beautiful little girl wearing glasses and an eye patch.

Teresa grew up and married R. D. Duzinske. They had two children, a girl they named Brenna and a boy, Greg. Teresa became a librarian and a painter—talents she developed herself.

The Crash

The information for this story came from the truck driver, who told it to friends, bystanders, and other people on the scene of the accident. I personally saw the wreckage of the car, dragged and left on the side of the highway. Uncle Kirk was a decent, honest person, known and respected by many people. Word of the accident spread quickly around Klamath Falls.

I was working in Seattle when I received some urgent news. I immediately caught a plane to Klamath Falls. I was twenty-nine years old and married with two children.

May 19, 1957, was a clear, sunny day, and traffic was light on Highway 97. The driver of the truck had left Doris, California, a small town a few miles south of the border, and headed toward Klamath Falls.

The driver had started his day in Redding, California, early that morning and was half a day from his destination. The forty-five-year-old driver was experienced and felt good. He could reach Bend by sundown and be done for the day. He looked forward to sitting down to a good meal, served by a pretty waitress at his favorite restaurant in Bend.

Suddenly everything changed.

On a straight stretch of highway, the truck driver was traveling comfortably at the posted speed limit. An older-model Ford sedan was coming toward him. The approaching driver, a forty-five-year-old divorcé, struggled with a female passenger who had her arms around his neck and was trying to pull his head around toward her to embrace him. The driver tried to push her away, but he lost control of the car.

The car swerved directly into the path of the eighteen-wheeler. The oncoming driver's eyes were wide, and the whites shone brightly. He was looking into the face of death as the truck and the small sedan collided head-on with an explosive crashing and crumpling sound, crushing and squeezing the smaller vehicle under the truck's front wheels.

The truck driver, having survived the initial impact, was fighting with the steering wheel to keep the eighteen-wheeler upright, while braking to stop the truck's forward motion. However, the steering wheel was useless; the truck's front wheels had climbed onto the top of the car and sat on the mashed hood. His heart was racing from the realization that he had almost died.

The truck driver stopped his rig, opened the door, and jumped to the ground. He ran to see the flattened wreckage and knew that no one had survived. He stared at the car's scattered wreckage—the remains mashed flat to half its former height.

He saw two people in the tangled steel and debris: a bloodied man crumpled on the floorboard inside the car, and an Indian woman crushed on the other side of the front seat.

The driver was my great-uncle Kirk; he was only fifty-five years old!

At the funeral home, I looked down into his coffin. Tears streamed down my face as I remembered how comfortable I had always felt in his presence. He was like a rock that was always there—like a father. Now he was gone!

At the graveside service, the preacher giving the eulogy went on and on with his bullshit; he did not really know anything about my Uncle Kirk.

I wanted him to hurry up and finish, and he finally did, with the closing words, "He was a good man."

You got that right!

After the ceremony, relatives and friends congregated in Aunt Co's parlor and kitchen. Many relatives brought an enormous quantity and variety of food. Everyone wanted to tell stories and anecdotes about Kirk's life to celebrate and say goodbye to a good, hardworking, selfless human being and mourn his or her individual loss.

I was uncomfortable with the soft cadence of conversations going on around me at the wake: murmured remembrances exchanged, kindnesses remembered, stories of every kind.

I had an explosive urge to cry out, "You're not dead—you can't be dead."

The absurdity of this thought subdued my urge to cry out.

You are dead … gone. I had never told Uncle Kirk how I felt about him. It just was not the way in our family—or in any other family that I knew. Now, I silently told him how much I loved him!

Not wanting to remain an hour longer, I said hurried goodbyes, left the house, and returned to Seattle on the first plane out.

Although Uncle Kirk worked full-time for the railroad for a living, he was a mountain man, a hunter, and a dog trainer. He was kind and gentle in his own way, but he had a few vices: he liked Van Dyke cigars and Shasta beer and had a more-than-occasional eye for women. Although he drank, he would not allow anyone to drive if they were drunk or had more than a couple of beers, including himself. He did not apply his rule to passengers, who were generally free to do as they liked. Kirk never tried to be the boss or tell people what to do. This may have led to his tragic death.

I remember when I was a kid, Uncle Kirk, Perry, and I went buck hunting about seventy miles east of Klamath Falls. Rimrocks formed from molten lava millions of years ago and provided lookouts to watch for deer in the brush and trees below. We hunted for a couple of days with great anticipation, but no bucks. Hunting was over for this trip, and we were back in camp, sitting around, sipping coffee, cleaning our guns, and generally resting our weary bodies.

As the sun set, Uncle Kirk said, "Boots, it's time to load up—we're going home!"

I remember his voice as if it were yesterday.

Jean and I had our third son, Allan Wade, who was born on November 18, 1957, in Renton, Washington. We moved there after Boeing transferred me from the plant in Seattle to the Renton plant. Allan was a happy baby and smiled a lot, but he gave the nurses a lot of trouble when he did not like what they were doing with him.

The Renton plant was producing the new Model 707, a four-jet-engine commercial passenger plane, and the KC-135 tanker to refuel bombers in midair.

In the summer of 1959, I decided to leave Boeing. I loved my eight years there and had a succession of enjoyable duties, positions, great bosses, and gracious, funny, and comradely associates.

Seattle was a great place to live and work, and there were great hunting areas available all over the state. Working at Boeing and living in Washington was a great experience. However, I realized that I was not going anywhere, and I needed to find a management position with growth possibilities to advance my career in the direction I wanted to go. I wanted to manage a company and have a financial interest in it.

I got word that Thiokol Chemical Corporation in Utah was hiring and sent them my résumé.

Chapter 8:
Up the Corporate Ladder One Rung
at a Time–The "Bad Boy" Days

Thiokol Corporation and the Minuteman Intercontinental Missile

In 1959, after submitting my résumé, undergoing a personal interview, and obtaining a security clearance from the FBI and CIA, I was hired as supervisor of industrial planning for Thiokol Chemical Company. I moved my family into a single-story ranch house that we purchased in Brigham City.

Thiokol's most important product was the first-stage rocket engine of the Minuteman Intercontinental Ballistic Missile, the strategic weapon with which to retaliate against a missile attack from the Soviet Union. The Cold War and the strategy of mutually assured destruction were in full effect.

The Thiokol facility covered several hundred acres of roads and facilities. A quantity-distance ratio determined the distances between buildings or facilities to prevent or minimize damage to other structures should an explosion occur.

The Learning Curve

When I got settled into my job, I projected the manpower required to meet the production schedule of the Minuteman.

The learning curve was based on the more efficient use and productivity of labor as the job became more familiar and the continual improvement of the methods and tooling used to increase productivity, as well as improvements in availability of components to eliminate delays due to the lack of components or materials on the production line.

All of these factors provided the measure of management's effectiveness in managing their workforce and staff.

These improvements over tens, hundreds, or thousands of units were substantial, requiring fewer people to produce more units—or more units without adding more people. Without utilizing the learning curve, there was no quantitative incentive for the production organization to improve its efficiency and productivity.

New orders for rocket engines declined, and more than a thousand workers and staff were dismissed, with virtually no other jobs available in the area. This tragedy largely resulted from management not being sufficiently indoctrinated in the learning curve to manage the staffing efficiently.

I vowed to not let the same thing happen in my future jobs by keeping close control of staffing and indoctrinating management to not let the employment rate surge out of control. Overstaffing could cause massive layoffs if the business declined.

Boeing had used the learning curve as a management tool and closely controlled their productivity and personnel staffing; they were very efficient and productive. Thiokol did not, and many of the employees were the victims since they were terminated when the workload decreased.

I enjoyed my work at Thiokol and looked forward to going to work each day. I also enjoyed taking my sons on weekend hikes to the top of the five-thousand-foot Wasatch Mountains behind our house. I also took the boys deer hunting across the Salt Flats to the Sawtooth Mountain Range.

The boys were not old enough to carry guns and hunt, but they made good lookouts while I took an occasional nap. Once I shot a buck over three hundred yards across an arroyo in the mountain using binoculars and my scope sight. The boys had awakened me and pointed out the buck. They did their job well.

David Allen, a supervisor in my department, was a Jack Mormon, meaning that he skimmed the surface of the Mormon religion. He was bright and competent and reported to me.

Dave loved to share his ribald, Mormon stories.

A woman from back East was visiting Utah and came upon a Mormon man. During their conversation, she asked him how many wives he had. He answered, "Twelve."

Disgusted, she said, "You ought to be hung."

"Ma'am," he replied, "I am."

Sam Packwood

Sam Packwood was a likable person and a competent, hardworking engineer, but his true forte was playing the piano and singing a prodigious repertoire of barrack-room ballads, sea chanteys, Scottish poems converted to songs, and English ditties.

Jean was friends with Sam's wife, Anne. Jean and I visited the Packwoods socially and once had dinner at their home. Later, after seeing his wife changing their infant son's shitty diaper on the dining room table, Jean gave polite excuses to avoid dining at their home again, but we continued as friends to visit them socially.

Sam played the piano with the gusto of an old-time saloon piano player. I eventually picked up the words and music to a wide variety of ballads and ditties and sang along with him for hours. We refreshed ourselves with Jack Daniel's and beer chasers. Our wives excused themselves and retired to the kitchen to chatter—away from the racket of our raucous voices and the heavy-handed piano.

Many of our songs Sam had no written song sheets for. Some of the songs were from Rudyard Kipling's poems from the British Army. "Danny Deaver" was one of the sad poems of a British soldier marched out onto the parade ground and hung for stealing from, and shooting, a fellow soldier.

What are the bugles playing for?
Says Files-on-Parade.
To turn you out, to turn you out,
The Color Sergeant said,
For we're 'anging Danny Deaver,
We are marchin' of 'im round.
We are 'anging Danny Deaver
For a sneaking, shootin' hound.

There was a poem about British troops marching in India:

Oh we're marching on relief o'er Inja's sunny plains,
A little head of Christmas time and just before the rains,
And if your 'eels are blistered and feels to hurt like hell,
Just drop some taller in your socks
And that will make them well.

There was a romantic poem of Mandalay:

By the old Moulmein Pagoda,
Looking lazy at the sea,
There's a Burma girl a waiting
And I hope she waits for me

And let's not forget the Scot's poems and songs:

Just a wee doc and doric,
Just a wee drop that's aw,
A wee doc and doric
Afore we gang awa.
Just a wee wifey waitin',
And a wee bock and bairn,
For if you can say 'tis a broad brict moonlict nigt,
Then you're all rict, you kin.

There were many other songs, ballads, and ditties. Sam kept
a bottle of Jack Daniel's on top of the piano, from which we kept

our drinking glasses refilled. Sam always knew when he had had enough–he fell backward off the piano bench onto the floor and fell asleep.

Many months later, one early Saturday morning at his house, Sam became belligerent, something that I had never seen in him before in the couple of years that I had known him. We were having a good time, with him playing piano and both of us singing raucously. His sudden aggressiveness toward me was completely out of character, perhaps from an excess of Jack Daniel's.

In an apparent calm, composed manner, he invited me to go outside with him. Although polite, his intentions were not peaceful, for reasons unknown to me. He wanted to fight, and I was not interested in accepting his challenge. Sam was a good friend and was on my staff. He was just drunk and I did not want to hurt him, but I went outside with him to attempt to talk him into coming to his senses.

Most of the homes in Brigham City had rock yards. No matter how many times you raked the rocks and planted lawn seeds, the only thing that grew was more rocks—not a very good arena for a scuffling match, let alone a fistfight.

A full moon lit up the ground and Sam's house. Sam and I went around to the large backyard. We were facing each other in the moonlight, and I attempted to soothe him and calm him down, but it was useless. I did not believe that he knew where we were or why we were there.

Sam suddenly lunged toward me. I grabbed the front of his shirt, took a quick step backward, and made a backward roll, at the same time kicking both my feet into his gut as I completed my roll. The maneuver sent him airborne, and he hit the ground on his back, his head toward me, faceup. Surprisingly, he did not seem to have any serious injuries, maybe a few rock dents in his back, but nevertheless, he got groggily to his feet.

Catching his breath, he asked, "What the heck happened? What are we doing in the backyard?"

I replied somewhat deceptively to avoid him becoming pugnacious again. "I was just demonstrating a maneuver to deflect a charging opponent. Don't you remember?"

Sam was coming to his senses, but had forgotten why we were in the backyard. I left it as it was.

He said, "Well, let's go back inside and have a couple of shots of Jack Daniel's."

"Can't," I said. "We drank it all up."

"And the beer too?" he asked.

"And the Coors too," I replied. "Good night," I said and started walking home. As I left, I saw him over my shoulder, looking around to find his front door.

Early on Monday morning, Sam was at his desk, working effectively, the weekend episode a faint memory. Sam was a good guy, and our episode never repeated nor did it affect our personal relationship.

Falling into Infidelity

A vice president's wife and I became acquainted at a cocktail party, enjoyed each other, and eventually set up a romantic liaison when her husband went out of town, which he did often. She was suspicious about his reasons for the trips and said that she was sure he was cheating on her.

I went to her home one evening at her invitation, and we sat at the bar in the remodeled basement drinking and talking. Her husband was off on one of his trips. She was a beautiful woman with light brown hair, hazel eyes, and a slim, sensuous body.

After a while, she took off her blouse and removed her brassiere, saying something about the heat, but I was not listening, I was looking with rising lust at her perfect breasts. We talked and drank, and after a short time, she got up and went to the door of a small bedroom with a double bed. As she walked slowly to the bedroom door, I watched her skintight short-shorts and followed her—I left a couple of hours later.

Our sexual liaisons continued for almost a year, until the vice president became suspicious and stopped his traveling.

Philandering

In my numerous travels and the many bars I drank in, there were women who indicated in a number of ways that they were interested in having sex. At first I declined their offers, but I eventually succumbed to my desires toward promiscuity. My philandering lasted over ten years and included many women, until I met Martina.

I knew that my wife, Jean, would be devastated if she found out what I was doing, and I tried to keep my trysts with other women a secret. I felt sorry for what I did and for Jean, but could not or would not cease my philandering.

I continued to love Jean, the mother of our five children, but Martina was the love of my life.

Shoot, Cut, or Drink

One Friday evening, I got a phone call from a friend of mine. Fred was as drunk as a skunk and pleaded for me to come to his house to help him. I went to his house and found him on a worn leather couch. Spread before him were a bottle of Jack Daniel's, a large hunting knife, and a .45 caliber automatic pistol with a loaded magazine beside it. He told me he wanted to kill himself—one way or another.

"To hell with it, Fred, let's have a drink." I poured him a glass of whiskey and myself a much smaller one. About two hours later, the whiskey bottle was empty, and Fred was sound asleep—passed out.

I took the knife, the pistol, and the ammo clip, and went home for the night.

On Monday morning, Fred came into my office, closed the door, and said, "You saved my life, and I am indebted to you. I will never pull that shit again; I have learned my lesson."

"Forget it—you do not owe me anything. You are going to be fine. You are right, though. Never pull that shit again! And by the way, I am keeping your gun and your knife until I feel confident that you will not pull the shit again."

He agreed.

The Ogden Flyers and the "Milk Bottle"

In 1959, my friend Rollie Berry and I rented a plane and took flying lessons. We received our pilot licenses while at Oregon State College. Later, after my family moved to Brigham City and I took a job with Thiokol Chemical Corporation, I joined with two other pilots to form "The Ogden Flyers Flying Club." We were based at the Ogden Airport, about thirty miles south of Brigham City. Our first order of business was to purchase an airplane. We found a six-year-old Cessna 172 for sale, and the owner agreed that we could fly the airplane to Las Vegas for a trial run. We needed to determine if we wanted to make an offer to purchase the plane.

The Ogden Flyers consisted of me as founder and president, Dave Powers, and George Nozdiez, all of us in our thirties. The three of us took off for Las Vegas the following morning. By mutual agreement, the members of the club chose me to be the pilot for the flight. Although I had only some thirty-five hours of flying experience, the others had less. A couple of us also had a few flying hours with Ziegler, the local pilot-instructor.

Ziegler qualified me for an FAA pilot certification where, among other things, I learned about what could happen in a high-speed climbing turn. Surprisingly, the plane flipped over ninety degrees from the direction it was actually turning, as if caught by a vicious crosswind, and he taught me how to avoid this dangerous maneuver.

The weather forecast called for scattered snow showers and reduced visibility.

I asked the others, "Anyone want to abort?"

The resounding reply was, "No!"

Shortly after takeoff, we were dodging snow showers, and they were only getting thicker. Upon reaching the first mountains, I descended to an altitude where I could follow the highway through the mountainous area, navigating visually with an ordinary road map.

We were below the line of sight of the OMNI directional navigation beacon and could not use the A/N beam either, since we were flying in a virtual winding tunnel. Both the A/N beam and the OMNI beams directed point-to-point in a straight line and were unusable in this situation.

Since none of us was instrument-rated, we were under visual flight rules, which meant the pilot had to see where we were going and keep the ground in sight at all times.

If I were to fly into the clouds, I could become disoriented and end up in the "milk bottle." The milk bottle was a metaphor for a whiteout, where the pilot does not know the orientation of the plane and, in a short time, begins a spiral into the ground. Conventional wisdom said that once pilot disorientation sets in, the pilot had three minutes to control it, or else the airplane would go into a downward spiral and crash into the ground.

That, folks, we did not need!

I had a problem with acrophobia, the abnormal dread of being at a great height. In tall structures, I not only have acrophobia, but also vertigo. I am drawn to the precipice like pieces of iron drawn to a magnet and see myself falling in the air.

However, when I am flying, I have absolutely no fears and soar in the air like a carefree bird.

The overcast sky had sunk below the top of the peaks and formed a thick cloud cap above the highway. I had to fly just above the highway and under the cap. The road was twisting and turning, and the sharp rocky inclines on either side formed a V, with the highway at the bottom and our plane in the middle. If anything filled the V, we were dead ducks—there was no place else to go.

Landing on the highway was not a viable option. It curved through the mountains, with few straight stretches to land on. It was reserved as the last resort.

Things were getting tighter and tighter by the minute, but I pressed on toward Las Vegas. We pressed on because we had no other options. We were boxed in, and I took full responsibility.

After what seemed like hours, we were finally through the mountains and into the sunny Las Vegas plateau.

We landed at the Las Vegas airport in one piece. I looked at the others and realized that I had not heard a peep out of them in the past hour. We looked each other over, expelled a mutual deep breath, and burst out laughing.

We made it with God's grace!

We took off home to the Ogden, Utah, airport. Although the plane got us home, we ended up finding a better airplane and bought it.

Airplanes and Houses of Ill Repute

Several months later, a group of us at Thiokol decided to fly to Ely, Nevada, for a weekend of gambling at the casino and visiting the four whorehouses in the town. Ziegler had relatives in Ely that he was going to visit and did not visit the whorehouses with us.

The next afternoon, we gathered at the airport to fly to Ely. There were five pilots—including Ziegler—and planes and six passengers. I was flying solo by personal preference. We took off more or less in formation and set our navigational OMNI beams for Ely. We arrived at the Ely airport in the late afternoon, gassed up the planes for the return journey, went into town, prepaid for motel rooms, and headed for the casino.

We spent a couple of hours at the casino and left to go into town. Some split up, going their own ways, but most of us ended up on the cross street that had three whorehouses.

Prostitution was legal, and business was thriving. Inside one of the houses of ill repute, we went to the bar for drinks, and several of the women swarmed over us, trying to entice us to take them to their rooms and get a little action.

Some of us visited all three houses and, in each, were surrounded by seminaked women breathing heavily in our ears, trying to convince us to go with them to their respective rooms.

We enjoyed drinking and talking with the women. Some were intelligent, some were pretty, and some were gorgeous, but all had a strong sexual attraction.

This went on for almost an hour as the men started to stray away with the women to their rooms or set off to look over the other houses.

I was attracted to a young, slim, pretty, very sexy woman. She was also intelligent—as I found out later. She had turned down invitations by the other guys. She was waiting for something or someone. I noticed her eyes on me and went up to her. She took my hand and led me down the hall to her room. We talked, sitting on her bed for quite a while, the meter ticking away.

She was from Ashland, Oregon, and had attended the University of Oregon for a year and a half. She had been through Klamath Falls. She married a drunk, abusive man—a lazy good-for-nothing who was good in the sack, but couldn't hold down a job. She divorced him six months later and ended up as a prostitute in a brothel.

We spent the rest of the night together. I was down to the loose change in my pocket, but I did not worry about it. My plane was all gassed up and ready to go.

As morning broke, I headed back to the airport, where we had all agreed to meet for breakfast. We pooled our money and had enough to buy six plates of scrambled eggs, sheepherder potatoes, bacon, toast, and coffee.

We asked the waitress for additional plates and split up the meals eleven ways. A couple of the fellows were so hung over that they could not eat their meals and gave them away to the others. I was not hung over, but was not in great shape since I had not slept at all. I was very hungry and cleaned my plate.

The pilots went to their respective planes, performed a visual check of their aircraft, and were ready to return to Ogden. We took off and formed a ragged formation, with Ziegler at the rear to make sure that there were no stragglers and to ensure that everyone stayed on course.

About a half hour into the flight, I nodded off. I heard Ziegler screaming, "Jerry! Pull up! Goddamn it, Watson, pull up, you dumb bastard! Your plane is going to go into a spiral, and you are going down!"

I awoke with a start and yelled into the microphone that I was okay. I grabbed the yoke, carefully pulled it back toward me, and slowly pushed the throttle forward, slowing the downward dive of the plane into a shallow, turning climb—careful not to let the plane slow down and go into a stall and spin out of control into the ground.

I moved the ailerons to bring the plane even with the horizon and righted it. I gradually pulled the yoke back and pushed the throttle forward to gain altitude to climb and catch up to the others and got back into the ragged formation. Whew! I was sweating like a stuck pig.

All of us landed safely in Ogden and returned to our respective homes weary and worn out—our wallets and pockets lighter.

Thank you, God!

Walworth Valve in Braintree, Massachusetts

One summer morning in 1962, Bill Gibson called me at my desk at Thiokol. Bill was a former associate and friend at Boeing and was now working as a consultant for the Walworth Company at their headquarters in New York City. He said that there was an opening for chief industrial engineer in the Braintree valve plant—with a good shot at the works manager job in a year or sooner.

Although I enjoyed my work at Thiokol, I knew that when the company's contracts ran out—and if no new contracts came in—there would have to be a downsizing of the workforce, as well as a reduction in management. Rather than wait for the extension of the current contracts or new contracts, I decided to go on the job market.

Bill Gibson and I had worked in different sections of the three-hundred-person industrial engineering department. From a professional standpoint, I may have stayed at Boeing too long. I should have been widening my horizons and advancing into line positions in smaller, growing companies rather than continuing in staff positions in a large corporation.

I had strayed from my goal of becoming a manager and eventually running a company—eventually having the top executive job and an ownership stake.

Several Walworth executives and managers interviewed me, including a Hungarian fellow named Louis Mihaly. I was offered, and accepted, the position of chief industrial engineer at the Walworth Valve plant in Braintree, Massachusetts.

Clarissa (Clari) Jean was born in Brigham City on December 7, 1959. A couple of months later, we wound up our affairs, put our house up for sale, packed our belongings, made the necessary arrangements with the moving company, and were off to Massachusetts.

On the road again for a two-day driving journey!

We found a house to rent in Randolph, about eight miles from the Braintree plant. While Jean arranged to get our kids in school and attended to other details of our relocation, I arranged to meet the works manager and visit the plant.

The Tour

Although the Walworth, Braintree plant was on a maintenance shutdown, the works manager came to the plant to welcome me and discuss the plant's operation and his goals.

Don Kane shook my hand with a firm grip and welcomed me. He was a young manager, about four or five years older than I was, but we were not far apart in education, intelligence, or temperament. He had earned a line position as works manager, whereas I was a member of the staff. My ambition was set on becoming a manager and managing operations.

Don was an experienced manufacturing professional and provided me with information on the plant, its managers, supervisors, and workforce. I was impressed with his managerial knowledge. We also discussed the competition, Crane Valve, the largest valve manufacturer and the biggest price discounter in the industry. Don believed that the most pressing issue for the Braintree operation was reducing product costs to compete effectively in the highly competitive valve market.

The plant manufactured small cast bronze valves and pipe fittings for the building trades and specialized copper-nickel marine valves for nuclear submarines.

The plant workforce totaled seven hundred people. It had a large modern bronze foundry and metallurgical laboratory, a well-equipped machine shop, assembly area, testing facilities where all valves were tested 100 percent, and related support and administrative services. The line management included the foremen, supervisors, and the superintendent.

Don said, "Due to the plant shutdown, you will be the manager in charge. We have a crew of maintenance people working, a small assembly crew, and a crew in the foundry snagging department to catch up on late orders. The plant is yours. Help yourself and look at whatever you like. You will learn a lot about what we do and how we do it just by walking around and looking."

I thought, *I am a line manager for the first time, although only for the weekend and not with a very large group of workers.*

Unbeknownst to me, before the year was out, Don would join a larger company in Cleveland as president, and I would fill his shoes as works manager of the Braintree plant.

All of the plant's products depended on the foundry producing quality castings. I toured the plant's foundry—a huge, high-ceilinged, dirt-floored section of the manufacturing building. It had only minimal lighting during the shutdown. I bumped into Bob Appleby, the foundry superintendent, who had come into the plant to check up on the maintenance people, who were working on some equipment. Bob was about ten years my senior and was an old foundry hand, having done almost every job in the foundry on his climb up to superintendent.

He told me the story of his early days in the foundry. On his first job in a foundry, the old, grizzled foundry foreman gave him some good advice: "Kid, don't ever pick up nothin' in the foundry until you spit on it first." It was good advice; the parts can be hot enough to give a person a serious burn.

He also used the phrase, "Eight for eight or out the gate," a straightforward way of communicating the necessity of doing what you are paid for or being canned.

I liked Bob Appleby and found him to be hardworking, smart, and highly respected by his peers, foremen, and the foundry workers.

He asked about my foundry experience. I admitted that this was the first company foundry in which I had worked and my knowledge was based on my experience at Oregon State College. I proceeded to tell him about what my industrial management curriculum covered in regard to foundry work.

Bob said, "It sounds like you have the foundry basics down pat. All you have to learn about now is the actual machinery and processes used in our shop. Anytime you need any assistance or have a question, just ask—I will be glad to help you."

I expressed my thanks, and Bob left to spend some time at home with his family.

I climbed up the steep, dust-covered steel ladders into the higher reaches of the dark foundry to look over the sand system. It was a little spooky and surreal, as if I were looking down on a ghost town. I looked over every piece of equipment used in making and testing valves and fittings.

After a full weekend of orienting myself with the machinery and processes of the plant, I felt confident to take over my duties on Monday morning when the plant would be back in full operation.

Louie and Gisele Mihaly

Louie Mihaly worked for Don Kane as a consultant and was installing an accounting standard cost system to cover each of the several hundred cost centers in the Braintree factory.

While spending time in social gatherings with Mihaly's wife and friends, I accumulated a personal profile of the man. Although Louie normally was closemouthed about himself, he filled in some parts of his life story for me. On some occasions at their dinner table eating Hungarian goulash or paprika chicken or *seikay kapusto*, I'd listen to the reminiscing between him and his Hungarian friends. When I asked him about the stories, Louie authenticated them.

He was born the same month and year as me, weighed about the same, but was four inches shorter. He had a large head, thinning blondish hair, and blue eyes. He had a modest accent and was brilliantly articulate. He spoke Hungarian, English, and Italian fluently and understood several other languages.

Louie's family was of the Hungarian aristocracy, and Louie was an educated university graduate with a doctorate degree. He was interested in sports—skiing, in particular—and had broken every bone in his body in various skiing and ski-jump accidents. In his twenties, he rose through the Communist hierarchy to head a thousand-person section of a bureaucracy responsible for worker productivity.

Louie and I became good friends, golfed together with other Walworth managers, and habited the local pub after golfing. Liar's dice was popular, and the constant rattling and clanking of the dice and boisterous emanations were a continuous background noise. A shot and a beer was a common drink; it consisted of a shot glass full of whiskey dropped into a mug of beer and chugalugged in one continuous swallow.

After several months at the house in Randolph, we moved to a village called Egypt in a wooded area a few blocks from the Atlantic Ocean. The house and surrounding woods were secluded and tranquil, and we liked it better than the more traditional house we had in Randolph.

Greensburg

One day, the manager of the Greensburg plant called me at my office in Braintree and asked me to assist them in solving some mechanical and managerial problems on their cast iron plug valve production line. I flew to Pittsburgh, rented a car, and drove to the Greensburg plant. Bob Sapp, the sales manager, arranged for my hotel room. After I checked in, Bob met me at the bar for martinis.

After drinking and conversing for a while, Bob asked me if I could use some company. I wondered what he had up his sleeve. Bob made a call, and twenty minutes later, his friend Bev saw us, walked over, and sat on a barstool between us. Bev was an accounting supervisor and was very smart, although she was only in her late twenties or early thirties. She had brown hair, brown eyes, and a nice body, but her main attraction was her sexuality, which she openly flaunted.

181

After another round of drinks, Bob suggested that we go up to my room, where it was less noisy and we could talk. We were playing poker and drinking and had switched to strip poker. When Bev and I were both down to our underclothes, Bob said he had to go and said jovially, "Goodnight! Have fun—I will see you tomorrow."

After Bob left, Bev and I quickly became intimate and spent the rest of the night enjoying ourselves. We ordered more drinks and a couple of rare steaks. We ate, drank, and frolicked to a late hour.

We continued our relationship each time I was in Greensburg until I left Walworth and accepted another job a year later.

When I returned to Braintree after the first meeting with Bev, I had several phone messages on my desk to call Sally So-and-So, a pseudonym used by my Braintree girlfriend. Her name actually was Jane, and we set a time to meet.

I had been to her father's Braintree mansion, where she lived, but we usually just drove around, picked up a bottle of scotch, and rented a motel room for an evening of pleasure.

Her father's mansion was designed like a four-sided box, with skylights in the ceilings, rooms around the outside, and gardens, walkways, streams, and waterfalls scattered in the center area. One could easily get lost in this place.

The first time she guided me through the inner area, we passed a scrawny old man with long gray hair and gray beard, sitting silently with closed eyes by a small pond with lily pads. He was naked except for a thin loincloth barely covering his genitalia.

I asked Jane, "What was that?"

She replied, "Just dear old daddy getting his rocks off again."

A beautiful fall came to Massachusetts, and the leaves turned colors in a bright array of brown, red, orange, and yellow.

I decided to take Ron and David deer hunting in Maine. We made the four-hour trip and found a campsite by a river, set up our tent, finished our supper, and settled in for the night.

It had been raining all day, but around midnight, it became a torrential storm. We held up the center tent pole to keep it from collapsing until the wind and rain let up and we could get a little sleep. Nevertheless, rain had entered the tent and soaked some of our bedding. The next morning was overcast and cold, with the temperature in the thirties. Using the gas stove, I fixed a breakfast of bacon, eggs, toast, and coffee.

Ron and David were still not old enough to carry guns. They just liked the three of us to be out in the woods together having a good time. We had to stop several times to thaw out Ron's feet. The blood in his feet did not circulate properly to keep his feet warm. Periodically, I removed his boots and massaged his feet to bring back the circulation. I took off my warm boots and put them on his feet until his feet thawed out. When his feet turned cold again, I removed his boots and massaged his feet again. We switched boots a number of times.

A freezing rain soaked our non-water-repellent wool jackets and trousers. After a while, I decided we should go back to camp, build a fire, and dry out. The temperature was falling fast.

We arrived back at our camp and tried to start a fire, but the wood was soaking wet and we could not get it started—even when we poured some gasoline onto the firewood. The rain increased in intensity and was starting to turn into large snowflakes that covered the campground and tent.

We gathered in the tent out of the snow and warily set up the Coleman stove. We opened the tent flap of the entry door to prevent a buildup of carbon monoxide. The storm rose in intensity with the ferocity of a blizzard. The tent was collapsing, and to avoid burning down the tent, we set the stove outside. We tried to keep the tent up, but it finally collapsed.

"Okay, guys," I yelled over the sound of the wind. "It is time for us to get the hell out of Dodge!"

I walked over to my station wagon to back it closer to the tent to load our gear and head for home. I turned the key, and the starter motor went Rrr-er, Rrr-er, and quit. I looked under the hood at the starter motor, checked the battery connection to assure that it was clean, tightened the nut, and rapped the cable connectors down with the butt of my knife while Ron turned the key. Still nothing.

We were dead in the water, soaked, and freezing in wet clothing. It was getting dark, and we were in the wilderness ten miles away from a little-used highway and thirty miles from civilization.

This was definitely not a good situation!

Although the bedding was soaked, I asked Ron and David to get the sleeping bags out of the collapsed tent and squash them into the back of the station wagon.

We could hike to the highway, which would take about four hours, to either try to get a ride or walk another eight hours to the closest town, a total of twelve hours.

Or we could stay where we were and bundle together in the station wagon that had been sitting for almost a day and was as cold as a whore's tit and wait. Unable to run the engine, we had no heater to warm up the car.

I decided that it was too dangerous to start out walking now with nighttime coming, snow falling, and the temperature at freezing. We would hunker down, stick it out until morning, and then go. When daylight came, we would walk to the highway to catch a ride. If we were unable to catch a ride, we would have to walk to the nearest town. We would have to depend on someone stopping and giving us a ride—a chancy proposition.

A third option, which probably had little chance of success, was worth a try.

I took my axe out to the access road that wound up the hill from our camp and down to the highway the other way. I had not seen a car since early that morning, but that did not mean there were no cars on it during the day.

I cut down two small cottonwood trees that had fallen on the road, partially blocking it both ways. I trimmed a small tree, sharpened one end into a long point, and put it in the crotch of a tree pointing in the direction of our camp in case someone came by.

I told Ron and David my plan. "Stay here tonight in the car and hike out early tomorrow. Also hope that a car comes up or down the road and sees our emergency signal."

I checked to see how much fuel was in the stove and lantern. We probably had enough fuel to run the lantern through the night. The stove would only provide a few hours of heat if the burner were turned down low, but we had to use it outside.

I decided to cook some food to build up our body heat and energy and save the rest of the fuel for when the cold became unbearable later on.

We huddled close to the stove while I prepared enough food to last for a couple of meals.

Ron said, "Sheesh."

We went silent and listened … nothing. Then we heard the sound of an engine, and we stumbled in the dark toward the road. When we got there, there was a heavy-duty pickup truck with a single individual inside, stopped in front of the tree-limb barrier in the road. He had on a Fish & Game hat and uniform and carried a large flashlight.

He called to us, "You boys having some trouble?"

I answered, "Yes, you could say that. We have a dead car, a couple of half-frozen kids, and a pile of soaked bedding, it is cold as hell, night is coming, and we need to get the hell out of here."

"Is that all? You're in luck; I am the last vehicle coming down off the mountain today. We can hitch your station wagon to my pickup, and I will tow you into town."

"Thanks, we would sure appreciate it. I would like to get these boys in a warm bed tonight—and I could use one myself."

We pulled the tree limbs out from in front of his pickup and stuffed our gear into the back of the station wagon.

I helped the officer hook up his towing cable to our station wagon, and we were off, heading to the highway and then on to the town. The boys were in the truck with the heater going full blast, no doubt, and I was in the station wagon, freezing my butt off. I did not mind—we were very lucky to get the heck out of Dodge.

The trip took over an hour because we were towing another vehicle, but it would have taken us twelve hours or more on foot, in a driving snowstorm, if we had not caught a ride. Had we set out on foot and become unable to walk due to frostbite or hypothermia, or in Ron's case, a lack of circulation in his feet, a passerby in the morning might well have found three snowy lumps frozen together along the side of the highway.

As we entered the small town, there was a motel with a vacancy sign. We unhitched the tow cable, pushed the car into a warm garage, and thanked the officer.

We had a warm night's sleep, and in the morning, the car started without trouble. We drove back to Egypt after breakfast.

The Gravestone

A couple of weeks later, David and I went deer hunting in Vermont. I tromped through the woods with David tailing along for several hours. We came upon a low stone wall. Some of the stones had broken, and some had spread out on the ground. Lichen and moss covered much of the stones' surfaces. We rested there for a while.

David got up to look around and was kicking the dead leaves around. He stooped and got down on his knees to look at something. He brushed away the leaves, scraped the stone with his fingers, and wiped the surface clean. He was looking warily at what he had uncovered. It was a very large gravestone, toppled over on the ground.

Chiseled into the stone in large letters was an inscription: David James Watson 1795–1816. David's face turned as pale as a shroud, and his breath came in slow, silent gasps as he looked at the chiseled words and numbers. The inscription struck me too; it appeared as if David James Watson, probably a member of a frontier farming family, had died young. I wondered what had caused his death at such a young age: Indians, illness, or accident? We would never know. David had a somber look on his face and was not talkative as we left the area.

We hiked back to camp and had some cold sandwiches for lunch. After we finished, I picked up my rifle, a lever action .30-30 Winchester model 94 carbine. As I started to leave camp for an afternoon hunt, David told me he was not feeling well.

I asked him what was wrong.

He said passively, "It is just a sick stomach—I will be all right."

"Are you sure?"

"I'm sure. Don't worry, Dad. I'll be just fine. Wasn't that tombstone weird? Do you think our running across that tombstone was just chance? Could it be an omen or something?"

"It is all chance, David—you finding that tombstone. The odds are probably one in a billion that we would find a tombstone with the same name as yours on it, and I agree that it was weird. However, unless we are going to start thinking like a supernatural cult, I think we had best just forget it."

I asked him if he wanted me to stay with him, and he said, "No, Dad. You go ahead and hunt. I will be all right hanging around the car until you get back."

"Okay. I'll only be gone for a couple of hours or so, unless I get a deer. If I shoot a deer, I'll wait about fifteen minutes and fire three shots evenly spaced so you'll know that I'm on my way back. I'll have to drag the deer back with me if I shoot one, which will take more time to get back to the car. Don't worry if I don't get back right away."

I handed him the car keys and told him not to lose them. I took off into the woods.

David called to me and said, "Just don't get lost, Dad."

I promised him that I would not get lost.

The afternoon was pleasantly cool. I moved quietly through the woods for about an hour and a half. I repetitively walked about ten minutes, stopped, and listened for the sound of deer grazing, carefully scanning the woods for a flash from the tail of a white-tailed deer. I sat for a while and smoked a cigar.

Surprisingly, I have had deer walk almost right up to me when I was quietly smoking a cigar, if the wind was right. I stood still and watched for deer on the upwind side of the trickle of cigar smoke.

A few minutes later, three does and a buck approached through the brush and trees. I judged the deer to be a six-point buck.

Slowly, I raised my rifle and aimed at the buck, which was almost concealed in the brush. When it moved, showing its head and the front part of its body, I squeezed the trigger. The buck leaped into the air, snorting, staggered ten or fifteen yards, and went down. The shot had blown his heart to pieces.

I rolled up my sleeves, slashed its throat, and slit open its belly. I reached inside the carcass up to my armpits and cut and pulled out the guts, testicles, and leg glands.

I fastened my deer tag to its antler as required by law and got ready to return to the car.

Fifteen minutes after I shot the deer, I fired the three shots to let David know that I was on my way. I hooked my deer-dragging shoulder harness to the buck's antlers and started dragging the carcass back to the car.

David was waiting expectantly to see the deer. We put a tarp in the back of the station wagon and loaded the deer into the vehicle.

Dave seemed very quiet, and I wondered what was on his mind. To draw him out, I said, "Dave, at least we did not almost freeze to death again like on our last hunting trip."

David was morose, and I asked him what was wrong.

"Dad, please do not tell anyone at home that I was sick and you had to drag the deer back by yourself."

"Dave, is that all? You have nothing of which to be ashamed. You were sick and voluntarily elected to wait in the car so I could hunt. I thought that was admirable on your part. Most people would want to go right home if they were sick, but you did not. You stuck it out. Don't worry—no one is going to hear anything from me. It is just between you and me. Let me give you a bit of free advice. Never pay any attention to what people think or say about you. You are the only one who really knows who you are—and their opinion is not worth a bowl of spit!"

David laughed, and his demeanor brightened appreciably. We drove back to our new home in Scituate, Massachusetts— one and a half blocks from the Atlantic Ocean.

Alloyco Valve Company

About nine months into my job with Walworth, Don Kane told me that there might be a works manager position coming up at Alloyco in Elizabeth, New Jersey—one of Walworth's several manufacturing plants.

Bill Gibson, now a consultant for Walworth, called me and asked if I would come to Alloyco for a few weeks and learn the ropes. He wanted someone to take over the operation. I agreed and, with Don Kane's blessing, packed a bag and flew to Elizabeth.

Alloyco specialized in manufacturing valves in a variety of stainless steel alloys for industrial use, whereas Braintree manufactured brass valves for commercial building construction. I studied the Alloyco plant's manufacturing operations, the various office organizations, sales and marketing, and became acquainted with the managers and staff.

Bob Sapp, who I had met in Greensburg, was on the phone, feet up on his desk, yelling at the top of his lungs. His dialogue, filled with expletives and laughter, could be heard throughout the office. Everyone liked Bob; even his customers enjoyed his raw jokes and likable personality. His expletives apparently did not offend them; there were no complaints from any of his customers, according to the manager.

Bob asked me if I would like to go with him to the Veteran's Hospital that he frequently visited to talk with the disabled or sick veterans. Inside the hospital, Bob went from room to room, visiting patients and telling jokes, which cheered them up.

There was one large room, however, in which no one spoke, with the exception of a few hospital staff. Bob and I entered the room, stood inside by the door, and saw a dozen or more patients strapped to narrow beds. The beds looked like teeter-totters swinging up and down through forty-five-degree arcs and were continuously rocking the patients back and forth. Bob could not tell me what sort of therapy it was and I never found out, but the scene stuck in my mind.

Bob was a very heavy drinker, and the last time that I saw him, he had suffered delirium tremens and was rushed to the hospital. Wide leather belts fastened his wrists, ankles, and waist to immobilize him.

He half-recognized me and kept saying in a whispery, conspiratorial voice, "Jerry, get me out of these handcuffs, and let's you and me go out and have a drink."

I tried to soothe him and said that he would be well in a short time and just to rest. When I finally left, the last words I heard were, *"Jerry, get me out of here, Jerry get me out—"*

He died a few months later.

I am not a thanatologist, but I have seen many managers and executives and others who were my age or younger, die from alcohol-related causes: cancer of the liver, alcohol poisoning, heart attack, stroke, dementia, suicide, or accident. I wondered about the effect my drinking might have on my own life expectancy. *Would I die from the excessive use of alcohol?*

There, but for the grace of God, go I.

On a Tuesday morning, the Alloyco conference room was filled. Bill Gibson found me and said, "Get the hell out of here quick, Jerry! Call Don Kane and see if you can go back to Braintree."

I asked, "What's going on?"

"John Collins, president of Walworth, whom you do not know since his office is in California, is here with some staff from the New York office, and they are slashing and burning the place. No one is safe from firing. They do not know that you are here, so go!"

I hiked up my trousers, went back to Braintree, and reassumed my position as chief industrial engineer, after confirming my return with Don Kane and getting a positive reply.

Italy and Sicily

Several months passed, and Don Kane announced his departure. He had accepted the position of president of a large manufacturing company in Cincinnati. He recommended me for the Braintree works manager position. Fred Spence, the chairman, and Louie Mihaly promoted me—effective immediately.

My hopes and dreams to be a manager of a manufacturing plant were being fulfilled!

Louie subsequently became the managing director in Rome. When he returned, he had a proposal for me. He really wanted to start a consulting business in Europe. He asked me if I would consider being his assistant at WAGI (Walworth, Alloyco, Grove, International), learn the business, and eventually take over as president.

He said I could learn basic Italian in a year and there were people in the company who spoke perfect English and could help me when I needed translations. He suggested that Jean and I go to Italy with him and his wife for a couple of weeks to see the sights, talk to the Italian managers about their operations, and visit their plants.

Although I did not know if I would accept the job in Italy, I decided to take the tour and learn more about WAGI.

Jean was excited, but nervous, when I told her that we were going to Italy. A week later, we met Louie and his wife and flew to Rome. We settled in our room at the Excelsior Hotel to recover from jet lag, ate dinner, and went to bed.

Louie and Gisele met us the next day, and we took a cab to the railroad station. We boarded the train to Reggio Calabria, the toe of the boot at the southern tip of the country.

The train ride was very long, and it was dark. Everyone but me was sleeping. When the train stopped at a small village, I decided to get off and get some sandwiches and cokes at a small store next to the station. I got the sandwiches and cokes with the last liras in my pocket and started out to reboard the train.

As I looked up, the train was moving out of the station. I ran desperately to catch the train as it started speeding up and barely made it. What a mess I would have been in with no money or passport and no ability to speak Italian. Since everyone in our party was sleeping, no one would know that I had gotten off the train at some desolate place along the way.

When we arrived at Reggio Calabria, Louie picked up a rental car, and we started out to the plant in Patti. We were driving on the outskirts of Messina when Louie sideswiped a motorcycle police officer, almost making him crash.

The officer was enraged, but neither he nor his motorcycle was hurt or damaged. Louie soothed the officer in perfect Italian. He told the officer who he was: "capo de capo" of WAGI. It turned out that the officer was from Patti, and several of his family members worked at the plant. His anger turned to comradeship as they shared their mutual interests. The officer shook Louie's hand vigorously and told him that there was no problem now that they understood each other. He let us go without further ado. Everyone knew that the local Mafia boss controlled Patti.

At this time, the Mafia was shooting, kidnapping, and holding people for ransom. In addition, a terrorist organization called *Brigada Rosso,* the Red Brigade, was assassinating people in Italy.

We had a delicious dinner, went to our hotel for the night, and visited the plant the next day. In discussions with the manager and his staff, Louie acted as the interpreter. The manager invited us to lunch, and he brought several of his staff along. We had a two-hour lunch of delicious pasta, salad, local bread, and about a half a dozen bottles of Sicilian wine.

We returned to Rome the next day, and over several days, Louie and I visited two more manufacturing facilities and talked to the managers. We visited Milan, had a sumptuous going-away dinner, and returned to Boston the next morning.

After returning home, I decided that apprenticing to become the managing director of WAGI was not where I wanted to be in my career and declined Louie's offer with thanks, which he graciously accepted.

As works manager of the Braintree plant, I needed to address a number of problems. Prices for copper ingot, the primary metal used in producing bronze valves, were rapidly escalating and represented a large expenditure increase for the production of bronze valves and fittings. This cost increase and a drop-off in orders in the valve industry due to a decline in housing, commercial, and industrial construction were serious profitability problems.

Additionally, a new vice president of manufacturing started his tenure as a micromanager, involving himself directly in the day-to-day operations of the plants. John Walters personally called each of the works managers of the several plants to arbitrarily cut the quantities of valves to be ordered to replenish inventory in half to reduce inventories. A heavy-handed approach would assure that our ability to obtain new business and meet customer delivery requirements would suffer, especially with the market already under heavy pressure.

At the Braintree plant, we reanalyzed our inventory formulae and changed the quantities selectively, on an individual basis, up or down depending on usage. This was the way to get maximum inventory reductions without sacrificing our sales volume and profitability.

In examining inventory, I found that many valves in the inventory were obsolete or slow-moving and would be carried in stock for five years or more. There were over 200,000 pounds of these valves, and I decided to have them thrown into the furnaces to remelt them into ingots for current production, which reduced the amount of purchased high-cost copper ingot. The cost of the melted valves was an accounting issue, whereas using the melted valves for current production increased current profitability while improving cash flow.

My actions did not sit well with John Walters, the new vice president of manufacturing. He undoubtedly thought that his directive should be obeyed blindly, like a private saluting a general, even though his dictum would adversely affect sales and profitability.

My method produced better results, which he should have initiated at all the plants, but he perhaps was an "If it wasn't invented here, it's no good" sort of a personality. I expected a second call to show up at his office in Harrisburg to read me the riot act or listen to me or fire me on the spot, but no call came.

Louie Mihaly, back from Sicily, called me, and I explained the situation in its entirety. He said he would look into it.

I'll Drink to That!

A few days later, Fred Spence's secretary called me and told me to report to the corporate office in New York at ten the following morning. Arriving on time, I noticed that the corporate office took up an entire floor.

Spence's secretary greeted me amiably and told me to take a seat. Louie Mihaly came out of Spence's office and told me that it might be a while. I read the *New York Times*, the *Wall Street Journal*, and anything else I could get my hands on for over an hour.

Spence's secretary finally came out and said, "They are finished here, Mr. Watson; you may go back to Braintree. Mr. Mihaly will call you in the morning at your office."

I wondered if the reason for the meeting had been to terminate me for the disagreement. I rode the elevator down to the lobby and exited at street level. There were high-class shops and an upscale bar on the ground level.

I decided that I could use a martini and took a barstool at the mahogany bar alongside a stranger slumped over a drink that looked like a Manhattan. Several uneaten maraschino cherries were on the bar by his half-empty glass, appearing as if he had already had more than a few drinks.

I ordered a martini—up with a twist of lemon—and lit a cigar.

As my martini arrived, the stranger turned out to be John Walters, the vice president of manufacturing. I had met him briefly and had talked with on the telephone when he called me about reducing inventory. He raised his head, extended his hand, and said, "I am surprised to see you here, Jerry. How are you?"

"I am just fine. And how are you?"

"Not so good. You had more influence with Fred Spence and Louie Mihaly than I would have thought. Spence just fired me!"

"No shit," I said. I raised my glass and said, *"I'll drink to that."* I tossed the drink down in a couple of gulps and got up off the barstool. I dropped a fiver on the bar and said, "Good luck." I left the bar to catch the flight back to Boston.

On my way out the door, I glanced back at the dimly lit bar. John Walters was still crouched over his drink, his head down, elbows on the bar.

Wilton Tool

Walworth was in turmoil, and the corporate office in New York was running amuck. I decided to protect my butt and in 1965 sent out résumés for a number of jobs, including vice president of manufacturing at Wilton Tool just outside Chicago.

After Alex Vogel, the president and owner of Wilton Tool, reviewed my professional résumé, he contacted me. He went so far as to fly to Boston to meet me. Something in my résumé must have caught his eye.

I met Alex at the Porter House Hotel, a Boston landmark. We sat in the café and had coffee and porterhouse rolls, along with a lengthy discussion about his job offer. I ended up accepting the position.

Walworth had become a hotbed of political infighting, and the executive office was changing operating management personnel right and left. It seemed like a good opportunity to leave. I arranged to move to Chicago.

I was as noncommunicative with Jean about this move as I was regarding our previous moves or any other topic.

When our family arrived in Illinois, we rented an unexceptional two-story house in Lombard, a half hour from the Wilton Shiller Park plant. Open fields surrounded our four-bedroom house on the edge of town.

Alex was obsequious toward Jean and me, perhaps to assure my devotion to him and my desire to be a long-term executive of his team—or perhaps to determine if we met his socially acceptable standard. Once he invited Jean and me to be his guests at the ballet.

Jean and I were both from working-class families and had never attended a ballet. We knew nothing about the pirouettes or the choreography and were unable to converse intelligently about the ballerinas' performances or the musical renditions. Nevertheless, we enjoyed the performance.

Roland, David, Teresa, Allan, and Clarissa (Clari), our five children, went to school in Lombard and were doing well, except Ron, who was having problems with mathematics, and David, who continued his mischievous pranks, doing wheelies on his bicycle in the middle of the street and other acts of juvenile bravado. He was moping around his mother to get her to buy him a motorcycle, which I forbade, knowing David and his devil-may-care nature.

I finally relented and went to Sears and bought a small moped. When David saw it, he said it was a kid's toy and would not touch it or even go near it. I decided to try it out myself. I put my two youngest children, Clari and Al, on the seat over the back wheel and took off. When I got to the thoroughfare a block from our house, I accelerated full blast to cross the street quickly, and the unbalanced moped's front wheel went skyward. The violent wheelie threw Al and Clari off the bike into the middle of the road.

I dumped the moped, snatched the kids up, and carried them safely to the side of the street. Fortunately, they were not injured. Whew! And I thought David was wild. *What did that make me?*

Although David had disassociated himself from the bike, he was pissed that I was riding it. He capitulated and eventually started riding the moped.

At Wilton Tool, I was working on streamlining the inventory storage management as well as overseeing the Toledo, Ohio plant and managing the Shiller Park manufacturing operation. Wilton Tool was a manufacturer of cast iron vises, hydraulic clamping tools, and woodworking machinery.

The company also produced "Carry Pack" paper handles, used by department stores such as Macys, Saks Fifth Avenue, and other well-known names, to apply paper handles to the customer's packages. Carry Pack designed and manufactured their own machines, giving them an edge on their competition.

Alex Vogel had inherited the business from his father, the founder of the company. Alex was a relatively young man, with thick dark hair precisely cut and combed. His dark, pin-striped suit was immaculately pressed, and his shoes were brushed to a sparkling shine. A crisp white shirt and blue tie completed his office ensemble. He was small and appeared to have something of an inferiority complex because of it.

He spoke quietly in a tight-assed manner, as if he had trouble with exactly how he wanted to communicate. Sometimes it made me want to say, "Just spit it out, for Christ's sake."

From what I had heard, Alex and his father were opposites. According to the old-timers, the Old Man was a company legend and a straight-out personality, who said what he wanted to say in a no-bullshit, straightforward manner.

He patrolled the offices and plant in his shirtsleeves—no coat or tie. He was a short, stout man, with powerful muscles. One day, on his tour of the shop, he saw a large vise on a "finished parts" collection bench with an obvious unacceptable defect. He picked up the hundred-pound vise and threw it down the center aisle, followed by a string of epithets.

Everybody in the shop knew his demanding posture on quality, and this demonstration emphasized it in a very graphic manner.

The Proposal

In the middle of my second year with Wilton Tool, Alex asked me to come to his home in the upscale Arlington Heights suburb on a Saturday morning. His home was a large, two-story brick house, with a beautiful landscaped yard and large lawn. The paint looked new, the bright green grass mowed, and the shrubs immaculately trimmed. It was a warm, pleasant day. He invited me to sit with him outside at a patio table on the lawn.

He asked me if I would like a cold drink, and I replied, "A cold beer would be fine if you have it."

He left for a couple of minutes and returned with two cold bottles of beer and two glasses. We sipped the beer, or I should say, I sipped my beer. His glass remained on the table untouched, as if he were in training for something or other. We talked for a bit about nothing, as if he were biding his time to drop something important but could not figure out exactly how to begin.

Finally, he asked, "How are things going?"

I replied, "Pretty well overall. Shipments are up, but we have to get a better handle on our on-time deliveries—as you know. I am working on some solutions right now."

He nodded his head and replied, "You know how important on-time deliveries are to the company and the urgency in getting it fixed soon."

I returned his nod and said, "We are making good progress on speeding up orders through the shop and eliminating bottlenecks—and we have added more personnel temporarily in the shipping department. I have spoken to both Bill Ferrick in marketing and Tom Wright in finance about these delays. We need to make sure that the records for late orders are correct, or we could go off on a wild-goose chase."

Alex said, "Okay. I want all three of you to work together to get the problem solved."

I replied, "I have it set up, and we meet together every day to review the progress."

"Good," said Alex. "What do you think of my plan for building a plant in Tennessee?"

Alex had already made plans to start production on the building in Tennessee, and he and Bill Ferrick were running the show without any input by me. It was a little late for the question to be asked of me.

I said, "Frankly, I think it is basically a good idea to establish a new low labor-cost manufacturing plant somewhere else to manufacture the Toledo woodworking machinery."

The plant in Toledo had originally been a Willy's Jeep plant in the war. It was old and had an intractable union, with all the attendant problems. Production was inefficient and required transporting parts and materials by elevators up and down three floors.

I said, "Also, moving the Carry Pack operation out of the Shiller Park facility to a new plant will give more room at the Shiller Park plant to set up additional assembly lines for producing vises. And it will eliminate some of the bottlenecks, as well as improving efficiency and reducing overtime costs. It is important, though, to get all the input you can from your staff if you expect it to be successful."

I was not privy to any cost-savings analysis or break-even analysis and cash flow for the project. He either kept them close to his vest or did not have the documentation. If he did have it, he did not share it with me. Do not get me wrong—his management weaknesses were his own, not mine. I was happy to perform the duties assigned to me—and do them to the best of my ability.

Alex scowled for a moment about my comment, but beamed with pleasure at my confirmation of his Tennessee project. "Good. I want you and Tom to coordinate with Wally and Dick to make sure everything goes right. I have a lot at stake here."

I thought, *And so do I.*

Alex leaned forward in his chair and said, "Now, I would like to get to the point of why I asked you to come here today. I want to make you a proposition: If you agree to stay with the company for five years, I will give you 5 percent of the equity stock of the company for a bargain price."

This was the most lucid, straightforward statement I had ever heard coming from his mouth, and I was surprised.

Alex receded as if he were waiting for an answer to his marriage proposal and slumped back in his chair waiting for my answer. After a moment, he asked, "How is your beer? Would you like another?"

"Another beer would be fine—if it is not too much trouble."

He left and returned with a frosty beer. His first beer had died flat in his glass without his having touched it.

I was biding my time while I considered how to reply to his offer. I poured a glass of beer, took a sip, and said, "Nice beer."

He was watching me closely to hear what I would say.

My thoughts becoming clear, I said, "Alex, I want to thank you very much for your generous proposal. I would, however, like to have some time to consider it. If you would provide me with a draft proposal, I will review it and give you my answer."

What I really felt in my gut was that there were several reasons for not taking him up on his offer.

The company was a closely held company, which brought up the question of nepotism and the accuracy of the financial statements. Everyone in business knows that many small, closely held companies do their accounting in such a way as to reduce reportable earnings, thereby reducing their taxes. In addition, in a nepotistic environment, what assurances did I have that the president would not replace me with his brother-in-law or some other relative on a whim?

The most important reason was that I did not believe that I could, or wanted to, work for Alex for the next five years. Alex was not a bad person; it is just that he was a pain in the ass and had not been through the school of hard knocks. He was like an actor playing company president and not quite making it. He was like a Charlie Chaplin character—without humor.

I was considering in the near future finding a position with a company with better growth prospects and opportunities, and I had little interest in making the commitment that he wanted.

After a long pause, he said, "Okay, then. We are finished here for now." He stood up to indicate that our chat was finished. Alex never forgave me for not throwing myself heart and soul into his verbal proposal, and he never brought up the offer again.

Just as well.

Nashville, Winchester, Toledo, and Pensacola

Alex had begun his plan to relocate the Toledo, Ohio, operation to Winchester, Tennessee. The normally hardworking male population in the southeastern tip of the state was mainly unemployed. It was real hillbilly country.

Early in the Winchester project, we took a tour at the invitation of the vice president of the Hat Corporation of America, which was the largest employer in town and had a working employee population of three hundred. All of the workers were women—all the supervisors and managers were men.

As we walked down the aisles through the main work areas, we heard low whistles, muted catcalls, and rowdy sexual remarks from the workers. It was a scene normally reserved for construction workers' behavior toward female passersby.

After the contractor completed the Wilton plant, I routinely received verbal and graphic offers of sex from a number of production workers—both black and white. I declined, but it did not stop them from making the same offers each time I returned. It would have been counterproductive to have their supervisor reprimand them. It would only create hard feelings by all the female workers, so I let it slide and excluded those parts of the shop from my tours.

Alex had allocated to himself the purchase of the land and the construction of the building. I was responsible for the start-up and operation of the facility. My staff—Wally Altgilbers, the plant manager in Toledo, and Dick Perry, the manager of the Carry Pack operation—were coordinating the necessary products, tools, machinery, supervision, and quality controls for the start-up and operation of the facility.

Tom Wright, a straight shooter and vice president of finance, was in charge of the financial and accounting controls. Jerry Pollack was assigned to purchase materials for the plant and oversee the manufacture of woodworking equipment.

The project required that I make frequent trips to the plant to coordinate the various efforts, assess the progress, and find solutions to problems.

I flew from Chicago to Nashville, rented a car, and drove to Winchester every few weeks. On my return, I drove three hours back to Nashville, returned the rental car, stayed overnight, and flew back to Chicago the following morning.

On my first visit to Winchester, the local chamber of commerce officials, the mayor, and his staff met our leased plane at the small airport and welcomed Jean and me to the city. On arriving at our two-story hotel, we stowed our scanty luggage in our room and went downstairs.

The chamber of commerce had arranged a jeep-driven tour of the wild, hilly country surrounding the town—dense woods, meadows, gullies, mountains, raccoons, polecats, possums, bear, and deer. Jean and I sat in the backseat of our assigned jeep listening to the dialogue from the front seat about the beauty of the area and the location's benefits to our company.

As we rode over the bumpy mountain roads, they passed a rectangular Ballantine Scotch bottle back and forth between the front and backseats. Jean was not a drinker and passed, but I took a large gulp from the bottle and gasped as the fiery liquid flowed down my throat. This was no Ballantine—it was 100 percent moonshine! There were still moonshiners in the hills of Tennessee making white lightning. I became used to the moonshine after a few more gulps and drank the rest of the bottle during our two-and-a-half hour ride.

Arriving back at the hotel, the mayor and his delegation and the entire chamber of commerce and their wives were waiting to greet us with a box lunch social on the grounds of the hotel.

I struggled out of the jeep, the road rolling like waves under my feet, stiffened my knees to stand steady, and announced loudly to the gathered local dignitaries and their wives, "Damn, my ass is sore!"

That was the last thing that I remember for the next fourteen hours. They carried me to my bed and called a doctor, who checked me out to determine if I was in an alcoholic coma.

However, I do not remember any of it.

I awoke the next morning and was ravenous. I saw a pill bottle with a note from the doctor beside a white cardboard picnic box with a red ribbon tied around it. I ignored the pill bottle and the note from the doctor, tore open the ribbon-tied picnic box, devoured the two sandwich halves and the tapioca pudding desert, and washed it down with a pitcher of cold water. I felt much better. It must have been the nap!

At two o'clock, I met with the appropriate people of the mayor's office and the chamber of commerce and concluded our discussions. A couple of the younger chamber of commerce members invited me to go with them on a mountain ride and barbeque the next time I visited. I accepted their offer, but thought that I would have to slow down on the white lightning.

A few weeks later, I had the opportunity to take them up on their offer.

There were five jeeps in the party. The entourage drove a couple of hours up a steep wooded canyon road to a large cave in the side of the mountain. The sandstone cave was about twenty feet high and thirty feet wide and looked out over the valley below. There was a twelve-foot-wide ledge along the base of the cave, sloping off on a steep downhill slope. From the cave, you could see for miles in the early evening: blue mountains, greenish brown hills, and billowing gray clouds.

One of the men brought a chainsaw, sawed down a tree, and cut it into five-foot logs. The rest of us unloaded the gear, shoveled out the fire pit, placed kindling and small firewood in the hole, and stacked the logs in the pit.

One of the men started the fire by sloshing a half-gallon of gasoline on the firewood and logs. He tossed a lit piece of pitch into the hole, singeing his eyelashes in the process when the gasoline exploded! You could smell his eyebrows from six feet away, and the suntan on his face turned a couple of shades redder.

When the fire had burned down to softball-sized red coals, the smoke collecting in the roof of the cave and floating out toward the darkening sky, the dozen men, including me, sat around on the ground or on canvas camp chairs. We drank moonshine from bottles with beer chasers and told stories about dogs, hunting, guns, cars, and women until darkness fell. The night was still and comfortably warm; the stars stood out sharply in the clear black sky, and a half-moon had risen.

As we continued to talk and drink, I noticed that a number of my companions were undergoing a metamorphosis in their speech, manner, and expressions—from sport-coated, golf-pants-wearing Southern businessmen into backwoods, moonshine-guzzling, hound-chasing, gun-toting, rednecks.

I was just about to find out how right I was.

One of the men had brought his dog along. It was downslope from us and was barking loudly and incessantly in the dark.

The man next to me stood up from his wooden chair and pulled a Luger-like automatic pistol from his waistband. I recognized it as an old Colt Woodsman .22 caliber automatic pistol.

As he waved the gun in the air, he said loudly, "If that damned dog doesn't shut up, I am going to shoot the sonofabitch!"

The dog's owner furiously grabbed the wooden chair that the man with the gun had been sitting on and tossed it down into the darkness below.

The dog's owner said in a loud, threatening voice, "If you ever even shoot near my dog, whether you hit him or not, I am going to kick the goddamned shit out of you and stick that peashooter you got up your ass!"

Unfazed, the gunman said drunkenly, "Okay! Go down and get my damned chair and bring it back and I will not shoot your dog. And while you are at it, get your fucking dog and put a muzzle on him."

The dog's owner said, "Bull-shee-it; get your own goddamned chair yourself. And don't try to tell me how to handle my dog!"

There was laughing in the background as the farce unfolded. Seeing the impasse—and being a little concerned about the waving gun, which I am certain was not the only gun there—I felt that I might have to act. I did not have a dog in this fight, but things could escalate and someone could get hurt!

I got up, slipped and slid down the dark slope, found and picked up the wooden chair, brought it back up, and said, "Okay, you guys, here's the chair. Now you can put the gun away."

The dog followed me back up the slope and curled up at its owner's feet.

Attempting to distract their attention from the dog episode and avert a second argument, I said, "When are we going to put on the steaks? Come on—let's check with the cook."

This cooled off the situation, and we all turned to the subject of the steaks. The cook removed the meat from several packages and displayed the huge steaks. They must have weighed two or more pounds each; copious blood permeated the butcher paper. My mouth was watering, and I am sure that eleven other mouths were as well. The fire's coals were just right, and the cook topped the metal grates on the coals with twelve huge steaks.

The cook hollered, "Who wants rare?" Several people raised their hands and were noted by the chef. "Medium rare?" New hands went up. "Well done?" A few more men raised their hands, and the orders ceased.

The cook was diligent in his duty, and the steaks came out dripping fat around the edges, cooked exactly as ordered, which was a good trick, considering that the only light he used was the moon, the flickering light of the burning coals reflecting off the cave's ceiling, and a Coleman lantern.

As I ate, I was amazed at the amount of meat before me. I had trouble getting it all down, but I did. It was the best steak I had eaten in a very long time.

After a while, everyone started packing up for the drive back down the mountain. The men shoveled dirt onto the coals until they were dead. Equipment was loaded into the jeeps, and we started our perilous journey down the mountain. We were lighter by four or five bottles of white lightning, several cases of beer, and thirty pounds or so of red meat.

We arrived back in Winchester at one o'clock in the morning. Having left at five the preceding afternoon, it was an eight-hour mountain ride and barbeque. The dog owner still had his dog, unshot, and no more guns had been drawn or brandished.

It was a trip that I really enjoyed and one that I was looking forward to repeating. However, it was probably just as well that it never happened again.

Returning from one of my trips, O'Hare and the nearby airports were shut down by a heavy blizzard, and no airplanes were flying in or out. The blizzard and its effects lasted three days, stranding me in Nashville.

I had a few drinks in the bar of my hotel with a young, good-looking blonde woman with a striking figure. We enjoyed each other's company continuously and amorously until the blizzard subsided, the snow cleared from the runways, and the airport opened three days later. We had a great time and never left our room except to go to the dining room for dinner or the bar for another bottle of scotch.

It turned out that Patricia was married to a pilot, a major in the air force. She was visiting her mother in Nashville, but her home was in Pensacola. Patricia and I were intimate whenever I was back in Nashville before she returned home to Pensacola, and she invited me to visit her at her home in Florida.

A few weeks later, I was on a business trip to Panama City and made it a point to drive to Pensacola to visit her. In her usual phone call, Patricia had said it would be all right. The major flew out to Germany and would not return for a week.

We were naked together in her bed when a car's lights flashed through her bedroom window. I awoke and was immediately aware of the possibility of discovery and decided it was time for me to hightail it out of Dodge!

I was out of bed, out of the second-story window, and onto the first-story roof in thirty seconds, naked but with all my belongings under my arm. I jumped down to the lawn, hit the ground running, and headed for my rental car, as a shot from a .45 automatic exploded the air above my head!

I knew the sound well—the pistol's steel slide ejecting the spent cartridge case and chambering another round—having fired the .45 Colt pistol many times.

No doubt the .45 Colt automatic was in the hand of the husband, but I did not look around to confirm it. I was too busy trying to remember where the hell I parked my damned rental car.

Damn! According to Patricia, he was supposed to be in Germany drinking steins of beer and glasses of schnapps and seducing the Berliner fraus and fräuleins.

On my visits to Nashville, I spent some evenings in Printer's Alley, where burlesque and prostitution once flourished. It was now a noisy, fun-filled alley full of country and western music, nightclubs, and honky-tonks, known for featuring such performers as Johnny Cash, the Carter Sisters, and many other knowns and unknowns. Eventually Printer's Alley became my regular hangout when I was in Nashville.

I became attracted to a female singer-pianist, who played the piano and sang in one of the clubs. She had a beautiful voice, and her piano was a perfect backup to her singing. We had a few drinks together between her performances and became friendly. She was about my age, very pretty, with a shapely figure, sexy brown eyes, and short brunette hair with waves and small curls. We became closer, and before the night was over, she drove me to her home in the outskirts of Nashville and we became amorously involved.

On my next trip to Nashville a few weeks later, I went to the club where she was working, sat at a table, and watched her performance. Caroline saw me in the audience and cut short the song she was singing and playing and segued into a medley of snippets of songs from her repertoire. Cheating hearts, true love, good-hearted women, blissful happiness, unrequited love, good times and bad times, glad times and sad times, cheap hotels and honky-tonk bars, and more.

When she finished her riff, the audience gave her an appreciative round of applause. I enjoyed her presentation and was sure that she meant her selection of songs for me—even if I was unable to unscramble the mixed metaphors. However, I like a woman who is a little mysterious, funny, and sexy, with a good sense of humor.

We delighted in each other's company and spent our time together in sensual pursuits each time I came to Nashville. She was intelligent, well educated, a good conversationalist, adventurous, and carefree; and we engaged in amorous interludes as well as foolish diversions. She was one heck of a woman and knew what made a man happy.

When we were not frolicking in bed, we enjoyed driving through the countryside and nearby small towns looking at the sights, going out on the town, visiting the Hermitage, the home of President Andrew Jackson, swimming naked in the several lakes in the area, and exploring the dark woods at night.

One night, we drove into the dark woods around Nashville and, at my suggestion—with which she foolishly agreed— explored the inside of a vacant ghost house. With me carrying a half-full bottle of Jack Daniel's as a weapon, we explored the two floors with only the moon and the occasional flicker of my lighter to see where we were going—and what or whom we might run into: dopers, drunks, killers, or maniacs—or just hungry bums sucking on empty bottles of booze.

We delighted in our escapades together and enjoyed each other's company and sensuality. As a young woman, Caroline immersed herself in feminine pursuits, education, and music— mostly classical, but her country and honky-tonk songs were my favorites.

Once we flew to New York, saw the sights, and at her suggestion, visited Greenwich Village, where an entertainer that she liked, Thelonious Monk, was performing. We enjoyed the weird, but fascinating, musical performance. The next evening, we had drinks and dinner at the Rainbow Room, a favorite spot for celebrities, show people, and would-be show people.

Caroline had not told me much about her sexual liaisons, nor had I told her about all of mine. I looked for adventurous escapades in my youth and still lived for them.

Once, after we had been seeing each other every couple weeks for over a year, she was in her kitchen preparing cucumber sandwiches for herself, her daughter, and me. I was in the kitchen alone with her, idly watching her make the sandwiches and sipping on a glass of whiskey.

We were making small talk when suddenly she looked up at me over the sink, looked me in the eyes, and said seriously, "Jerry, I love you, but I am not in love with you."

While eating the sandwich, I thought, *Things, they are a-changing.*

Caroline and I drifted apart over the next six months, both somewhat reluctantly I believe, and she eventually remarried.

We did meet again, however, twice after she married— once in Nashville and a second time in New York, where I was attending a convention. We said our final good-bye in bed.

Later, I realized that of the many women that I had encountered and been involved with up to this time, Caroline was the only one I could not forget. I have been with too many women for my own good—most of them unmentioned, and their mention will have to wait for another time, if ever.

It had become as if I were living three different lives. Preeminent in importance to me was my job. My second life was drinking alcohol, spending my time in bars, carousing with women, and bedding them.

The last was the prosaic, everyday routine of the family: a dutiful, loving wife and mother of our five kids and the rewarding weekend family trips, picnics, hunting, camping, and other recreation.

Jack Watson

Jean was a beautiful bride. She was a fine woman, a wonderful mother, and a dedicated wife, but we unfortunately had little in common except the children, whom we both loved very much.

We were both very young when we married. I was a virgin, having been burned several times in my romantic quests in my youth, and she was a virgin by choice. Perhaps we were too young, inexperienced, and ignorant of the long-term needs for a successful marriage.

We had different intellects, interests, and ambitions. She was content with the simple things in life: home, children, and friends. It was difficult for her to realize that there was a big world out there. She was content without making it a significant part of her life. I, on the other hand, looked for challenges and adventure.

Her life with me had not been easy, but like a saint, she had never complained. She lived through moves with me to different states, different jobs, different friends, different houses and neighborhoods, and different schools and playmates for our children.

I was involved in the heady pursuit of grappling with new problems, opportunities, and challenges, broadening my knowledge, honing new skills, learning new things, and drinking and cavorting with women. The distance between us widened, and we started to drift apart. More accurately, I drifted away—and she remained where she was.

Before we were married, Jean was not ready to consider marriage. I was the one who insisted that we marry. She had reservations, which I had finally overcome. Sadly, I believe that Jean would have been happier had she not met or married me, but who knows? The fact is that we had five fine children whom we both love.

A Stolen Quarter

The Gulf of Tonkin incident happened in 1964. North Vietnamese PT boats fired torpedoes at the USS *Maddox*, causing a furor in Washington. Congress passed the Gulf of Tonkin Resolution with overwhelming support of both parties,

210

and President Johnson received authority to wage all-out war against North Vietnam.

From 1964, the Vietnam War escalated; the troop level of 200,000 in 1965 rose to more than a half-million servicemen and women in 1968.

Conscription was in effect; however, education deferments reduced conscription of the ranks of the upper class, and conscientious objectors protested induction and did everything they could to stay out of the war.

The antiwar movement was strong and becoming stronger as the casualties mounted on the battlefield. Protestors burning draft cards and some potential draftees fled to Canada or other draft-evader havens. Marches and gatherings to protest the war swelled to the thousands as the war dragged on. With all these problems, there was a continually increasing demand for more soldiers to fight the war.

It was a dreary, overcast Saturday afternoon in late March 1969 in Lombard. Jean came into the kitchen where I was having a cup of coffee. David moped along behind her as if he would rather be anywhere else but there. David had been out all night and had just gotten home. Roland had covered for him.

Jean said, "David, come over here so your father can see you."

She looked at David, and said to me, "David wants to tell you something."

I looked at David and said, "Go ahead, tell me."

He reluctantly replied, "I was picked up by the sheriff last night for burglarizing the Lombard airport office. I broke the door to the office and went in."

"Well, what did you steal?"

"A quarter that was in the desk drawer."

"What?"

"The district attorney is going to file charges. Breaking and entering—burglary," he said.

"What?" I said even more incredulously. "The DA is going to do what?"

"He also said that if I joined the army and went to Vietnam, he would drop all charges, and I would not have any record against me in the file."

I leaned back against the kitchen counter, stunned for a moment. Jean and David both looking at me intently.

After a while, I looked at David and said in a tough, macho tone, "David, it looks like you are going to join the army." I would later regret that statement—forever.

David enlisted the following week, and a couple of days later, I drove him to the huge Chicago Army Induction Center to be processed for transport to boot camp to start his tour of duty. David had attended a going-away party the night before, hosted by a number of his friends, and had a terrible hangover.

We arrived, and he proceeded through the induction process. He looked like warmed-over dog shit and probably felt even worse from an excess of booze, hardly any sleep, and an enormous hangover. Knowing the torment he was going through facing the grueling induction process in his sorry state, I felt bad for him and my heart was saddened.

Two and a half months later, Jean and I and David's brother Allan and his sisters, Teresa and Clarissa, loaded into my station wagon, and we drove to Fort Leonard Wood, Missouri, to see David graduate from boot camp.

Roland did not go with us; he had joined the navy in May 1968 and completed boot camp at the Naval Training Center at Great Lakes, Illinois. He was assigned to the USS *Rankin,* based in Norfolk, Virginia, which was somewhere en route to, or at, one of a dozen or so international ports of call.

We proudly watched the crisp military formations on the parade ground and listened to the patriotic music, drums, and bugle calls. After the graduation ceremonies, David joined us in the park on the base, and we enjoyed a picnic lunch together. David looked splendid in his uniform and appeared amazingly healthy, strong, and well fed. He was beaming with pride as his mother and two sisters doted over him. I was also very proud.

Eventually, he had to return to duty; and sadly, Jean and the kids all kissed him good-bye. I shook his hand.

We received mail from him, or I should say that his mother and maybe his two sisters and his two brothers did. I never personally received any mail from David. Perhaps he figured that his letters to his mother were for the whole family—I do not know. In his letters to Jean, David recounted where he was or where he had been, as much as the censors permitted or as much as he wanted to talk about, including a Vietnamese girl with whom he was in love.

Jean and I were in Toledo—me to visit the plant, and she just to get out of the house and go somewhere for a couple of days.

I had to be somewhat careful since I had had a number of escapades with a Toledo society woman and a merchant seaman's wife, and others, on my trips to Toledo. I wanted to avoid any unpleasant incidents that would spoil Jean's holiday—not to mention mine.

We dined in the hotel restaurant and ordered our meals. I decided to order the matzo-ball soup, and Jean said she would have the same. The waitress returned with our order and set the soup bowls in front of each of us. I looked over my soup—it looked like Rocky Mountain oysters floating in a light brown broth.

As I stirred my soup, I asked the waitress, "How large is a full-grown matzo?"

She shrieked a high-pitched laugh and headed to the kitchen, probably to tell the cook what I said.

A couple of months later, Tom Wright came into my office and closed the door. He said, "Jerry, I have bad news."

I waited for the next shoe to fall.

"Alex heard rumors about you having an affair with someone in Nashville, but he doesn't know her name. He asked me if I knew about it, and of course, I told him I didn't."

Tom and I had previously discussed what was going on, and being a good friend, he knew about my affair with Caroline—as well as other women. Tom would not betray my trust; he was closemouthed, and the information that Alex had could only be gossip.

The next morning, Alex's secretary called me and said that Alex wanted to see me in his office.

When I entered, Alex rose from his chair and closed the door.

He said nervously, "It's just not working out. I want you to resign."

I replied, "I agree. It is not working out for me either." Peremptorily I said, "I am prepared to submit my resignation effective immediately—providing severance issues are agreed."

Alex said, "What do you suggest?"

I replied, "One year continuation of salary and benefits and moving expenses is fair. I will take care of all other miscellaneous expenses myself."

Tom's heads-up had given me advance warning and time to plan my exit strategy. Alex had no issues regarding my job performance over the last three years, which he had told me was exemplary. He had nothing to support an outright termination for cause and, at best, had only unsupported rumor and gossip about my personal life that was none of his business. My performance on the job was what mattered.

Alex said, "Then we agree."

"One hundred percent," I replied.

Alex, after a quizzical glance at me, took a sheet of letterhead, wrote down the severance agreement, and handed it to me.

I looked at it and said, "If you would have a signed copy made for me, you may have my resignation, effective immediately. There is one thing I would ask, however. I would like you to call my managers together as a group. I want to compliment them on their performance, encourage them to continue to strive for excellence, and say good-bye to them personally."

The paperwork was completed, and the meeting with the managers concluded in good spirit. Later that evening, I went to the plant, cleared out my desk, and left the building without looking back.

Medalist Industries in Oshkosh, Wisconsin, 1970

After my resignation "firing" at Wilton, I started sending out my updated résumé and combed the newspapers for professional openings in my field.

After several weeks of searching and sending out résumés, I had an offer of employment from Medalist Industries in Milwaukee. Although athletic clothing was Medalist Industries' major focus and represented the bulk of company sales and profits, they had two orphan-like manufacturing facilities in Oshkosh, Wisconsin, producing machinery, boat engines, and pumps. The Oshkosh operation had two plants and 350 personnel. I accepted the job as vice president and division manager for the Bell Machine Company plant in Oshkosh.

The only suitable family residence that I located in Oshkosh was an apartment in a two-story, multiapartment building under construction, which would be complete in four to six weeks. Jean, Teresa, Alan, and Clarissa remained in Illinois for the time being. Roland was in the navy, and David was in Vietnam.

I took up temporary residence at the Pioneer Resort Hotel on the south end of Lake Winnebago. The Pioneer had outdoor and indoor swimming pools, three bars, two restaurants, a dance floor, and women all over the place.

I caroused with more women than I would have ever anticipated. Out-of-state, single, divorced, or lonely married women—even a traveling saleslady who brought tons of dresses on a wheeled hanging rack to her room at night, the young blonde-haired woman at the reception desk who liked to go to Packer games in Green Bay, the local young married woman who liked to swim and frequented the Pioneer while her husband was at work on the evening shift at a factory, even renting a room, and the dark-haired Italian woman who lived in Milwaukee—all ended up as available, amorous girlfriends.

215

I was fully aware that God would not look favorably on my indiscretions, but I just didn't give a damn. God's wrath, however, would punish me in the future for my transgressions.

In spite of my amorous diversions, I was dedicated to my job at Medalist and found it interesting and rewarding.

The division had been an orphan in the corporation and had less-than-competent management. The former management had ignored, or failed to recognize, obvious impediments to profitability and the necessary actions.

My work was cut out for me.

The original company, Bell Machine Company, produced a line of machinery for manufacturing specialized wood parts by furniture manufacturers such as Thomasville, Broyhill, High Point Furniture, and other furniture manufacturers in North Carolina and other locations. The second division produced pumps and related equipment.

Over the years, the Bell Machine Division had acquired other specialized machinery manufacturers—Dyken, Challoner, Nash, and Peerless—with diverse product lines.

The acquired product lines had different drawing formats, standards, and part numbering systems. Tooling, jigs, fixtures, and foundry patterns were often inefficient or outmoded, and their numbering systems were different from each other—and from Bell's system.

Repair parts, a significant portion of the company's sales, were priced from different formulae—or no formula at all. Prices for spare parts sometimes had not had price increases in several years—even pricing that would, at a minimum, keep abreast of inflation.

The factory's production machines used to make the woodworking, textile winding and wrapping machines, and metal cutting saws were aged and inefficient. The production and inventory control and quality control were archaic, especially with five different part-number identification systems.

Plant housekeeping was practically nonexistent. Skids of parts filled the aisles and restricted movement of product from machine to machine and into and out of the store areas. The scrap bins were full of scrapped parts—without assessment of the defect or reason for the defect or the individual responsible, providing no basis for corrective action.

It was just my cup of tea!

My job was to find solutions and to develop and act on action plans to produce positive results. The union, however, did not always see problems in quite the same way as I did. *Productivity* was a word seldom used by the union, and when mentioned, was used more often in combination with an expletive.

As manager, the staff and I made numerous improvements in efficiency, productivity, and marketing, which substantially increased profitability. The corporate office, however, severely restrained capital expenditures for cost reduction, new machine tools, and other productive equipment, which would have further boosted profitability.

I updated and expanded the data processing department at the specific direction of Norman Fischer, the chairman of Medalist Industries, delivered to me by my boss, the president of Medalist Industries: "Perk" Perkins.

I reluctantly agreed to spend the money to upgrade the data processing, but I thought it should have been a lower capital expenditure priority than the acquisition of profit-enhancing productive machinery. However, there was a method to their madness at the corporate office, of which I was to become acutely aware in 1972.

Skydiving

I often thought about skydiving, and I decided to learn to jump out of an airplane. I drove to Milwaukee, stopped to pick up my local girlfriend—the dark-haired Italian one—and had a few beers and a romp in the hay before we left. In the car, she opened two beers from a six-pack, and I drove to the airport where the skydiving school was located.

I took the short course on how to exit an airplane and practiced jumping off a platform and rolling as I landed to minimize the shock of hitting the ground.

After I completed jump-and-roll training, I made my first parachute jump with a tether attached to the airplane, which automatically opened the parachute when I jumped out.

The next week, I brought my Italian girlfriend and a six-pack of beer, and we each had a beer before we reached the skydiving school.

I practiced pulling the ripcord attached to my chest to release the parachute from its pack on my back. I thought I was ready to make my first jump without the tether attached to the airplane.

My adrenaline rushing, I jumped out headfirst. I pulled the ripcord, and my legs momentarily caught in the lines of the parachute. I was diving straight down, my head pointing to the ground at 3,500 feet!

This was no way to land—on my head!

After a few seconds, the parachute lines unwound from my legs, and I was floating down under the open parachute. It was a wondrous feeling. In the three and a half minutes while I was descending, everything was dead quiet, except for the sound of cows mooing far below and the buzz of miniature cars and trucks driving down the highway.

I finally saw my instructor, who had jumped right after I did. His parachute floating fifty yards or so away, he called to me with a voice as clear as if he were standing beside me. I realized that he had been talking to me over the two-way shortwave radio that I carried on my belt. I can remember his exact words when I was diving for the earth headfirst: "#$@Z%&!"

I jumped out of airplanes eight more times over the next two months. Once I landed on a rock pile and got a sore butt from it, and once I landed in a four-foot-deep swamp. I hit the surface of the swamp, knocking my feet out from under me and submerging me under the swamp's turbid water with a water-drenched parachute on top of me.

It took a while to drag the soaking parachute over three hundred yards to the skydiving shack—much of it up to my waist in swamp water.

At the skydiving shack, the owner was reading my instructor the riot act for not seeing the low clouds around the landing zone and telling me to jump, which I did, when I could not see the landing zone and landed in the swamp.

I enjoyed skydiving and wanted to continue, but my work led me in a different direction.

"Dago Red" and Fried Peanut Butter and Jelly Sandwiches

The middle of winter arrived, and Joe the welder invited me to go ice fishing on Lake Winnebago. Ice fishing was a popular sporting activity for Oshkoshians in the winter. Hundreds of vehicles drove and parked on the frozen lake to ice fish. Ice up to more than a foot thick covered the fifty-mile-long lake.

There were hundreds of ice-fishing shanties all over the lake, each seating two to four—and sometimes more—fishermen. The ice fishermen drilled and sawed a hole in the ice about three feet by six feet in the center of the ice-fishing shanties and arranged chairs or benches around the hole for the long wait. The ice fisherman held a three-pronged trident spear and enticed the sturgeon to the hole to spear it by using a fish decoy with lead weights hanging on a fishing line from the ceiling down into the water.

All an ice fisherman needs is lots of time, patience, and luck that a sturgeon will be attracted to his decoy and swim under the hole in the ice and be speared with the trident. Sturgeons can be a hundred or more pounds and over six feet long.

Joe made a tradition of hosting other ice fishermen on the lake. His hosting repertoire consisted of continuously providing toasted peanut butter and grape jelly sandwiches and large paper cups of "Dago Red" wine from gallon jugs for all who came by his shanty—until the food and drink ran out.

In the late afternoon, I was full of red wine, stuffed with sandwiches, and in the ice shanty drinking "Dago Red" and watching the hole, hoping for a sight of a sturgeon.

As I moved around in the crowded shanty, I slipped and fell fully clothed into the hole, into the ice-cold water. My boots and clothing were heavy, and I sank under the water. There was about a six-inch breathing space between the bottom of the ice and the surface of the water. Although there was translucent light filtering through the ice, a feeling of extreme anxiety swept over me.

The cold water refocused my mind, and as I assessed my situation, a thought entered my head. What would happen if I were to backstroke under the hole of another ice shanty and get a three-pronged trident spear in my belly from a trigger-happy ice fisherman?

Not likely, I decided, but I was cautious nevertheless, and soon arms reached into the cold water and pulled me out. The whole thing lasted maybe a minute or so, but it seemed like a lifetime to me.

I drove home to our apartment and parked in the carport under the building. The winter sun had been down for some time, and it was getting dark and freezing cold.

After a short while, Jean came out of our apartment and tried to get me to come inside, but I felt just fine—even cozy—and rebuffed her pleadings. After a while, she gave up and left me asleep in an ice-cold car on a freezing black night.

Hours later, I awoke to find that my wet clothing had started freezing on my body. I managed to exit the car and, as if I was the Tin Man, climbed the stairs stiff-legged from my frozen trouser legs, to our apartment, where I stripped and fell into bed and was asleep minutes later.

The sheriff had pulled Joe over on his way home from the lake. The officer said that he was driving erratically and issued a citation for Joe to appear at court the following week. Joe explained to the officer that a piece of his ice-fishing equipment was under his foot and he was merely removing the equipment so as not to interfere with his driving. He admitted that he might have wobbled a bit for just a second or two in moving the equipment, but that he was not driving erratically nor was he drunk. When I heard his story, I wanted to believe Joe.

I volunteered to be a witness in court on Joe's behalf and showed up in a pressed pin-striped suit, starched white shirt, conservative tie, and shined shoes. It turned out that I was the only witness for Joe—except for Joe himself. The session lasted only a few minutes. The police officer was the first to testify and testified straightforwardly. Joe was next, and his performance was adequate but lacked appeal.

I was next. The judge asked my name and occupation.

I replied, "My name is Jerry Jack Watson, and my profession is industrial manager."

The judge asked, "Where do you work, Mr. Watson, and how do you know the defendant?"

I answered, "Your Honor, I am the vice president and division manager of the two Medalist Industries plants in Oshkosh, which provide employment for several hundred people in Winnebago County. The defendant is a master welder in our welding shop and has a reputation in the shop for honesty and humor. I know Joe personally; he is a model employee and has nothing derogatory on his record. He has never come to work with alcohol on his breath—as have some others in the shop. He is honest and dependable, and his word is his bond."

I could feel a drop of sweat rolling down my neck.

The judge nodded his head and asked me, "And what was the defendant's demeanor at the lake before he drove home?"

"*The last time I remember seeing him,* he was outside by his stove socializing with some fishermen and was as sober as—if you will excuse me, Judge—as a judge."

The judge smiled at my attempt at wry humor, thought for a moment, tapped his wooden gavel once, and said, "Case dismissed—the defendant may go."

The judge shuffled his papers into a stack, picked them up, and as the bailiff intoned "All rise," got up and left the courtroom.

Joe came over to me, grabbed my hand, shook it heartily, and said, "Thanks."

I replied, "Don't worry about it."

The sweat on the back of my neck had dried.

Months later, the company and the union were negotiating a new labor contract. The negotiations came to an impasse, and the union declared a strike against the company.

To counter the strike and to continue as much of our production and shipments as possible, I had previously, as a precaution, suggested to our managers to poll their staffs and determine who was willing to work part-time or full-time in the shop and also to find out the skills available to continue production during the strike.

The results were encouraging. We found many in our management group had hands-on manufacturing skills. Some of them had been promoted to staff or supervisory positions from the shop floor and knew how to do the jobs of the workmen they supervised.

I pulled on a pair of jeans and a long-sleeved work shirt and went to work in the machine shop on the Kearny & Trecker milling machine, machining aluminum meter castings for a very profitable order from a large Wisconsin meter manufacturer.

After I spent a couple of weeks working on the milling machine, the welding shop foreman asked me if I would consider working in the welding shop since they were short of help and there were only a few people in the office who could weld.

He told me that he had seen an article on a paper I presented to the Lincoln Foundation for Technical Welding Publications in an old copy of a welding publication. I had won third place nationally in the Lincoln contest with a paper on "fabricating welded turret lathe tools from scrap metal."

I accepted the welder job, but told the welding foreman that I was going to need a lot of help from him.

Ironically, I ended up doing Joe's job during the strike, but not nearly as fast. I did not have the experience of a qualified welder and was learning on the job.

Negotiations with the union continued, but tempers flared after the strike continued for several weeks. On the first few days of the strike, the strikers were elated, and their spirits were high—it was almost like a picnic or a holiday for them.

However, as the strike wore on, they became discouraged, restless, resentful, and often aggressive toward the company.

The strikers attempted to block the company gates with a human barricade to stop trucks from shipping out the finished products and trucks from coming into the plant with raw material, parts, and supplies. Some strikers did not use good judgment and ran in front of the trucks, narrowly avoiding a serious accident and injury.

Someone was going to get hurt.

I had our lawyer get a court order barring strikers from gathering in front of the company gates, which substantially reduced the risk of an accident. It also kept our shipping and receiving operations functioning.

Negotiations continued, but were making little progress. The federal mediator assisted both parties to come up with solutions and mediated the negotiations. I thought about ways to break the impasse and devised a plan that I discussed with the federal mediator—an incentive plan that would pay a special bonus to the hourly and salaried personnel based on productivity improvement of the hourly workforce.

I presented the plan to the federal mediator, who after reviewing it, deemed it fair to both sides and said that he would recommend it to the union. After several hours of explaining the plan and answering questions from the union, the approved plan became a part of the labor agreement.

A few days later, the strike was over, and everybody was back on the job. The union and the shop employees knew about the productivity bonus plan, but they were reluctant to increase their productivity voluntarily or to identify potential cost improvements due to their antagonism toward management.

After a few weeks of informing and discussing with the workforce and the union how they would benefit, what they needed to do, and the company assistance available to help them, we saw the employees start to realize the benefit in their paychecks, and the program started getting traction and was eventually successful.

Artist: Deb Bartelt
Martina's Oshkosh House

Chapter 9:
Redemption–Meeting Martina

Oshkosh, Wisconsin

One evening, after work, I was sitting at the bar at the Town House and Restaurant in Oshkosh—my favorite place to drink and cavort with women.

A motherly woman at the bar was having a martini. She looked in my direction and said squeakily, "So you are a martini drinker too?"

I smiled and affirmed that I was.

Taking my expression as a willingness to converse, she asked, "Where do you work?"

"I manage one of the two Medalist Industries plants here in Oshkosh."

"Is one of them the old Bell Machine Company on Jackson Street?" she asked.

"Yes, that's one of them. But it is now called the Medalist Automated Machinery Division."

"And does it still make woodworking machines?" she asked.

"It still manufactures woodworking machinery, but also textile winding and wrapping machines and metal-cutting band saws."

She nodded her head knowingly and asked, "And the other company?"

"Universal Motors—on New York Avenue on the east side of town. It assembles pumps and generator sets and produces diesel-operated pumps and the Atomic 4 auxiliary sailboat engine."

She seemed to be interested in, or at least conversationally knowledgeable of, the subject. She said, "Do you know Ted Urban?"

I replied, "I have not met him personally, but I know that he owns Lamico next to our building on Jackson Street."

She stuck out her hand and said, "My name is Eleanor Urban—Ted Urban's wife."

"No kidding," I said as I extended my hand and shook her hand. "My name is Watson—Jerry Watson. It is a pleasure to meet you. I heard that your husband was the largest manufacturer of laminated wooden crutches in the world."

"Yes, he is—and it keeps him very busy traveling to Canada, Asia, and South America to get exactly the right wood for laminating and calling on his sales agents, who are spread all over the world. He also manages the plant here in Oshkosh and a smaller one in Appleton."

Eleanor was 100 percent Polish—as was her husband. Their grandfathers had emigrated from Poland.

Ted Urban was an imposing figure and a workaholic, learning the toolmaking craft and working as a toolmaker during the war. This led eventually to his ownership of Lamico, where the right cutting tools were essential for the production and quality of laminated wooden crutches.

Although he was seldom at home for very long, he was authoritarian by nature and temperament and attempted to control his wife and five daughters. He also controlled the pocketbook with an iron hand, putting as much money as he could into his business.

When Ted was working at night and the daughters were grown, but some were still living at home, Eleanor went to the Town House to be around other people, have conversations, and sip a martini or two. She was good at starting up conversations, enjoyed the vivacity and boisterousness of the bar patrons, and kept up the back-and-forth with the best of them.

Tonight, she had been talking to three salesmen who were pretty well into their cups. I was relatively sober. She suggested that we all take a short walk to visit her oldest daughter, Martina ("Tina"), at her antique shop just a block or two away.

Martina was a curvaceous, slender, young woman with blonde hair and blue-green eyes. She had the poise of a model and sat on a high wooden stool near the side of the room, a cigarette held gracefully between her fingers.

The tightly packed shop displayed antique furniture and a wide variety of other items. There were silver items, flatware, dishes, furniture, cooking utensils, framed pictures, and clothing.

Eleanor was introducing the three besotted salesmen to Tina. A surprising surge of jealousy warmed my face, and I hesitated in joining the introductions. Eleanor saw me, pulled me over to Martina, and introduced us.

Martina was even more beautiful up close. She was wearing a short-sleeved pink top, a short skirt, and boots. My heart skipped a beat—she was the most beautiful woman I had ever seen!

Martina and I made small talk, and eventually Eleanor herded the salesmen back to the bar. Martina and I talked about her antique shop, which she had affectionately named "Nana's." She told me how she named the shop after her grandmother and showed me the variety of articles for sale as I followed her around.

However, what I was really interested in was admiring her beautiful face and slender body and how gracefully she carried herself. I was smitten with love, but I was hesitant and did not clasp her hand in mine nor touch her cheek to feel and sense her beauty, which was my true desire.

Martina needed to close her shop and go home. We agreed to see each other again the next day. I was entranced and completely absorbed in our brief time together. In short, she was a knockout. I could not wait to see her again and maybe touch her—or even hug and kiss her, if I were lucky.

The next day, we had an informal date at a restaurant. She ordered mashed potatoes and gravy—and nothing else! I kidded her about it in a light, noncondescending way—not wishing to offend her.

Our love was blossoming by the day and growing stronger, and we had our first sexual episode. It was lovely and passionate. Martina and I dined together at various restaurants and frequented bars almost every evening. Sometimes, however, we did not go out together for an evening for whatever reason. One of these times, I got out of work late and was sitting alone at the Town House drinking martinis. I looked up to see Martina on the dance floor with some man I had not seen before. She was a great dancer, and she noticed me at the bar and put on a show of dancing to make me jealous—and it worked!

I was pissed and got up and left the bar. I found out later that the man was a visiting salesman from Stockholm. Martina hated salesmen, and I later teased her about the salesman every so often—just for fun.

Martina sure knew how to make a man jealous, though, and eventually to get him to marry her.

Jean and I had legally separated. She filed for divorce, and we went to court and finalized the papers.

I was looking for a place to stay. After surveying rooms and apartments to rent, I was disappointed with the results. Martina asked me if I wanted to move in with her and her two children (Maelee, who was twelve years old, and Joel, who was eight), her grandmother ("Nana"), and her sister Michaelene. Three of my five children still lived at home with their mother.

I moved my few belongings into her bedroom on the second floor, along with a new record player as a present for sharing her room—and her bed—with me.

The second day her son, Joel, spit on my head from the balcony at the top of the winding stairway.

"Welcome to Madison Street," I said to myself as I raced up the stairs to catch the little culprit, but he had already slipped away and disappeared.

A few nights later, at about one in the morning, I went downstairs silently in the dark so as not to disturb anyone. I was hungry and thought I would check out the refrigerator to make a sandwich. I was barefoot, and as I entered the kitchen, I stepped on something soft and squishy that came up between my bare toes.

Reaching in my pocket, I found my lighter and illuminated the floor. I was standing in a pile of dog shit in my bare feet. I noticed several more piles of it on the kitchen floor. It seemed as if one of Martina's sisters, Sheryl, had left her dog for her to take care of. No one had thought to walk the dog so it could relieve itself in somebody's front yard or sidewalk—or front porch for all I cared—rather than on Martina's kitchen floor.

Since I was a guest in the house—and was up and wide-awake—I decided to clean up the mess and forget about a snack—I did not think my stomach could take it now.

Even after I picked up and disposed of the dog shit, the whole kitchen floor was a mess of shitty dog tracks and puddles of urine. I turned on the chandelier and spent the next few minutes quietly looking for a mop, bucket, dustpan, and soap, and then spent the next half hour scooping, mopping, emptying the bucket, and remopping until the wood floor looked clean.

The dog was innocently curled up in a corner—either asleep or ignoring my presence and his culpability in the mess.

At about two o'clock, I turned out the light, climbed the stairs, slipped into the bathroom to scrub myself, and hit the sack. As I closed my eyes, I wondered, *What's next?*

A few days later, as I came in the front door, I happened to glance into the living room before I started up the stairs. Joel was squatting on top of a high bookcase, with his arms hanging down at his sides like a chimpanzee in a tree.

"Martina!" I yelled plaintively. I repeated it several times before she answered.

She came down the stairs, and we looked at Joel. She was getting little response to her pleading with him. He eventually slithered down the backside of the bookcase and disappeared again.

As I passed Nana's bedroom door, I saw that she was busily pushing orange peels under her bed. She gave me a pleasant, quizzical look and returned to her orange peels. I proceeded on my way, thinking that I should mind my own business.

Martina had decorated her bedroom with several classic antique valentines hanging from the ceiling by strings. She also had several record albums, including Bob Dylan and Chicago. I enjoyed Dylan's songs and almost became addicted to them, falling asleep at night listening to his music.

My appetite for alcohol continued unabated, and I stacked empty Scotch bottles around the sides of the bedroom. An early Wisconsin winter fell, with almost a foot of snow covering the roof. I placed a six-pack of beer in the snow on the roof outside our upstairs window to chill.

Later, when I reached out the window to get the beer, it had slid farther down the steep roof. Naked, I slithered out on my stomach. When I reached for the beer, I started to slide downhill, inch by inch. I visualized myself sliding headfirst down the roof like a toboggan on a ski slope and off the roof like a ski jump.

I called out to Martina, but she must have been in the bathroom or somewhere, and there was no answer. I yelled for Martina about every minute, but not too loudly; the last thing I wanted in my present situation—especially in my naked state— was a helpful female neighbor. After two or three minutes that seemed like a lifetime, Martina finally saw the situation, reached out, grabbed my ankles, and pulled my naked ass back through the window.

What a woman! I love her, and I am glad she is mine.

To thaw out, I had a couple of slugs of Scotch and a cold beer chaser.

The Message

A year later, after Martina and I were married and living in Texas, the Swedish salesman intruded again. An opened and discarded Christmas card addressed to Martina with a return address on the envelope was on our floor.

I was able to locate his office in Stockholm and called his phone number. I talked to his secretary, who spoke fluent English, and ascertained that he was married. Since he was not there, I asked her to give a message to him. "The next time you try to contact my wife, I will call your wife and let her know what you are up to. And if you try again, I will come there and cut off your goddamn balls."

I asked his secretary if she got it, and she said that she got it and asked me if I were one of those "wild Indians" in America. I smiled to myself at the thought and said, "I might be—you can never tell."

She asked, "Who should I say called?"

"He will know—it's the guy he does not want to meet."

My Whole World Changed

On Monday morning, I arose as usual to go to work. It was November 1971, and I was at my office on Jackson Avenue, meeting with my management staff around a small conference table. I was standing in front of my desk when the telephone rang. I picked up the phone, and an army master sergeant introduced himself with an official tone.

"Is this Mr. Jerry Jack Watson?"

I felt the muscles tightening in my throat. I swallowed and hoarsely affirmed my identity.

"I regret to inform you that your son, David James Watson, is deceased."

The telephone slipped from my hand to the floor, and I gripped the edge of the desk as a dizzying cloud smothered my mind.

After several moments, I regained my composure, retrieved the phone, and asked the sergeant to hold on as I waved my staff out of the room. The sergeant finished with a few terse words of condolence and gave me his telephone number.

Alone in my office, I continued to grip the edge of my desk as I stared into nothingness. Disbelief, grief, and sorrow crept into my brain. *David is dead?*

I refused to believe it. The army had made a mistake. I ticked off the points in my mind to refute the news of his death. Wrong name—a mistake of Daniel or some other name—perhaps the wrong middle or last name. Perhaps John or Jason instead of James—perhaps Wilson or Watkins in place of Watson? A misread dog tag? The points were endless, but I continued until suddenly I realized the futility. David was dead!

Jean received an official notice a few days later. David had died in Quang Tri, South Vietnam, on November 8, 1971. He died on his second tour of duty, which he was not required to serve but for which he had volunteered, in a strange land in a distant war far from home.

They found David at night, his back against a truck in an army vehicle park in Quang Tri, a few clicks north of Hue. He had died from an overdose of drugs. I could not—would not—believe them. David was the most carefree, cheerful, happy-go-lucky, life-loving human being whom I had ever known. The last thing in the world he would do was kill himself. It had to have been a tragic accident from a corrupted drug or an inadvertent overdose.

David was barely twenty-one and had almost completed his second tour. He had fallen in love with a young Vietnamese woman, Sandy (Tranti Ngoc Ho), who had a son named Terry. He was trying to get permission to marry Sandy and to get her and ,Terry, whom he treated as his own son, to the United States. David was almost in a panic. He was concerned that the army would ship him off and he would never see his wife or son again. He would never have killed himself and left them stranded and alone.

He loved both his wife and son and only wanted to take them home with him when his second tour was over. Instead, he died alone on a dark night in a dark place—thousands of miles from home. Illegal drugs of every kind proliferated in Vietnam. They were cheap, available, and deadly. It was a virtual plague.

David traveled to many firebases and other active locations and was in many dangerous places and situations—including Khe Sanh during Dewey Canyon II—and many of the firebases. He also risked sneaking alone at night into the small village where his girlfriend lived, which was a hotbed of Viet Cong soldiers at night.

Maybe he would have made it home, but he died—as surely as by a bullet or shell fragment—by drugs. I am to blame for his having been there.

I clearly remembered the day that he told me that he had been picked up by the sheriff. I will never forget the words I told him: "David, it looks like you are going to join the army!" I cursed myself when I thought of those arbitrary, macho words. I would give anything in the world to have never spoken them. He stole a lousy quarter, and now he was dead—because of me.

It finally sank in over the next week, like a worm in my gut gnawing at my insides—and there was no way to stop it. The army informed us that David's casket would arrive in Oshkosh by air and provided us with the date and flight information for its arrival.

Our oldest son, Ron, had received his discharge from the navy six months earlier and returned to Oshkosh after spending some time visiting friends in Illinois.

Ron, his cousin Robert, and a friend of his from Illinois, and I met the plane carrying David's coffin at Klamath Falls Airport, Oregon. It was a dark night, and stars covered the heavens. We watched reverently as the honor guard removed the coffin from the airplane and loaded it onto a hearse to be driven to the funeral home.

It was late and we were in a very sorrowful state, so we decided to salute David with a round of drinks. We stopped in the Pioneer Inn and went to the bar, ordered our drinks, and raised our glasses in a toast to David. This kept up for a couple of hours—until the bar closed and we dejectedly returned to our respective homes.

Pastor Thomas Asuma of Saint John's Lutheran Church was a fine human being and assisted in the funeral arrangement at Seefelds Funeral Home—as well as being by Jean's side and comforting her and the children at the funeral and gravesite.

Roland contacted his and David's friends in Lombard—their old stomping ground—and they came to Oshkosh to honor David. They showed up for the viewing, filling most of the space available, and spent time paying their respects to David.

They were an outrageous group, most riding Harleys and wearing every kind of motorcycle getup you could imagine. Some looked like Hell's Angels—David would have loved it!

The army provided an unasked-for honor guard for the funeral. I am sure that they have their own rules and regulations, and I respected their decision and was glad that they were there. David had done everything asked of him, did not hesitate in placing himself in harm's way in life-threatening situations, and voluntarily signed on for a second tour of duty. He did his duty.

At the cemetery, a six-man honor guard carried the casket from the hearse to the gravesite. A firing detail fired a salute of three volleys, and the bugler played the mournful notes of "Taps." The notes drifted sadly over the coffin and those attending the ceremony.

Two of the guards removed the flag from the top of the coffin and ceremoniously folded it. The head of the burial detail rendered a few words honoring David and placed the folded flag into Jean's hands. He saluted and retired as David's coffin was lowered gently into the ground.

David's body rests in the veterans' section of the Lakeview Memorial Park cemetery in the Field of Honor on Algoma Boulevard on the northwest side of Oshkosh, but his soul is

HOMER'S SON

in heaven. He was twenty-one when he died—and will remain twenty-one forever.

A dark cloud of unbearable grief and sadness overcame me; empty scotch bottles littered the bedroom floor as I tried to drink myself into oblivion. I played sad, depressing Moody Blues music for hours on David's wire recorder, and the grief and loss got worse.

I repeatedly took my revolver and put the muzzle in my mouth with my finger on the trigger. I was no stranger to the oily, metallic taste of the barrel of a loaded and cocked .38 caliber revolver.

My drinking out of control, I fell asleep sprawled and passed out on the floor.

During an infrequent minimally sober phase, something disconnected the continuous film in my head and brought me a sense of clarity and reality. I could see the faces of my four remaining children and thought about what would happen to them. *What will my selfish act to end my pain, remorse, and guilt do to them?*

They would not only have lost a brother, but also a father, who in a selfish, uncaring, and unthinking manner would double their grief and create anger in their souls.

And what would happen to Martina? She would lose a future husband that she loved and who loved her.

I felt sure that God would not forgive me for what I was set to do to my kids and Martina.

I must not, cannot, and will not do this to my children and Martina!

Some of Martina's sisters, seeing a way to disturb their older sister and carrying the seeds of their father's negative demeaning attitude toward Martina, said, "You can forget about Jerry! He will go back to his wife for sure now." It was a disgusting thing for them to say, but I think they enjoyed—in a perverted way—the pain they caused her.

But Martina kept her feelings to herself, as she always did.

Christmas 1971

Martina had placed a skimpy Christmas tree in a corner of the living room, and her children were trying to select ornaments to place on the tree from a small assortment of worn and cracked ornaments.

Martina was cross-legged on the floor, trying to repair a string of lights with Band-Aids. Her face was radiant and intent; she was beautiful, and I observed her with pride and love.

Jean filed for divorce two days before Christmas Eve. Christmas came and went.

For several nights, I awoke around two o'clock in the dark morning, threw on my clothes, and drove to David's grave. I stood at his grave and saluted him—the "Christmas Boy." I sensed that he knew I was there, although I know he had left this mortal coil to be with God in heaven.

I was pained that I had never told him that I loved him, and I said, "I love you, David. I am sorry." I hoped that he would hear me.

I returned to my car on the graveled cemetery road facing a massive oak tree. Its branches spread like arms reaching out to the gravesite, and the moon was silhouetted by dark shadows.

As I sat in my car, I could see the mischievous grin on David's boyish face—his blue eyes and tousled light brown hair that once had been blond. I started to weep silently. *Why? Why David and not me? A child should not die before his parents! Where were you, God?*

My thoughts turned to the Christmases that he had always managed to peek into the wrapped Christmas packages when the family was sleeping. Sometimes he opened them carefully to examine the enclosed present, and sometimes he ripped off the wrapping paper and brazenly hid the present in his room. He loved Christmas, and I called him the Christmas Boy during Christmastime.

On one of the nights that I visited David's grave, something was there that had not been there before. I flicked my lighter on the object on his grave. It was a single, shiny, silvery Christmas tree ornament hung on a twig by a string at the head of his grave. I wondered who had left the tribute on David's grave, but I never found out.

Martina wrote an elegy—a memorial of David's tragic death—but as was her usual inclination, she did not tell me of it at the time.

The Recruit (An Elegy for David)

A quarter stole
A thief, he said
As they rode side by side
On a sick day—after morning
Chicago building—looking gray
As they shook hands—parting

Five thousand miles—and blue skies
Different eyes—and glad smiles
Warm hearts—and cold corpses.
Rolling green, bloodied jungles
Pieces and smoke—a quarter paid
But no receipt requested.

Nights waiting by the Christmas tree
Nights waiting …
Waiting forever
… on a truck
… at Quang Tri
Waiting for a Christmas he'll never see.

Martina Watson, December 1972
(From the collected writings of Martina Watson)

David was always in the back of my mind and in my heart. Sometimes I felt as if my stomach were empty and hungering, but food did not assuage the terrible emptiness. I finally decided to find renewed energy at work and put my mind to it fully to try to divert me from my constant thoughts of David.

The following week, at my office, I assessed things and found that most were fine. Orders for the month were as planned, and manufacturing had achieved its scheduled delivery performance for the period. Quality, production, efficiency, and productivity were above plan. We could always do better, and the managers and I continually looked for ways to improve operations.

Something Is Brewing at Medalist

As the weeks went by, I sensed something brewing at the Medalist corporate office in Milwaukee. Six months earlier, I had agreed to hire the chairman's twenty-four-year-old son as data processing manager of the Oshkosh operation. I did not actually agree, but my direct boss, Perk Perkins, gently shoved it down my throat.

About two months later, Perk asked me to meet him at his office in Milwaukee at nine o'clock on Saturday morning. Something bad was up; I could sense the outcome in my bones.

Perk was ten or fifteen years my senior, had an excellent professional reputation, and came to Medalist from the Kearny & Trecker Company, a Milwaukee icon.

On the Saturday morning of my meeting with Perk, whom I considered a mentor and friend, I think I knew what was waiting for me ahead—or more accurately, my gut was signaling what was waiting for me ahead: trouble!

It was an overcast, foreboding, rainy day. As I approached deserted downtown Milwaukee, I heard a thumping noise and knew that I had a flat tire. I was not dressed for rain, but I still got out in the pouring rain, jacked up the car, and installed the spare tire.

I entered the Medalist office, went to the men's room, dried myself off with paper towels, and brushed my hair back with my fingers. I was still sopping wet when I entered Perk's office.

Perk rose behind his desk and said, "You look like a drowned cat, Jerry. What happened to you?"

"Nothing much—just a flat tire in the rain," I said cordially.

Perk replied sincerely, "That's a tough break, Jerry. I'm sorry you got soaked."

Perk returned to his chair, his face tight, and said, "This won't take long, Jerry, and you can get back to Oshkosh."

I took a seat and waited patiently for what I already knew was coming. I could sense the water in my shoes, my soaking wet socks, and my suit pants clinging wetly to my legs.

"The chairman and the board of directors are making some changes at the Oshkosh division."

It was not a question, so I said nothing. Perk was obviously uncomfortable and fussed with the papers on top of his desk as if they held the clue to his next remark.

"We are putting in a new vice president and division manager at Oshkosh, and I would like for you to submit your resignation."

His eyes were down, and he was not looking at me as he finished.

I said in a false, upbeat manner, "Who are you going to put in to take over my job?"

"The company has not announced that at this time."

"What is the severance plan?"

"You did an excellent job running the division, and I convinced the Medalist board to continue you on full salary and full benefits for one year—or until you assume a new position, if sooner."

"That's fine by me," I said. "Do you have a resignation letter prepared?"

"Yes, I do," he said, sliding a one-page resignation letter across the desk.

The letter said that I was resigning effective immediately for personal reasons. I signed it and handed it back.

"And the severance agreement?" I asked.

He slid the paper over, which I glanced at, signed, and returned.

The mundane severance details out of the way, I said, "Perk, I have always respected you and consider you a mentor and friend. Just between you and me, I know that my so-called resignation was not of your doing, and I bear you no ill will. You have always treated me fairly. You have taught me a lot about business, and I am grateful. I will always remember you as my friend, regardless of this decision, which I know that you had no control over."

Avoiding my comments, he mumbled, "Thanks, and good luck to you, Jerry. I know that you will succeed in anything you do in the future."

We shook hands, and as I left, I turned and said, "Please give my congratulations to Fischer's son."

He said, "You knew all along?"

"Yes—all along."

I strode to the door and exited the office.

I said to myself, "Nice way for the son to get ahead: Skip the hard work and the corporate ladder, take the private elevator to the top, and have your daddy at the elevator controls."

That evening, Martina and I splurged on a dinner of savory northern pike, a bottle of wine, and drinks at the Pioneer Inn. In a macabre salute, I made a toast to the promotion of the chairman's son, and we touched our glasses together and gave each other supportive smiles.

I began my job search and sent out dozens of letters to prospective employers as well as to a few headhunters.

Allis Chalmers in Wichita Falls, Texas

In 1972, after weeks of searching, I applied at Allis Chalmers in Milwaukee to be plant manager of a new electrical equipment manufacturing plant in Wichita Falls, Texas, a town near the Oklahoma border with a population of 100,000.

Some call Wichita Falls the "asshole of creation" due to its position in Tornado Alley, its blistering summer heat, and its freezing winter winds—not to mention its copious quantities of rattlesnakes and other venomous creatures in the desert around the town.

Peter Wargo, the corporate senior vice president, invited me for an interview at the corporate headquarters in West Allis, Wisconsin.

I completed three days of interviews with everyone at Allis Chalmers who made over $200 a week, and I had a final interview set up with the chairman. If my interview went well with the chairman, I would report to work at Wichita Falls on the first of the month.

The interview was bizarre, to say the least.

I arrived twenty minutes early. Vince Lombardi always said, "If you are not fifteen minutes early, you are late." I parked across the street from the entrance. At a quarter to nine, the chairman's limousine pulled up, his chauffeur opened the back door, and David Scott got out, adjusted his tie, brushed out a wrinkle in his suit, and entered the building.

I trailed in after him at a distance and announced myself to the receptionist. At nine o'clock, the receptionist told me that I could go in. His door was open, and I stood in the doorway to his office for an instant, waiting for him to recognize me and invite me in.

He was sitting alone at the head of a long conference table that could seat at least twenty people. He glanced up from his papers and silently waved me into a chair at the opposite end of the table.

I waited, and after a couple of minutes of picking through his papers, he said in an accusatory voice, "What makes you think you can run the Allis Chalmers plant in Texas?"

Ignoring his tone of voice, I briefly outlined my experience and accomplishments.

He asked no questions and expressed little interest.

He said, "I understand that you may be getting married— first or second?"

"Second," I replied.

He stood up to leave and said, "That's all—call Peter Wargo's secretary tomorrow."

The interview was over. He turned to me on his way out the door and said officiously, "The jury is out, Watson!"

I assumed that meant that he had hired me—at least until the jury came back in.

I stood in the vacant conference room for a moment, reflecting on his cryptic last words, and then proceeded to the exit with mixed emotions. At the same time, I was looking forward to the new challenge and opportunity.

I contacted Wargo's secretary the next day, and she told me to report to Wichita Falls to start work on the first of the month.

Redemption

The following day, Martina and I were driving down Main Street in Oshkosh. I was in love with Martina and trying to think of how I should propose to her.

Suddenly, I turned to her and blurted out, "I do not want you for a week or a month or a year—I want you forever! Will you marry me?"

Although somewhat surprised, she agreed to my proposal— even though it was likely not quite what she expected. She decided that we should get married in New Orleans in a week. It was all right with me, as I would drive her sporty, 1964 two-door, Pontiac and leave my old gas-guzzling Oldsmobile behind.

Martina laboriously sewed her own beautiful wedding gown from some cloth that she had bought. I thought that it looked great, but just before the wedding, she decided that she did not like it and purchased a lovely, white, full-length gown in New Orleans.

Before we left for New Orleans, we drove around in the countryside because it was a nice day. I found a wedding jacket hanging on a line with other used clothing at a farm yard sale. The white seersucker jacket with pale blue stripes—which fit perfectly—cost me eight dollars.

The next day, I bought a pair of comfortable white polyester trousers and a pair of inexpensive white shoes and socks to complete my wedding ensemble—a total of eighteen dollars. The day before we were to leave for New Orleans, someone at Allis Chalmers called and asked me to come in the next morning.

The person said, "Something has come up that needs clarification—it will only take a few minutes."

Martina and I arrived the next morning at the headquarters all packed to head out after I finished whatever business was on their mind.

Martina drove off to pick up a couple of six-packs of beer for the trip, and I proceeded into the building. Fifteen minutes later, Martina returned with the beer, and I joined her in the car.

"What was that all about?" she asked.

"One of the suspicious staff guys at the corporate office heard a rumor that I had just gotten a divorce, which was a big deal because they were reluctant to approve a single guy running one of their remote operations."

Martina said, "But you did just get a divorce."

"That's true, but I told them not to worry about it. My new bride-to-be and I are on our way to New Orleans to be married. From the way he acted, it looked to me like he had wanted to catch this new guy in a lie and enhance his standing with the brass, but my answer blew his plan out of the water. Tough, wouldn't you say?"

Martina dismissed my query as was her usual habit and said, "Everything is settled then—we can get on the road."

I drove a few blocks, parked, broke out the beer, popped two caps, and we toasted the start of our journey to New Orleans.

We drove from Oshkosh to the "Big Easy," a nickname for New Orleans, with only one breakdown. A fuel pump went out on her Pontiac, and we found a garage that had the part and installed it, losing only a couple of hours.

We decided to detour to the Mississippi coastline and stopped outside of Biloxi for the night at a quaint old hotel, which sat on the slope of a hill above the shoreline of the Gulf of Mexico.

While Martina made herself comfortable in our room, I went out to explore the grounds and the beach. I was surprised to find a large number of faded, discolored concrete foundations along the beach. I found out later that they were the remnants of buildings wiped out by the devastating Hurricane Camille, which had struck the coastline at 190 miles per hour only three years earlier.

We ate our delicious Creole dishes and went for a swim in the evening in a lighted pool. The water was warm, the weather hot and muggy, and we could smell the sweet aroma of gardenias in the light breeze. It was a very pleasant evening, and we both enjoyed the graceful Southern ambience and cuisine of the hotel. We were very much in love.

Early the next morning, we drove to New Orleans, but decided to wait until June 14 to avoid starting our marriage on a traditionally bad luck day.

To kill some time, we took a paddle-wheel riverboat ride on Lake Pontchartrain and its bayous. While I enjoyed the ride, the scenery, and the beautiful day, a blue sky with delicate drifting white clouds, Martina busily cleaned out her purse, blissfully unaware of the moss-hung trees, birds, and quaint shacks and fishing camps along the shoreline.

After the boat ride, we explored the French Quarter and Bourbon Street's music, drink, and food, with a Satch Armstrong-wannabe blues musician playing the cornet. I ordered a dozen oysters on the half shell at the oyster bar and ate most of them since Martina was not hungry. We finally returned to the Cornstalk Hotel—a quaint, small hotel not far from the French Quarter, with a unique picturesque ironwork fence in the form of cornstalks.

We will always remember the Cornstalk Hotel. In the middle of the night, the bed broke down, and we were on the floor, laughing. We spent the rest of the night on the mattress on the floor.

The next morning, on June 14, 1972, a justice of the peace married us in a civil ceremony at the courthouse. After the ceremony, we started out on the trip back to Oshkosh.

Martina was twenty-nine, and I was forty-five years old. It was a difference of sixteen years, but we both were so happy that we felt like a couple of kids.

Marrying Martina was my redemption. I became a new man with the grace of God. Martina was the most jealous person I had ever known, and I could not transgress even if I wanted to—which I did not.

I felt redeemed in God's eyes and felt that God had come back into my life. But God was not done with my transgressions just yet. I had not given up drinking, but I was working on cutting down on it with Martina's support.

One day, after Martina and I had married, I came upon this poem addressed to me but which I had never seen. Martina hid her writings and poems because she thought that they were not of the quality that she wanted to achieve.

For You, Jack

You're Jeff Chandler, Gable, Geronimo
Warrior
Your face flings possibility
Women speculate
Rave, oh do they rave,
Errol Flynn, Valentino
The possibilities are endless,
Romance reborn
They simper, gush,
Giggle.
You're the last of the lovers
They know it,
Run to you
Offer themselves.
You're lucky I'm here to stop them!

(From the Collected Writings of Martina Watson)

Salvation

Marrying Martina was my salvation. I was in love with her and very proud of her. I have never violated our wedding vows and never would, in spite of my many previous sexual transgressions. She was gorgeous, intelligent, and wise beyond her age, and really knew how to make a man walk the line.

We have our different viewpoints due to our difference in age—just the differences of the times and our individual circumstances growing up. However, we did not quarrel about them, and they were not a threat to our marriage.

At this time, I did not know about Martina's recurring depression brought on by her father's brutal verbal abuse and turning her four sisters against her. Beginning when she was young, he told her she was ugly and no good. He continued demeaning her until she and I were married.

She kept it to herself throughout our whole marriage; I did not have a clue. My drinking bouts must have exacerbated her depression. Had I known, perhaps I would have been more loving to her and cut out the bouts with alcohol. She lived with recurring depression without telling anyone or seeking professional help for almost her entire life, including the whole time we were married, until her premature death.

Oshkosh Bar

The evening after we returned to Oshkosh, Martina and I celebrated our marriage with one of her four younger sisters at a shabby bar. The only other patrons were eight young men in their twenties, who were sitting at a couple of tables on the far side of the dance floor having a boisterous time. We avoided them and seated ourselves at the bar.

One of the younger men became piss-faced drunk and repetitively came up to our party at the bar, jabbering incoherently and slobbering his words indecipherably. He would not go away although we ignored him completely.

Entreaties from the bartender to "Let these people alone" did not dissuade him.

Finally, my patience worn thin, I reached out and grabbed him by his shirtfront, spun him around, and sat the idiot on the floor.

"This is a private conversation we are having, so go on back to your friends and leave us alone," I said in a nonthreatening way.

He got up from the floor unhurt and staggered back to his friends.

At closing time, we left and found ourselves in the dimly lit parking lot facing the young men from the bar. They were not happy campers; they had an axe to grind. Their mood was ugly—and becoming uglier.

Cheryl was loudly calling them cowards, strings of invectives spicing her speech. "What a bunch of chickenshit cowards—eight guys picking on one guy."

Her verbal abuse was holding them off—temporarily.

Martina got a three-foot iron pipe from the trunk of her car and tried to put it in my hand as I faced them down. Having imbibed five or six martinis celebrating our marriage, I told her that I did not need it, and I would not take the pipe.

A few moments later, as the mob of young men were closing in, Martina came roaring up in her car into the throng. She was yelling at us to get in and almost pulling us into the car. Cheryl jumped in, and I followed. The noisy mob started to surge on all sides as Martina jammed down the accelerator without regard to anyone in her way and stormed out of the parking lot.

A smart-thinking, quick-acting wife and a determined sister-in-law with a withering mouth and expletive-laced vocabulary saved me—in spite of myself in my alcohol-fueled combativeness—from a beating at the hands of an angry, drunk mob of young men.

"Thank you, ladies," I uttered under my breath and leaned back comfortably in the seat for the short ride home.

The next morning, I pulled on a pair of running shorts, a T-shirt, and tennis shoes and rode my bicycle to the same bar to have a beer or two and see who did not approve of my being there. None of the young men from the previous evening were there.

Wichita Falls, Texas

A couple of weeks later, we completed our plans for moving to Wichita Falls to begin my new job. Everything was packed, and the moving van had left. We started out early in the morning, taking only our clothes and personal effects that we needed on the trip.

Off we went to a new life!

Nana, Joel, Maelee, Martina, and I left Oshkosh and headed for Chicago. Traveling through Chicago brought back memories to Martina of her life there. She was born in Chicago, lived there with her two children, and worked in a securities firm and as a nightclub dancer before she returned to Oshkosh.

She got mixed up with the Chicago mob, called the Outfit, and ended up married to a member of the Outfit—only to have it annulled many months later through the good graces of her father, who was threatened with death by the mob. It was the one good thing he ever did for her.

Before she married the Chicago gangster, she was in love with a handsome young man whom she wanted to marry. It turned out that he also was a member of the Chicago mob and a drug runner, smuggling drugs across the Mexican border into the United States. He got involved in a shoot-out with the US Border Patrol and was shot to death while trying to kill the border agents and escape.

Our next leg on the journey, Saint Louis, included an entertaining ride for all to the top of the Saint Louis Arch. The passenger car inside the arch moved up and simultaneously sideways following the curvature of the arch, causing subtle movements, shivers, vibrations, and noises as we traveled to the top. Martina hated it and was screaming to be let out, which obviously was impossible hundreds of feet in the air.

After Saint Louis, we got on Route 44, which goes all the way to Wichita Falls. We stopped at a Holiday Inn in Oklahoma City, and the kids swam in the pool and got vicious sunburns. We resumed our journey the next morning.

We drove south for a little over two hours and crossed the Texas border. The land was desolate: undulating prairie, sagebrush, tumbleweeds, and few if any trees. There were few settlements or buildings of any sort along the road. The only animals we saw were a flattened rattlesnake in the road and a squashed armadillo curled up on the berm alongside the road.

After a while, Maelee needed to go to the bathroom. I stopped the car at a desolate Phillips 66 gas station, pointed to the outhouse twenty-five feet behind the station, and let her out of the car.

Maelee returned a few minutes later screaming at the top of her lungs, "What are you doing to me? That place was filthy and stinks, and all they have is old newspapers for toilet paper—and no toilet seat. There were big, ugly, shiny, black insects with wings on the ceiling—and grasshoppers hopping around on the floor by my feet. You are never going to get me into one of those again!"

The primitive conditions had obviously traumatized and offended her.

She added, "If this is the way it's going to be in Texas, you can just buy me a one-way ticket on the Greyhound and put me on the next bus back to Oshkosh."

I said, "Welcome to Texas, y'all."

We purchased our first home for $32,225 in July 1972 with a down payment of $1,700, including closing costs. It was a charming ranch-style house with air-conditioning, a large living room, a nicely laid-out kitchen and eating area, a dining room, recreation room, and four bedrooms and three baths. It also had a garage, with a tornado shelter under the concrete floor.

I lifted the trapdoor of the tornado cellar and looked into the pit. I could not see any snakes, but I did not plan to use the tornado cellar anyway. I hated snakes, which could have been a major problem had we stayed there. Four years later, after we left Wichita Falls, many homes, including our previous home, were devastated by a tornado, wiping out the entire neighborhood.

We settled in Wichita Falls, and our family took on some of the Texas way of life. Martina tried growing roses, with disastrous results. The rosebushes she planted withered in the blazing sun, and the blossoms burned to a crisp and scattered to the ground.

Martina and I explored the desert to bring home some of the variety of large cacti that grew in clumps close to the ground for landscaping our empty backyard. The fresh breeze and the vast outdoors surprisingly made us both horny, and we made love on the open ground (between the cacti). Welcome to Texas—where the deer and the antelope and lovers play.

There were five main restaurants in Wichita Falls, Pioneer #1, #2, #3, #4, and #5. They served great fried chicken and mashed potatoes and gravy, topped off with apple, peach, or berry pie—often sporting a large lump of ice cream on top. They also served Tex-Mex dishes. Our family favorites were the fried chicken and the chalupa, a variation of the Mexican tostadas, as well as the Tex-Mex enchiladas.

The Snake Pit

Rattlesnake roundups were a popular attraction in parts of rural Texas, and they attracted adults, families, and children alike. One weekend, I took Martina, Joel, and Maelee to a weekend rattlesnake roundup. At the roundup in a large tent, the snake handlers poured plastic garbage cans filled with live, venomous, writhing tangles of rattlesnakes onto the floor of a ring encircled by a low barricade. The snakes, captured in snake dens located in rocky cave formations in the desert with as many as two hundred snakes, were coiled together or crawling all over the place.

The sound of hundreds of rattles vibrating permeated the air—a cacophony of viciousness and death.

The snake handlers used short poles with small hooks on the ends to catch and move the snakes. The handlers demonstrated milking the venom from the snakes by grabbing hold of the back of the snake's head, placing the exposed fangs over the lip of a glass beaker, and squeezing—or milking—the venom into the jar. Medical laboratories used the venom collected in this manner for the production of antivenom for snakebites.

There were many uses for expired rattlesnakes, and little was wasted. They hung the snakes on nails and removed the heads and entrails or skinned the snakes to make belts, hatbands, boots, and other decorative items. They cut the rattle off the tail and used it as an ornament or token.

The flesh of an expired snake was used in the same manner as most other meats—and even used by the sandwich shop at the event to make burgers. I bought snakeburgers for Maelee and Joel, but Joel was not hungry and did not eat his. Maelee was hungry and ate her snakeburger. When she found out later that she had eaten snake meat, she never forgave me.

To this day, I still do not know what snakeburgers taste like.

The Wichita Falls plant manufactured high- and low-voltage electrical motor controls. It was a new facility, recently dedicated, and was still in the throes of start-up problems, employee training, and inexperienced supervision.

The electrical controls division in West Allis was responsible for sales and prices of all electrical controls at the Wichita plant. The manager of the West Allis operation was a relatively young engineer and had not previously been involved in sales or marketing.

In my initial assessment of the situation at the Wichita Falls operation, I deduced that pricing of the product was going to be a difficult problem. The corporate office measured my performance on profitability, but I had no control over the volume of sales or the price of the products.

The former manufacturing vice president, who was responsible for the corporation's investment in the Texas plant—and the corporate staff who were also involved—were optimistic in the profitability forecast for the new operation and sold the projections to top corporate management. The manufacturing vice president left town for another job and left the mess for the next person, me!

I regretted that my efforts during my hiring interviews to obtain pertinent data and understand the basis for the forward projections for the plant's sales and profitability had not been successful. Unfortunately, I accepted the job without an understanding of the probabilities of success—either by intentional deception or from ignorance by the higher levels of management or myself.

Due to my newness in the company and the remoteness of my location, I had zero clout with the officers, managers, and particularly the staff at headquarters. I could not depend on them for any support. It was a clique of self-serving staff people that I, not being a member, could not persuade or depend on to be on my side of any issue.

I should have stayed on the job market longer and found a different job, but I had felt restless, wanted to get back to work, and accepted the first job offer I got. I took the job on faith that I could fix whatever was wrong, and I was committed to seeing the job through. Somehow I failed to follow my own adage: "Don't stick your head in where you can't get your ass out."

I worked on a program of pricing our products in a manner that would produce a suitable gross margin based on our plant's specific cost data and order quantities. I sent it to the young manager of electrical control products, with a cover memo suggesting that he review all of our prices compared with their actual gross margins and make whatever positive adjustments were feasible.

It was a simple Profits 101 request. I know that the market set the price, not the cost—but there was always some wriggle room to make some price adjustments that could add up to big bucks.

One of my mottoes is "If you don't try, you cannot succeed."

However, the corporate office apparently had a procedure for approving such requests from the division plant managers. They stonewalled any request until it died.

In the meantime, I was working with my managers and supervisors to come up with savings from better methods improvements, training, less scrap and overtime, and improvement of our on-time delivery.

Our profitability initiatives were beginning to bear fruit and were starting to improve the profitability of the plant. However, we were still far below the original crazy projections.

Martina, her two kids, and her grandmother, Nana, seemed to be surviving the Texas climate and environment pretty well— at least I hoped so.

Martina went to an evening school program, where the kids on the stage all sang "The Yellow Rose of Texas." Tears came to Martina's eyes as she saw and heard Joel and Maelee singing on the stage.

She told me later that evening, "What have I done to my kids? They are turning into Texans for God's sake!"

On weekends, I often took ten- or fifteen-mile rides on my bicycle—sometimes when I had been imbibing scotch or gin, with swigs from long-necked bottles of Lone Star as chasers. I enjoyed biking and took off to bike whenever I felt like it—the devil be damned.

One weekend, I was wheeling down a hill on a road by a golf course, and the front tire hit a crack in the pavement at a fast speed. The front wheel jerked violently sidewise, and the bike and I made a complete flip. I skidded on my bare right shoulder, and the bicycle ended up in the middle of the road.

Fortunately, the cars behind me were able to swerve and not grind me farther into the ground or leave tire tracks on my body. The skin and flesh on the top of my shoulder was ground down to a bleeding abrasion the size of a shoe heel, with grains of sand ground into the open injury.

I got to my feet gingerly.

The bike's fork was crooked and off center. I twisted it into shape and did not see any other problems. I got on, blood still oozing down my shoulder in small rivulets to my rib cage, and tried out the bike. When I was confident that there were no other problems, I headed for home, seven miles away.

When I arrived home, I got a mixed reception, ranging from "Let the bastard suffer!" (thought, but not spoken) to "Oh my God, we have to do something!"

I solved both problems, telling Martina, "Get the bottle of rubbing alcohol and pour some on the scrape."

She did, and I almost jumped out of my sneakers from the burning sensation. It felt like a blowtorch, but it only lasted a short time. The injury turned into a giant scab, and years later, I was still picking grains of sand out of the flesh of my shoulder.

Martina's Thirtieth Birthday

I wrote a poem for Martina's thirtieth birthday on October 29, 1973. I had previously been to Australia and learned something of the aboriginal concept of death, called dreamtime, which had an effect on me and gave me a theme for a poem to tell Martina how much I loved her.

For Martina,
Write Me a Poem

Write me a poem
For my aboriginal dreamtime
Write me a poem
That makes me dance the ancient ceremonies
That puffs out my chest ...
Like a strutting prairie chicken
That fills me with your warmth and makes me glow
Like a firefly on a summer night
That touches my soul with your love
Write me a poem
I will hear it in my dreamtime
And sing it back to you

Jack Watson
October 29, 1973

"Beats Me—I Don't Work Here Anymore"

I had been working at the Wichita Falls plant for eight months when I got a telephone call from one of the Allis Chalmers honchos. He informed me that Peter Wargo would be visiting me at the plant on Tuesday in the early afternoon. The corporate jet would arrive at noon. Wargo and three of his idiot corporate staff needed ground transportation to transport them to the plant.

I had first met Wargo at my initial interview for the job and later at the monthly dog-and-pony show in Milwaukee. Wargo was not a man that you could have any empathy for. He had an arrogant personality that was off-putting and struck me as a cleaned up hunchback of Notre Dame.

The dog-and-pony show was a monthly meeting of corporate management with the operating plant managers. Each plant manager displayed a chart projected on a large screen for all to see and reviewed the performance of his operation on a number of calculable metrics, shipments, gross margins, and prices.

It was a useful management tool—a report card on critical metrics of each operation. It was, however, on more than one occasion used by David Scott to humiliate and verbally degrade managers in front of their colleagues—a practice that even the dumbest young executive knew was wrong.

Just before noon, I drove to the airport in my company car, which could accommodate the four visitors and me. I chauffeured the entourage to the plant and led them to my office. Wargo asked me if someone were available to take his three staff people on a tour of the plant.

No doubt, I thought, *to survey the nest they want to crap in.*

I knew what was happening and prepared myself to meet the challenge and negotiate a favorable severance package. I promised myself that I would not hurt Wargo—not even a little bit.

I set up the plant tour with my chief engineer.

Wargo, his staffers, and I sat at a round conference table in my office, facing each other. They had more eyeballs at the table than I did, so I focused my eyes exclusively on Peter Wargo. This seemed to bother him, and he started looking out the large window, at the trees "blowing in the wind."

I said, "What can I do for you?"

"Jerry, we at the corporate office are not satisfied with the Wichita Falls plant's performance."

"Who is *we?*"

"Myself and my staff, and approved by the chairman, David Scott."

I realized that accepting the position in Wichita Falls had been a monumental error on my part. It was obvious that the corporate staffers who worked on the original optimistic justification for the plant would never admit that they had been wrong nor share any responsibility for the failure of the plant to meet their lofty, irresponsible expectations.

They would save face by developing a lower, more doable turnaround plan, and replace me with one of their unscrupulous henchmen to run the plant with the lower expectations. It was a no-lose plot for them to avoid any responsibility for their grandiose original plan, dodge the bullet, and save their own asses.

I sensed in their uncomfortable mannerisms that they were not as confident in firing me without repercussions as they might have thought. This was a "tell" in poker jargon for me to take the initiative and negotiate an aggressive severance package. I said to myself, "Let the game begin!"

I asked Wargo, "Do we need these guys around—or would you like them to tour the facility while we settle our issues?"

Wargo waved them out.

After an hour of haggling, Wargo agreed on the severance package. One-year salary and benefits continuation, whether or not otherwise employed. Job search costs, including headhunter fees and travel expenses. All moving and travel expenses for relocating my family back to Wisconsin. Reimbursement of any loss on the sale of our home in Wichita Falls and covering the closing costs on any new residence purchased in the next twelve months, not to exceed the actual closing cost of our home in Wichita Falls.

Not too bad, considering the middling poker hand dealt me.

I gave the agreement to my secretary, who typed it and placed it before us. We reviewed the agreement and signed it. He got up, collected his staff members, one of whom signed the severance agreement as a witness, and left the building to go to the airport.

I did not bother to shake their hands.

Wargo, finding no transportation waiting to take him and his entourage back to the airport, returned a couple of minutes later, stuck his head in my doorway, and asked, "How do we get to the airport?"

I answered, *"Beats me—I don't work here anymore."*

Just a small retribution, but otherwise I might have given him a bloody lip.

Wargo turned on his heel, red-faced and incensed, and departed, his three flunkies trailing behind like ducklings paddling behind their mother duck.

That evening, Martina and I went to the plant, packed my personal effects, and returned home to start preparations to leave Wichita Falls.

We put our house up for sale, finished up other details, and packed up. The movers loaded our furniture and household items in a van, and they were on their way. We left for Milwaukee three days after the firing—excuse me, the *resignation.*

We were on the road again!

Milwaukee Gear—A Happy Worker of the Working Class

We found a condominium to rent in Milwaukee and moved in the next day. I began my job search, sent out numerous résumés, and answered some advertisements in the *Wall Street Journal* and the *Milwaukee Tribune.*

Martina and I flew to Houston for an interview with a headhunter. After looking at my résumé, he complained about the number of jobs I had held. He would not tell me if he had a specific position in mind; I personally doubt that he had one, and he was just playing the tough-guy recruiter character. As it turned out, he was worthless, and my time was wasted—but Wargo paid the bill and Martina and I enjoyed the ride.

In the meantime, I decided to get a job—any job—while I continued to look for a management position.

I applied for an hourly job at the large Milwaukee Gear plant across the street behind our apartment. I did not want my résumé to include a low-level, hourly job in the gear plant, which could be detrimental to my future professional career, so I applied as J. Jack Watson rather than Jerry Jack Watson.

The superintendent hired me right off the bat as the night-shift tool-crib attendant, and I showed up for work at four o'clock the following evening.

As I was getting ready to cross the street to the gear company, a police cruiser screeched to a halt in front of an individual who had started to cross the street. The officer jumped out of his cruiser and grabbed and threw the man down onto the street. After a short scuffle, the burly cop pulled a small revolver from the man's clothing, tossed it aside, handcuffed him, picked up the gun, shook out the shells, slipped the gun and shells into his pocket, loaded the man in the backseat of his cruiser, and took off. The whole episode lasted maybe three minutes. These Milwaukee cops did not mess around!

Inside Milwaukee Gear, the toolroom was located in the large machining bay, where a variety of gear cutters and other machine tools were machining gears and related products. Production was mainly in small quantity lots, which required a tooling change for every machine setup, providing plenty of work for the toolroom attendant.

Machine operators came to the tool-crib window with their shop orders, which listed the jigs and fixture required for the job, and the toolroom attendant located the jig or fixture and placed it on the counter for the operator to take to his machine to set up the job.

I found the job to be physically demanding, but surprisingly, not boring. The first thing I noticed was that my shoes were stretching out on the side from carrying the weight of the steel fixtures. I sliced open my shoes on the sides by my small toes to relieve the pressure. Before going to work each evening, I put Band-Aids on my blisters, gulped down a half-glass of bourbon, and walked across the street to my job. It was a nice commute.

The tool crib was hot, with little ventilation, and sweat ran into my eyes when I crouched down or bent over to get at the tooling on the lower shelves. My reading glasses slipped down or off my face as I tried using a flashlight in the dim light to read the numbers identifying the tooling locations.

Often there were machine operators lined up at the tool-crib window waiting for their tools. The tool crib was dark, and the lighting inadequate. The first-shift tool-crib operators had not returned jigs and fixtures to their proper locations or put them in the wrong locations. Wiping rags overflowed their containers, debris was scattered everywhere around the tool crib, and the aisles were blocked with tooling. It was a goddamn mess!

During slack periods, I went to work fixing the mess. I borrowed a powerful flashlight from the maintenance department and methodically found and read the numbers on each tool or fixture in each bin. I also found tools and fixtures that were in the wrong location or had been lying loose on the floor and placed them in their proper locations.

I cleaned up all the debris and threw it in the garbage, picked up wiping rags, moved the filled wiping-rag containers to the rag-washing area, and replaced them with clean wiping rags. After a week, I had cleaned and organized the tool crib and all but eliminated the waiting line of the machine operators for tools.

The shop superintendent, whom I had met when I first started the job, came to visit me in the tool crib one evening during the thirty-minute lunch break at eight o'clock. He was very friendly and walked around the tool crib, noticing the improvements.

He said, "Jack, you have really done a superb job cleaning up and organizing this tool crib. I wondered what had happened when I started noticing that there were fewer gear operators lined up at the counter waiting for tooling. What did you do?"

"I just made sure that everything was where it should be, which makes it easier and quicker to find the tools. Like my Granny said, 'A place for everything and everything in its place.' But I do have a couple of suggestions. The lighting in the tool crib is piss-poor and needs to be upgraded. Not only does it take longer to find the jigs and fixtures, but mistakes are often made in deciphering the bin number and the wrong tool is given out, which has to be returned to the crib and another issued, wasting even more time."

He said, "I will get that fixed."

Encouraged, I said, "You also need to get some discipline in the first-shift tool-crib operations because if they do not do on the first shift as I have done on the swing shift, my work was for nothing, and the crib will go back to its unorganized, inefficient state."

"I will take a look at that situation," he said.

"And when you get the first shift disciplined, you can get rid of one of the unnecessary first-shift tool- crib attendants and save some money."

"We'll look into it," he said.

He thought for a moment or two and then asked, "How would you like a promotion now that you have the tool crib in good shape?"

Trying for humor, I facetiously asked, "The president of Milwaukee Gear has resigned?"

He chuckled and said, "No, not exactly, but I have an opening for a gear cutter. It's not that hard to learn. It would be a promotion, and the pay would be better. It could also lead to you becoming a supervisor."

This tool-crib job was definitely an interim position, which gave me something to do while I was searching for a professional management position. I was getting used to the tool crib. I replied, "No, thanks. I like my job, and I am satisfied." *I felt like a happy hourly worker of the working class!*

He said, "That is too bad, Jack. You would make a fine gear cutter—and even a supervisor. If you change your mind, come and see me."

Pressed Steel Tank Company

In 1972, I received a phone call from Ed Mytkowicz, vice president of Norris Industries in California, which owned Pressed Steel Tank Company. The discussion regarded the résumé that I had sent to apply for president of Pressed Steel Tank Company. He said he liked my credentials and had a few questions to ask me.

I said, "Shoot. I will answer them as best I can."

"Have you worked in a union environment?"

"Yes, in several companies, including Walworth Valve, Wilton Tool, and Medalist Industries."

"Have you worked in a labor standards incentive environment?"

"I started out my career setting labor standards at Boeing. I have had management responsibility for incentive standard-hour plans at Walworth Valve and am fully knowledgeable in standard incentive systems."

"Tell me about your work in metal forming operations."

I reviewed the varied metal forming operations of which I was responsible for setting labor standards, and my metalworking, foundry, and metallurgical background at Oregon State.

"Thank you. I appreciate your answers and would like you to be interviewed by the president of Norris Industries. Would you mind going to the headquarters of Norris Industries in Vernon, California, to talk with the president, Jack Meany?"

"I would be pleased to go see Jack Meany—and anyone else you might decide. When would you like me to go?"

I flew out a day later to visit Jack Meany. Jack was an extraordinary man. He was intelligent and knowledgeable in manufacturing and a wide variety of other subjects. He immediately put me at ease, and we conversed for two hours about Pressed Steel Tank and my experience and qualifications for the position. Ed Mytkowicz sat in for the last half of the session.

Jack Meany asked me if I would mind waiting in the reception area for a few minutes. After about five minutes, Jack's secretary asked me to come in.

Jack Watson

Jack Meany met me at the door and said, "Welcome aboard, Jack. [I had converted my name to J. Jack Watson.] You are the new president of Pressed Steel Tank Company!" He and Ed Mytkowicz both shook my hand warmly.

"You will report directly to Ed Mytkowicz, who will not be in your hair all the time—except his routine visits every month or two unless there is a problem that requires him to be there. He will also prepare your annual performance review."

I said, "Thank you. You can count on me to do my very best for Pressed Steel and Norris Industries."

I was elated and eager to start on my new job. I showed up for work early the following morning after taking a red-eye back to Milwaukee.

Pressed Steel Tank had its executive and administration offices in the original manufacturing plant in West Allis. In addition, there was an executive parking garage across the street from the executive office—a throwback to the old days, but a convenience and a perk, nevertheless.

Our family moved into a two-story house in Whitefish Bay, Wisconsin, and the commute was only twenty minutes, which was like an extra bonus. Later, we moved to Fox Point and had our first swimming pool. The home was completely surrounded by trees. Lake Michigan was about a mile away, and I jogged along the beach each morning. It was a wonderful, invigorating setting. Living here also made it easier for me to visit my children with Jean, who still lived in Oshkosh, Wisconsin.

"Oh, Boy! Problems Galore!"

The company manufactured high-pressure and low-pressure steel compressed-gas cylinders, accumulators, and other containers for the distribution of compressed gasses, chemicals, and liquids, and was a leader in the industry for the quality and breadth of the products offered. Pressed Steel Tank produced more popular types and sizes of compressed gas cylinders than any other manufacturer in North America.

Pressed Steel Tank had two plants. The main plant in West Allis was three-quarters of a century old and encompassed two large square blocks of old metal buildings, which contained the production shops as well as the executive and administrative offices. This plant manufactured compressed-gas cylinders from rectangular steel sheets or large steel coils, using squaring shears, circle shears, presses, and spinning machines. A hot-spinning operation closed the open end of the cylinder to form a head and nozzle for installing the pressure-control valve into the end of the cylinder. It also had testing facilities for pressure testing 100 percent of the cylinders to US Government Department of Transportation standards.

The West Milwaukee Billet plant had a different product and manufacturing process. They used steel billets—solid fifty- or sixty-pound blocks of steel—in their production process to make heavy-wall, high-pressure gas cylinders. They also used a large forging press line incorporating magnetic induction heating units to heat the billets to forging temperature, a forging press to extrude the billet into a cup shape, and a long line of extrusion dies to form the cylinders to size. The operation had a downtime rate of over 35 percent.

Going into the shop at Pressed Steel in August 1973 was like going back a century in time. The company, founded in 1902, was seventy-one years old. In the early days, the company manufactured acetylene lanterns for wagons and coaches and, later, for automobiles, in the original West Allis plant.

The buildings were old, the factory shop dimly lit, and the floor dirt. There were countless stacks of steel cylinders and finished tanks or cylinders in every place imaginable. Overhead cranes and fork trucks constantly moved steel coils, stacks of steel sheets, unfinished cylinder parts, and finished cylinders from location to location. I said to myself, "Oh, boy! Problems galore!"

There were seventy-five-year-old water-hydraulic presses and fifty-year-old oil-hydraulic presses in the pressrooms. A continuous parts handling and transferring chain ran through a portion of the building's ceiling trusses and down and around again; parts were loaded and unloaded at each station on the fly. The chain conveyor clanked, squeaked, and rattled overhead—a cacophony of sounds of poorly lubricated metal scraping on metal. This line also had an average downtime of over 35 percent.

Frederick W. Taylor

I fell in love with this old shop; there were a zillion things to fix everywhere you turned. I almost felt as if I were back in the time of Frederick W. Taylor, the original proponent of the use of scientific methods to improve labor efficiency. He organized these principles in his 1911 treatise *The Principles of Scientific Management,* which was the paradigm that spawned the industrial engineering profession.

Taylor's management system used the scientific method management technique, rather than the use of the empirical rule of thumb used by all of the factories of the time—and even now in many factories. An example of his work indicated that through measurement and the scientific method of analysis, you can improve the most rudimentary work and make it more efficient.

Taylor, in the early 1900s, studied shovelers in a steel mill— one of his many examinations and analyses of manual work. He determined the optimum shovel load for maximum efficiency. He then determined the most efficient shovel type and size for shoveling loads of different materials—iron ore, ashes, coal, sand—and positioned the most efficient shovels at the sites where the various materials were, rather than having the men carry one inefficient single-type shovel to the various shovel sites.

Just as I was in 1973 walking through the Pressed Steel factory with dirt floors and ancient machinery, Taylor at the turn of the century walked the dirt floors in the steel mills of Pennsylvania and identified inefficient labor practices and their remedies. I felt like a throwback in time.

I observed a man in the shop pulling a small wooden toolbox on roller-skate wheels carrying a few general-purpose tools and asked him what he was doing. He said that he was going out back to the acetylene cylinder welding line to fix one of the production conveyors—a three-hundred-yard round-trip on a dirt floor. He was one of seventy-six people in the maintenance department. It brought an idea to mind similar to the shovelers' study by Taylor. I thought, *Labor savings are all over this place*— and they were.

The plant looked as run-down as an aging, decrepit dowager with arthritic hands and limbs, but to me it was like a matriarch, growing old gracefully, her inner beauty untouched.

I set up a regular morning meeting where the shop superintendent, his lead foremen, and I met to analyze and act on recurring productivity deficiencies. The shop routinely collected detailed statistical data on production. Every operation in the shop recorded the cumulative total of pieces processed— and the number of press strokes—for every operation on each shift.

But the foremen did not make any use of it as far as I could see. I changed that and identified problems that the data uncovered, immediately following up to get the problems fixed.

I hired a supervisor for the maintenance department who, under my direction, completely revamped the maintenance organization. He purchased a fleet of three-wheeled golf carts, eliminated the backseats, and installed a metal box to carry tools and materials to the jobs scattered throughout the shops, which eliminated the walking time to the job sites. It also eliminated the back-and-forth to the maintenance shop for tools and materials.

The maintenance supervisor estimated the time to complete each job and used it as a guideline to schedule the jobs and assess the efficiency of the maintenance men. He also made up a list of the most frequently used tools and secured them in each of the carts. The maintenance supervisor got his own supervisor's cart to go quickly to the job sites and check on the maintenance men, at their job sites, and assist them with any problems.

In less than six months, the new system reduced the staffing of the maintenance department from seventy-six people to thirty-seven—a whopping 49 percent reduction in staffing, a major cost reduction—and the quality of the maintenance work improved.

The foremen and superintendent continued to come up with many new improvements, and productivity continued notching up.

David Scott

After almost a year as president of Pressed Steel, I received a letter addressed to "president." It was an invitation sent by one of the Allis Chalmers corporate staff, inviting the Pressed Steel Tank president to attend a cocktail party and presentations for the "West Allis Leaders of Industry," hosted by David Scott, President of Allis Chalmers.

I naturally marked an X in the "Will Attend" box and gave it to my secretary to mail.

When the day came, I joined the cocktail party and enjoyed the irony. Although I tried not to, I could not resist basking in my triumph over Scott after surviving the firing in Wichita Falls and subsequently taking over as president of Pressed Steel Tank.

The cocktail party was held in a hotel just two blocks from Scott's corporate office, where I had my introductory meeting with Scott and his last words—"The jury is out, Jack." It was, but in reverse, because here I was!

I schmoozed and sipped cocktails with the same idiotic sycophants that had accompanied Wargo to the Wichita Falls plant on the day of my firing. They asked about my new job and were interested in how I got it. I figured that it was none of their business and was starting to get irritated.

They persisted, and losing patience, I ignored them and turned away to survey the room behind me. I caught a glimpse of Scott on the other side of the room; he was facing the other way and did not see me.

I walked over to him, and as he turned to face me, I said, "Hi, Dave," a contraction of his first name that no one in the Allis Chalmers staff would dare use. It was just a small barb to rattle his conceit.

He was like a startled deer in a headlight, with an amazed expression on his face as he recognized who I was. It turned into a nervous, obsequious half-smile as he limply shook my offered hand. I said loudly, "How ya doing, Dave?"

His face could not hide his seething, submerged rage, and he no doubt was thinking about what he would do to punish the unfortunate persons on his staff who had invited me. Scott looked as if he had decided on "drawing and quartering"—and including me in the process.

I took an offered glass of champagne from a server, raised it high, and gave a loud toast for all within earshot, "To you, Dave!" He turned and slunk out of the room without touching his drink. My glass was still up as I watched him go, a buzz of people murmuring in the background.

He died a couple of years later and I am sorry for his family, but I did not mourn his passing. He was one less ass corrupting the power of his high position, trampling hopes and ambitions and damaging or ruining the lives of innocent, hardworking people.

God would have to deal with him now—as Granny would say.

I wondered how many more of these individuals I would run into in my professional years ahead, and I renewed my personal commitment to the people who worked for me. To be "fair, firm, and consistent" is the motto I have used throughout my management career—and will continue to use in the future. With God's help.

Spinning

It came time to negotiate a new labor contract with the steelworkers' union; discussions had been in progress for more than a month, but they had broken off and negotiations were at a standstill.

Several weeks later, the negotiations continued to be at an impasse, and the union declared an immediate strike. We quickly acted on a management plan to keep producing and shipping products for our customers and also receiving materials and supplies to keep the factory in operation.

Most of the managers and supervisors and nonunion office and shop personnel were splitting their time between working in the shop and performing their regular duties. Managers, accountants, production control, engineering, and other nonunion personnel were producing the products and shipping them to our customers.

I chose to work in the spinning department. The spinning room foreman taught me how to spin the end of heated metal cylinders into a finished compressed-gas cylinder. I clamped the cold-drawn cylinders in the holding jaws of the chuck on a special lathe, heated the open end of the cylinder in a small furnace, and shaped the open end of the cylinder into a closed spherical cone. The lathe's control wheel, operated manually, shaped the cylinder head by moving a thick, three-inch carbide block fastened to the lathe saddle against the heated cylinder while the cylinder was rotating at a high speed and produced the form desired—a tricky job, at best.

Infrequently, but dangerously and possibly catastrophically, sometimes the carbide tool caught on the surface of the heated cylinder and the cylinder violently tore apart, hurling pieces of jagged hot steel across the room and into the ceiling like shrapnel. Only a hard hat with a plastic visor and a spot-burned denim shirt shielded the operator. The maintenance man removed jagged pieces of cylinder that had pierced the ceiling—just in case one were to fall and injure someone—and the spinners continued their dangerous jobs.

The spinners considered themselves a special breed—the cream of the crop—and saw themselves a step higher up over the heavy press operators. However, the heavy press operators considered themselves on top of the shop totem pole.

Before the strike, Norman Swartz, the industrial relations manager—now called human resources—and management personnel were negotiating the new standard times for spinning the various sizes and shapes of cylinders.

The spinning department foreman designed and installed a new fixture, a method for handling the cylinder in and out of the heating furnace into the chuck jaw of the special spinning lathe, which reduced the time to spin the cylinder. The new standard times were one of the subjects of a grievance filed by the union before the strike.

I decided to make a film of the new operating method that was at issue with the union. Norm procured a suitable camera with a split screen. One screen filmed the operation, while the other filmed a ticking stopwatch. I decided to operate the spinning machine myself to demonstrate to the union that the new standard could be met—even with a novice spinner, such as the company's president, operating the lathe.

After the strike, we gathered the union leadership in the conference room and showed them the film. They were not happy campers, but they dropped the grievance and reluctantly accepted the new standard.

Several years after I left Pressed Steel, a violent incident occurred between a large press operator and several of the spinners. One of the large press operators brought a bag of loaded pistols into the plant and shot several of the spinners, two fatally. Norm Swartz bravely interceded and convinced the shooter to give himself up without further injuries or deaths. There definitely was serious bad blood between these two groups.

If Norm had not intervened or the spinners had had access to firearms, I believe there would have been a shoot-out, and there would have been bodies all over the place. Each of the parties had their everyday animosities that could explode at any time.

At the end of my first year at Pressed Steel Tank, Ed Mytkowicz sat down with me to discuss his evaluation of my performance. He gave me an A-plus overall rating, with a comment added at the bottom of the review: "I have never in my career seen a more profit-conscious executive at his level than Mr. Watson."

I welcomed his favorable review, especially his comment on my profit-consciousness, a trait that I had studiously developed in my prior jobs. He was tough and we did not always agree, but he was a damned good manager.

The US Justice Department was pressing Norris Industries to divest a substantial portion of the company. Jack Meany asked me to come to the office in Los Angeles to meet with him on the subject.

He said Norris was trying to sell the old company—the original plant located in West Allis—so that Norris could retain the newer facility in Milwaukee and he needed my help. He asked me if I would agree to stay with the company during the process, meet with prospective buyers, and assist in the sale.

I told him, "Of course, I would be happy to do what I can to help sell the company. You and Ed Mytkowicz and the other executives at Norris have always treated me more than fairly."

"I thought that you would, Jack, and we will give you a $50,000 bonus for helping to sell the company."

"Thank you. I appreciate the bonus; however, I would have helped out anyway, but I have a question."

Jack said, "Shoot."

"What if I get financial backing of my own and buy the company myself?"

"That would not be a problem for us. Go ahead and try a management buyout if you want to, but the deadline on bids is only four and a half weeks away, which will not give you much time to find financing."

We shook hands, and I returned to Milwaukee.

Jack Rishel and Jay Jordan

The strike continued, and I had been seeing a stream of potential buyers. It seemed as if I was usually working on the lathe when potential buyers appeared, and my secretary paged me to come in from the shop. I entered my office and tossed my helmet in a corner, sat at the small conference table in a denim shirt with burn holes, sipped a cup of black coffee, shook hands, and answered the potential buyer's questions.

One day, I came out of the shop and met Jack Rishel, a potential investor, and John Jay Jordan, an investment banker.

Rishel was the former president of the In-Sink-Erator Company, and Jordan was an investment banker from New York.

I decided to try to buy the company myself. The Milwaukee capital market was tight, and an unknown in the financial circles such as me was finding the banks to be uninterested and unwilling, although praising the financial statements I showed them. I was not knowledgeable in investment banking and where and whom to contact—and time was short. I was performing a full-time job, which limited the time I had available to go to New York or Chicago for financing.

In the end, I was unable to secure the necessary financing to purchase the company—a considerable personal letdown.

Norris Industries sold Pressed Steel Tank Company to Jack Rishel, but kept the West Milwaukee billet cylinder plant. Jay Jordan and the Carl Marks Investment Bank provided investment and financing services to Rishel.

In addition to the $50,000 for helping sell the company, I also received warrants from Jay Jordan. I thought I was onto something. I didn't know it at the time, but Jay Jordan was going to have a pivotal effect on my future professional and financial success.

Grandmother Edna "Coffman" Stover and Joseph Stover married in 1899 in Gallup, New Mexico. Grandfather Joseph, born on June 18, 1879, in Arkansas, died in January 1915 at the young age of thirty-six years of spinal meningitis, contracted from an infected mosquito bite. He left three children: my mom, Estallee, my Aunt Ethelene, and my Uncle Alva. Granny Stover never remarried.

Photo 2: (Left to right) Homer Watson, Estallee Stover, Aunt Corrine (Co), and a friend, in a circa 1920 touring car. They were driving through the New Mexico Badlands on their way to the Carlsbad Caverns in southern New Mexico.

(Left to right) Aunt Judy, Mom (Estallee), Aunt Co, and Aunt Eve, cutting up together in 1937. Aunt Co was the one who built the Log Cabin Roadhouse.

Aunt Co's roadhouse and diner was built by a number of relatives under Aunt Co's direction. Aunt Co paid the workers by cooking for them and their families. The roadhouse was referred to by some as "The Little Whorehouse," but Aunt Co put an end to the rumor by running off two prostitutes who rented a room while posing as freelance writers.

Our grandmother, Granny Stover, with her mother (our great grandmother), Margaret "Maggie" Coffman. As a young girl, Maggie patrolled the herds of her father's cattle at night to keep the mountain lions from killing them.

Homer King Watson in 1917 at seventeen years old. Homer's mother left her husband, Walter Watson, and took Homer to her mother's home. Homer's grandmother, Emily Crutchfield, moved with Homer to El Paso on the Rio Grande River, and she cared for Homer until he was old enough to care for himself. Homer sold papers on the streets of El Paso and learned to read and write Spanish from the Mexican families he spent time with there. Homer left high school in the middle of his second year.

*(1922) Homer Watson at twenty-two years old in Gallup, New Mexico.
Homer worked in a coal mine in Gallup and met Alva Stover, Estallee's
brother. Alva introduced Homer to Estallee, who was helping her mother,
Edna, run a boardinghouse for single men.*

*(1923) Wedding photograph of Homer and Estallee, taken in Albuquerque,
New Mexico. Estallee was sixteen, and Homer was twenty-three years old.*

(1930) Me (Jerry "Jack" Watson) at three years old and my brother, Perry, five years old, in Oklahoma City. There was a tornado, and we had to go to the root cellar under the house for our safety.

Oklahoma City, 1932. Perry and I on the Spirit of Saint Louis. Perry wanted to sit in the seat, but the photographer would not let him.

(1933) My brother and I with our new jackets outside the Colorado Springs Day Nursery.

Uncle Kirk Coffman. Uncle Kirk was my great uncle and was a surrogate father for Perry and me when our father abandoned Mom during the Great Depression.

Uncle Kirk was a great hunter, hunting dog trainer, and marksman. This picture is of Uncle Kirk (left), fellow hunter Axel Floren (right), and Kirk's three hunting dogs that "treed" the cougar.

(1934) Granny's farm, Lennox Addition, three miles from Klamath Falls, Oregon. Granny, as shown, raised vegetables of many kinds in her small garden and raised rabbits and chickens to feed Perry and me and our cousins, Maqulene and Billie Jean, and herself.

(1934) My dog, Gypsy, with me on the right and my brother, Perry, on the left. Gypsy and I ranged through the Juniper Woods, the mountain behind our house, and the swimming hole down by the Klamath River. She was the best dog in the world and did whatever I wanted her to do until she was run over by a car. I buried her under a tree in the Juniper Woods.

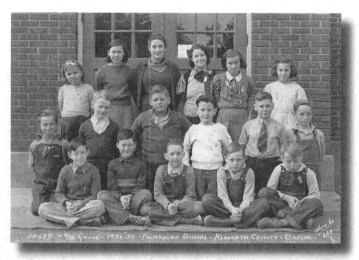

(1937) Fourth-grade class at Fairhaven Elementary School. I am in the second row, wearing a white shirt. The school was located about a half mile "as the crow flies" over the top of "Jack's Mountain," which I claimed as my own. I often ran over the mountain to get home to Granny's place, rather than take the school bus, where I was vulnerable to getting beaten up when the bus stopped and I got off and had to start running.

My cousin, Billy Jean, and me circa 1934. Billie's mother, Ethelene, bought us new clothes for the picture. Aunt Ethelene and her husband, Mack, brought me to Crescent City on the Pacific Coast to spend our summertime together roller-skating all over town and having fun. A number of years later, Aunt Ethelene vanished and was never found. The family agreed that something bad had happened to her, but did not have a clue as to what that was.

Jack Watson

(1940) Seventh-grade class at Fairhaven Elementary School with a few boys and a zillion girls. The principal, Mr. Robbinet, is in the top row, second from the left. I'm on the far left of the first row, getting ready to run home over the mountain. Ed Schultz, to Jerry's right, was nicknamed "Ickybod Crane" for his stature and large head.

Main Street in Klamath Falls, Oregon, in 1937. It was the largest town in southern Oregon, with a population of 16,000 people.

Klamath Falls, Oregon, 1945. (Left to right) My best friend, Calvin Worley, me, and Bob Kennedy before joining the US Navy.

Perry King Watson, my brother. US Marine Corps in Tiensin, China, in the fall of 1945.

Mom, me, and Perry's 1936 Ford convertible at Pelican City. The same car Perry drove down the Green Springs Mountain Road, sitting on the top of the seat and steering with his bare feet.

(Left to right) Unknown, Calvin Worley, me, and Bob Kennedy at the Owl Bar in 1945 while in Navy boot camp.

(1945) Estallee was in Oklahoma City with a businessman and invited me to dinner. I was stationed at the Aviation Ordnance School in Norman, Oklahoma, about fifteen miles from Oklahoma City.

(1946) I am on the right, with two buddies and a girl to my left, having a beer in Seattle on a weekend leave from Sand Point Naval Air Station.

Me and my 1934 Chevy, overheating as usual, at Oregon State College.

(Left to right) Cliff Brandt, mathematics genius, Rollie Berry, civil engineer, and me, Jack Watson, industrial administration and industrial engineer, Oregon State College. At the swimming hole and boat dock in Corvallis, Oregon, in 1948.

*Rollie Berry and I at Oregon State College,
working on my 1930 English Midget.*

*Me in my taxicab, working the night shift for an average of twenty-five cents
per customer. I didn't plan on getting rich, though I held three jobs while
going to school.*

Mom and I on the day I graduated from Oregon State College in June 1950.

Me at twenty-five years old and working at Boeing Airplane Company in Seattle, Washington. My first wife, Jean, was twenty-three years old; our beautiful little girl, Teresa, was three, Ron was eight, and Dave was seven.

MEMBERS OF DIVISION FLYING CLUB STAND BEFORE CESSNA WHICH THEY HOPE TO PURCHASE. LEFT TO RIGHT ARE DAVE POWERS, JERRY WATSON AND GEORGE NOZDIEZ.

The Ogden Flyers club members (left to right): Dave Powers, Jack Watson, founder and president of the Ogden Flyers, and George Nozdiez. The Club's Cessna 175 airplane is in the background.

(Left to right) Ron, Jack, Estallee, and Al Watson. Photo was taken in our home in Kent Woodlands, Marin County, California, about 1978.

My mother and I at a hotel for lunch in San Jose, California, before she went completely blind from a fall. She lived to be eighty-nine years old.

Martina and I were married by a justice of the peace at the New Orleans Courthouse in a civil ceremony on June 14, 1972. Martina was twenty-nine years old, and I was forty-five years old, a difference of sixteen years, but we were both so happy and in love that we felt like a couple of kids.

Martina and I (front) in Rio de Janeiro, Brazil, at a dinner party given by the owner of several companies under the CBV name and our distributor in much of South America. He, his wife, and his four sons and their wives occupy the table. The Brazilian food was sumptuous.

Martina on a camel in front of the Great Wall of China, in her Siberian red fox coat.

Jean and my second son, David James Watson, at age sixteen. David joined the US Army at age nineteen and was sent to Vietnam to fight the Viet Cong of North Vietnam, who were trying to take over all of Vietnam. He had volunteered for a second tour of duty at barely twenty-one years old. David had a Vietnamese wife and baby boy and was trying to get permission from the US Army to allow him to take them home with him when his second tour of duty ended. Instead, he died of a drug overdose, alone, on a dark night in a dark place, thousands of miles from home. He had six months to go before his second tour ended. Illegal drugs of every kind proliferated in Vietnam. They were cheap, they were easy to obtain, and they were deadly. It was a virtual plague. God rest his soul.

David and his Vietnamese wife, Tranti Ngoc Ho ("Sandy"). He was twenty-one years old and in the US Army in Vietnam when this photo was taken.

Martina at San Francisco Fisherman's Wharf.

Martina and I at the Hotel El Mirador in Acapulco, Mexico.

Martina and I in Venice, Italy.

July 1983, Houston, Texas. (Left to right) Torpe, Grove Valve's attorney, Watson, John Jeffers, our lead attorney from the firm of Baker Botts, and two unidentified Grove lawyers. We won the lawsuit brought by the distributor, Flo Control, against our company and had a celebratory dinner. After a few drinks, we slipped on our matching T-shirts, paraded by the Flo Control table, and displayed the backs of our T-shirts, which read: "We Knocked Their Dicks in the Dirt." They were definitely not amused.

John Jeffers displaying our special T-shirt.

293

On the right, Jack enjoying Jamaica. The other gentleman is Captain Dennis, a Jamaican, a writer, and Martina's friend.

Martina's son, Joel (Hartman) Watson, and her granddaughter, Chelsea Watson. Chelsea was one year old in the photo.

Chelsea, Martina's granddaughter, at about six years old. She was shooting targets with a .44 magnum pistol on the Winchester Shooting Range in the mountains near our home in Montecito, California. And she's hitting the targets!

(2009) Martina's daughter, Maelee, whom I adopted.

*(2009) Chelsea Watson, Martina's granddaughter,
just after she turned eighteen.*

*Martina on her last visit to Paris, a city she loved very much. Her children,
her granddaughter, and I were not aware that she had cancer,
which she died from nine months later. Our small family was devastated.
God rest her soul.*

Martina at the Shakespeare City Lights Bookstore in Paris. Martina was very familiar with the City Lights Bookstore in Sausalito, California. She received her bachelor's degree in English and creative writing and graduated cum laude from San Francisco State University. Martina started and owned the Sausalito Soap Company. Her daughter, Maelee, also worked in her store.

Our son, Allan Wade Watson, and his wife, Diane, with their two adopted Russian children, Nate and Emily. I was happy to be able to provide funds for their adoption. The Russian adoption bureaucracy tried their best to squeeze every dollar from Americans seeking to adopt Russian orphans, but it was well worth it. Nate and Emily are happy in their home, with a loving mother and father.

Ron Watson with his 1932 Chevrolet five-window coupe with a supercharged 1967 Camaro 327ci engine. The paint job is "plum crazy purple." Ron did a tour in the US Navy during the Vietnam War and is an outstanding mechanic with all types of machinery.

Ron's daughter and my granddaughter, Erika, and her husband, Tom Grenfell, with their daughter Justine and son Tristan.

My grandson, Broc (Ron's son), with his girlfriend, Heather, and me. We attended Broc's US Army boot camp graduation. I had a stent installed in a heart artery two days before, but I did not want to miss the ceremony for Broc and hundreds of other soldiers.

Jean and my daughter, Teresa. Teresa and her husband, R. D. Duzinske, are the mother and father of Greg and Brenna. R. D. is a farmer and entrepreneur who builds condominiums in Florida. Teresa is a librarian in Ripon, Wisconsin, the town that started the Republican Party. She is also an artist who paints primarily in watercolors. Brenna is teaching her son, Eddie Jack, to like the water.

Teresa's son, my grandson, Greg Duzinske, enlisted in the US Army.

Clari Watson and her husband, Rory Hasselquist. Rory is in the insurance business and also manages a thousand-acre forest with several summer homes. Clari has a real estate license and works in insurance. She also clog dances, hunts deer, turkeys, and ducks, fishes, and is a Taekwondo black belt and kickboxer (so watch out, you might get hurt). She is the most physically active member of the family.

(Left to right) Chelsea Watson, Nicole Spiegel, a close family friend, and Maelee, Chelsea's mother. Nicole Spiegel, thankfully, took on the task of organizing and preparing my book for publication— a demanding job, which she did well.

Chapter 10:
Awakening

Grove Valve and Regulator

L ouie Mihaly called me in 1977 about a possible new professional position that might be of interest to me.

He started by saying, "You appeared to have vanished off the face of the earth." He said that he had to contact the FBI, the CIA, and the Internal Revenue Service to locate me. I thought he must have been making a joke, but knowing Louie, he probably had used those contacts to locate me.

He asked me how I was doing and how I liked my present job.

I replied, "Just fine. I like my job, but as president, I have nowhere to advance except to another company. Jack Rishel, the buyer and owner of Pressed Steel, is now chairman of the company."

I explained my attempt to buy the company.

Louie said, "If you are interested, we should talk. It could be a challenging and rewarding situation for you."

He asked me to meet him in Washington at the posh Watergate Hotel complex where he was staying. It was the same building where the Democratic Election Campaign Headquarters was broken into in 1972, culminating in Richard Nixon's resignation.

We met and talked as we strolled along the public walks in the National Mall and Memorial Parks. We saw various monuments and park icons: the Washington Monument, the Lincoln Memorial, the World War II Memorial, and the Jefferson Memorial. We enjoyed the symbolic architecture, historic vistas, and landscape.

We walked for two or three hours, Louie doing most of the talking. The subject was the eight-hundred-mile Alyeska Pipeline in Alaska, and a valve manufacturing company in Oakland that provided large steel gate valves for the pipeline. Grove Valve and Regulator Company was formerly a subsidiary of the Walworth Corporation and was now owned by the Alberta Pipeline Company.

Louie talked about the difficulties in constructing the pipeline, how the elevation of the pipeline on supports above the ground accommodated the caribou on their migrations, and protecting the permafrost from the heat of the oil in the pipeline. He discussed the number of barrels of oil that the pipeline would transport for each of its planned expansions.

He described how the oil was stored at the Valdez terminal located on the shore of the Gulf of Alaska and was shipped by gigantic oil tankers to the United States, and covered many other details that held my interest. If I were to accept the position with Grove, I would have a chance to visit the pipeline and see its wonders for myself.

At the Watergate Bar and Restaurant, Louie told me the story of Grove Valve and Regulator Company over several martinis, a bottle of not-too-heavy French Bordeaux, and a rare New York cut Porterhouse steak for him and Chateaubriand for me.

He outlined the sales and financial projections for Grove's major market, pipeline valves, fittings, and regulators, which demonstrated that Grove was doing well. The other Grove product line was aerospace regulators, which were a small portion of total sales, less than 7 percent. It was a mature product line and sales were decreasing, but the profitability was high, primarily due to Grove being the sole provider of the technology and having pricing power on the declining product line sales.

Although Grove obtained some aerospace regulator business for the space shuttle, it was an insignificant part of the total regulator business. Sales of aerospace regulators had been declining for several years, and very little marketing expense was required for the regulators. The product line would not be a hindrance to the overall success of the company. The companies might eventually phase out or sell the mature product line since it was not essential to the company's strategic plan.

Louie said, "The job we are talking about is the top job—president of Grove Valve and Regulator Company—reporting to Bob Blair, the chairman of Alberta Pipe Line Company, in Calgary.

Louie asked me to give it some thought and said that he would call me the following Monday.

"Sounds good," I said.

Early on Monday morning, I was at my desk preparing to go to a meeting when Louie's call came in. I stepped outside the conference room into my office and took the call.

He said, "Jack, what do you think?"

I replied, "I like the sound of it, and I would like to pursue it."

That afternoon, I received a second call from Louie. He said, "Can you go to Calgary tomorrow afternoon for an interview with the president of Alberta Pipeline Company?"

"Sure," I said. "Let me check the airline reservations."

I flew to Calgary and met Bob Blair, Bob Pierce, and Dianne Narvick. They knew that I had run the Braintree plant for Walworth and had done a good job, and I was sure that Louie had put in a few good words for me.

They asked a few questions, going through the formalities, and told me the salary, which was more than I made at Pressed Steel. I presented a proposed single-page employment contract that set forth the amount the company would pay me if I were terminated with or without cause and a list of items that could constitute a termination for cause and showed it to Blair. He looked at it for a moment, started laughing, enunciated "moral turpitude," and handed the list back to me.

His response was strange. I left him the one-page proposed employment contract to review at his convenience.

The meeting lasted about twenty minutes. Blair wanted me to meet one more person, Arthur Child, president of Burns Foods, a large food company also headquartered in Calgary, who was a member of the Alberta Pipeline Company board of directors, as well as a director on the Grove board.

I went to Arthur Child's office, and we talked. He was a very pleasant man, and I immediately took a liking to him. He asked me about my experience, and I briefed him on Boeing, Thiokol, and so on, while he listened, politely waiting, until I mentioned Walworth.

His eyes lit up then. "So—Walworth Valve—that's the key to your being considered for the Grove Valve position. I was wondering what your other jobs had to do with Grove, and now I understand."

After the interview, we said good-bye, and on my way out, Arthur said, "Jack, I think you will do very well at Grove, and I will give Bob Blair a positive recommendation on your appointment as president."

I said, "Thank you; I appreciate your support." We shook hands, and I departed.

A few days later, Bob Blair's secretary called and said, "You have the job, and Mr. Blair would like you to start in three weeks—or sooner, if you can. You will receive an employment agreement in the mail in a couple of days."

Back in Milwaukee, I gave notice to the chairman, who handled it in stride.

Arriving at the Emeryville, Grove Valve & Regulator offices for my first day, I met with Bob Blair and Dianne Narvick, who had flown down together from Calgary on the company plane to introduce me to my job. We gathered in the conference room, and Bob Blair introduced me to the executive staff and spoke a few words. It was a short meeting, and everyone left after a few minutes, leaving me alone in the conference room.

Where the hell is my office? I started opening doors in the short hallway by the conference room. There were three closed doors: the first was to an executive bathroom, the second was to a closet, and the third turned out to be the president's executive office.

One problem solved, I thought to myself as I tried out the desk chair.

Having not had the chance to see the factory yet, I lit up a Rothschild cigar, proceeded into the shop, and spent a couple of hours touring the facility. The factory was on one large floor, separated by walls between the machining operations and the press shop, and welding, assembly, and testing. The shop had, in addition to the normal machine tools and presses, large Bullard vertical boring machines and an imposing thousand-ton-capacity hydraulic press used for forming large valve components from thick steel plates.

The company manufactured large gate, globe, and check pipeline valves and fittings up to forty-eight-inch inside pipe diameter, a line of regulators up to 5000 psi, including the aerospace regulators, and up to twelve-inch surge relief valves. Surge relief valves were vital pieces of equipment on a pipeline. These devices protected a pipeline from shock damage in an abrupt line shutdown, a situation similar to the pipes in your house hammering when a faucet is closed suddenly. The surge relief valves eliminated this problem, which could cause a pipeline to rupture and cause a nasty, costly, and environmentally sensitive oil spill.

The shipping and receiving docks and office were located at the back of the building, inspection and quality control was near the assembly area, and production control was located on a mezzanine over the shop. Engineering, human resources, accounting and data processing, purchasing, and the executive office occupied the main office area.

At least I knew my way around. As was my practice, I expected to spend substantial time on the factory floor talking to the workers and supervisors and observing the operations.

Later, I called the executive staff together to hear their problems. Although many of the managers were capable and outgoing with their thoughts and ideas, there were obvious changes required.

Prior to my arrival, the company had been in turmoil. According to some of the managers, there had been a mutiny by several top managers against the former president. As their conspiracy unfolded, each of the members was disposed of—not in the Russian way with a bullet to their heads—but by quietly leaving the company.

There were also unsupported allegations that the previous president and one or more of his managers were operating another business on the side—and that one of the employees was drawing a salary at both companies. However, who knew what the real facts were? I decided to find out.

I was particularly concerned about the vice president of finance. He was very close with the previous president, who had left the company under circumstances that I heard were not fully of his own volition. I was particularly concerned about the integrity of the accounting. There was talk that the former president allegedly increased the value of his final bonus through manipulation of the sales.

After months of wrangling, I replaced the vice president of finance with Richard Morton, a graduate of the University of Oregon. It was open-market recruitment, and Dick was a solid financial professional and worked as corporate controller and chief financial officer for the BEPEX Corporation in Santa Rosa. Dick and I were to have an excellent professional relationship that continued until my semiretirement in 1997.

Grove also had a manufacturing facility in Sparks, Nevada, and the main sales office in Houston. The Sparks plant was adjacent to Reno and manufactured small pipeline valves twelve-inch bore size and under. Chip Weeks was the Sparks plant manager, but I soon replaced him with George Dodson, an older, straight-shooting veteran. Dodson, before he went to Sparks, promoted Brian Warren, a top Grove manufacturing supervisor, to manufacturing superintendent of the Oakland plant, and later became vice president of manufacturing for the company and a longtime associate of mine.

Over the next few months, I hired or promoted several managers to the team. I hired John Tesher as vice president of sales and marketing, which, as it turned out, was a monumental mistake. Much later, I found Tesher to be a deceitful, Machiavellian personality and a tyrant.

I transferred Dick Golomb, the Oakland sales manager, to Houston to run our US sales office and accelerate our sales efforts.

I also hired Walter Connelly, an effective manager and professional engineer and a Grove veteran, to be vice president of manufacturing. Walt was working for M & J Valve Company in Houston for Red Grove, the founder of Grove Valve and the owner and president of M & J Valve, a competitor.

We set up a new assembly facility for surge relief systems in a vacant manufacturing building in Berkeley, a few blocks from the Oakland plant. With the availability of the new facility and our time-tested surge-relief technology, we were able to obtain new profitable orders for large skid-mounted surge relief systems.

Grove had been working on a new product for measuring liquid and gas flow in pipelines. Orifice plate technology was a common industry methodology for measuring flow in oil or natural gas pipelines. A technician calculated the flow from the differential pressure produced from an orifice plate in the pipeline.

We started limited production of the new, fabricated, flat plate orifice meter in the Oakland plant, but needed more space to go into full production. I spent time searching around the Houston area to find a suitable site for the new plant. I chose the land and constructed the plant in Brookshire, Texas, thirty miles west of Houston. We equipped the shop with the necessary

machines, cutting and welding equipment, tooling, and offices
and began hiring the workforce and started production.

The United States oil and gas industry and the suppliers
that serve it were sensitive to world events both positively and
negatively. They were booming due to the oil embargo against
the United States, and there was a priority to increase domestic
production.

The nexus of the energy crisis began with the 1973 Arab
oil embargo. Oil-producing countries in the Middle East,
including Saudi Arabia and other OPEC countries, embargoed
all petroleum product shipments to the United States.

The United States, which had been self-sufficient in energy
in 1950, was now importing 35 percent of the country's crude
oil needs from foreign producers. Because of the embargo, the
price of oil escalated to a new high of $35 for a forty-two-gallon
barrel of crude oil—from $12 a barrel at the end of 1974, almost
tripling the price.

The embargo posed a significant threat to the US economy,
but was a windfall for the petroleum and natural gas industry.
Oil and gas production in the United States surged to meet
the nation's energy needs to fill the supply gap created by the
embargo.

Grove Valve shared in the boom, and sales and profits rose
dramatically. Grove's overall sales and profitability went from
good to very good!

The boom of the oil and gas industry in the 1970s resulted
in an oversupply of American gas and oil production and excess
capacity of the facilities to provide it. This situation eventually
became a backbreaking bust in the 1980s and left the industry
in a major crisis.

Production of new petroleum and natural gas equipment
took a nosedive in the United States, Canada, and offshore Gulf
of Mexico. The oil and gas companies delayed or cancelled the
search for new oil and natural gas producing fields, drilling

rigs shut down, and few new drilling rigs or pipelines were constructed.

Some companies producing equipment for the energy industry shut down, and others restructured and had massive layoffs. Grove faced the same draconian choices as many of the other US oil and gas equipment companies.

Our company's production capacity and personnel were over two times greater than its incoming order rate, which required eliminating over one-half of our current personnel and staff as well as other costs. We had already implemented cost cutting and pulling in our belts, and these programs were ongoing but were insufficient to solve the problem. The oil and gas market represented over 90 percent of Grove's sales in the mid-1980s, and Grove's new orders were down by over 50 percent.

The outlook for Grove was bleak. A major restructuring was required—plant shutdowns, drastic layoffs, consolidations, and a complete reorganization of the company were mandatory.

At the same time, we were in negotiations with the United Steelworkers Union for a new labor contract. After weeks of negotiating, the company and the union came to an impasse, and the negotiations ceased.

Two union individuals, Tom Sullivan, reputed to be a card-carrying Communist, and David Means, a reputed radical of the Black Panthers, headed up the negotiating committee for the union.

When I laid the facts on the table that showed that incoming orders had fallen by over 50 percent and the company was deep in the red, the black militant's response was, "Shut it down!"

I vehemently responded, *"No, I will not shut it down—I will shut you down!"*

The federal arbitrator asked if the company would open its financial books to the union, headquartered in Pittsburgh, and I affirmed that I would be willing to go that far to reach a new contract. We provided the financial information, and the steelworkers headquarters agreed after a thorough review that the company had been forthright with the local union in everything we had said.

Regardless of our proactive efforts, the local union ignored the true situation and continued the strike.

Bricks Can Burn

Several months into the strike, Dan Wilson, my vice president of human resources, excitedly came into my office after a perfunctory knock on the open door. He said, "There is a man outside the hydraulic press room door, and he says he wants to talk to the top honcho of the plant—and he wants you to get your ass out there right now!"

I asked, "Who the hell is he?"

Dan said, "Says he is the boss of the union for the east side of the San Francisco Bay."

"Okay," I said. "Let's go see him."

The strike against the company had been in effect for several months, and we had brought in replacement workers to temporarily replace the union workforce. The National Labor Relations Board representative confirmed the company's right to hire temporary replacements for the strikers since we had made our final offer of settlement of the strike and the union rejected the offer.

Company management, including my staff and I, and supervisors and nonunion office personnel worked in the shop and performed their regular functions on a part-time basis, so the company could continue to produce and ship products to our customers.

I worked in the factory operating a numerical control milling machine, and Dick Morton, vice president of finance, assembled and tested high-pressure, 3000 psi regulators—a dangerous job if you did not know what you were doing, but Dick was competent in the job. We were able to find enough qualified or trainable office and management personnel to maintain production at the existing incoming order level.

Dan Wilson, my right-hand man for negotiating with the union and maintaining plant security, as well as his regular human resource functions, was an important member of our executive staff and strategy team.

Dan and I walked out through the factory to the open hydraulic press room door to the outside and came face-to-face with the individual who had talked to Dan.

"Who are you?" I asked.

Over one hundred strikers filled the streets alongside our buildings. Many union supporters also had come from all around the Bay Area to show solidarity with the strikers.

"I'm the union boss."

"Boss of what?" I replied.

He said, "I am the boss of all of the steelworker chapters on this side of the Bay."

"Well, okay," I replied. "I have never heard of you, but go on and say what you want to say—I'm listening."

Dan and I listened to his diatribe of incorrect "facts" and how his union was going to break the company.

Continuing his nonstop speech, he made a veiled threat. "Bricks can burn," he said.

"I doubt it," I replied.

He said, "You know very well what I mean!"

I stepped out into the street and looked up to one of our security guards that Dan had posted on the roof. He was manning a video camera and filming and sound recording everything that was going on below.

I shouted up to the security guard on the roof, "Did you get that?"

He gave me a thumbs-up sign. Dan and I turned our backs on the crowd and went back inside the building, leaving the crowd murmuring outside.

As we walked back to my office, I asked, "What do you think, Dan?"

Dan replied, "Looks like they are losing and know it."

"It sure does," I agreed.

After fifty-two weeks, there was a vote of the workers supervised by the National Labor Relations Board for or against having a union. The union lost and was decertified, and the company officially terminated the striking union workers. If they desired to come back to work, they had to do so the same as any new employee without seniority, filling out an application for work. These were the NLRB rules—not the company's.

After the union was officially decertified, the two official members of the union were too embarrassed to apply for work at Grove. My statement to them that I would shut them down succeeded.

The bricks did not burn—and Grove was not put out of business.

I regret that many people on both sides suffered during the strike and the drastic changes made to save the company, but we had no choice. If the union had won their demands, the company would have been out of business, and *all* of the workers and Grove employees would have been unemployed.

A few months later, the Grove purchasing manager died of an illness at a relatively young age. The vice president of manufacturing promoted John Litherland to purchasing manager. Later, John was stricken with throat cancer and had an operation; his voice box was surgically removed. When he came back to work a week later, he had a small hole in his throat. He also had a handheld, battery-powered, electronic voice box. He held the electronic gadget to his throat and spoke; the words coming out sounded like a ghost in a tunnel, but were understandable, allowing him to return to his job.

Two months later, John and I flew to Seoul, South Korea. I drove a rental car to Inchon to discuss the low-cost production of machined components for our small ball valve product line with the owners of a small South Korean business.

Inchon is located on the Yellow Sea, in the northwest corner of the country, a few miles from the demilitarized zone between North and South Korea, armed-to-the-teeth relics of the Korean War. In Inchon, General MacArthur's assault landings had turned the tide of the Korean War.

Jack Watson

We were greatly surprised when we visited the supplier's shop to see a fully assembled ball valve. Their authorization was for the manufacture and sales to Grove of only valve components—not finished valves. His contract was not for a competitive finished valve, which he likely intended to sell in the market competing against us. I made this clear to him during our discussions. He agreed not to compete with us and continued producing valve parts for Grove.

We returned to Seoul and stayed at the Lotte Hotel. John and I sat in the huge bar and restaurant and ordered drinks. A hostess clad in a long, colorful kimono took our drink order, and as she turned to leave, John said something to her using his electronic voice box. His voice almost made her jump out of her wits in fright.

She recovered and went to fill our drink order. She returned with our drinks—and several other hostesses—to hear John and his electronic voice box. They swarmed all around him to hear his voice—as well as using the device themselves, uttering giggles and shrieks. This went on for some time as additional hostesses dropped by to hear John and themselves.

We had lunch the next day at an authentic Korean restaurant in the southern suburb of Seoul. In typical Korean fashion, it had a scalloped roof and intricate moldings; the inside was dark wooden beams and walls, with wooden tables and chairs situated throughout the restaurant. The aroma of barbequed meat and roasted garlic filled the air.

The next morning, I had meetings with Hyundai, a major Japanese corporation involved in many industries worldwide. I traveled to Pusan, a rundown, sewage-laden city on the southern tip of the Korean Peninsula, to inspect an industrial facility producing valves.

In the Korean War, Pusan had been the last-ditch stand of the US Army—and our United Nations allies—in the fight to save South Korea. The North Korean Army pushed US and NATO troops all the way down from Seoul to the Pusan perimeter before MacArthur's strategic attack from the sea stopped the

314

North Koreans' offensive and pushed the North Korean army back to the Chinese border.

Later, after we had returned from South Korea several months earlier, John Litherland took a medical leave. One day his wife called me. She said John had returned to smoking cigarettes, using the hole in his throat to inhale the chemical-laden smoke, and he had died of throat cancer.

Beijing and Shenyang, China

Grove had been negotiating with the Chinese government on a license for China to manufacture Grove valves. Walt Connelly, vice president of manufacturing, was adamant on inspecting the Chinese manufacturing capability and quality controls before making a decision. This would be a very important trip. The decision whether to grant the Chinese a license to manufacture Grove valves was a decision that could be either favorable or unfavorable to the future of Grove.

I discussed the situation with Louie Mihaly. He agreed that we should look at the Chinese factory in Shenyang, review the manufacturing processes and the quality controls, and get a sense of their strategy for selling the product.

We wanted to restrict their sales to China and the Asian market, with the United States reserved to Grove. We also needed to define their pricing policy for purchases of Chinese valves by Grove for sales by Grove outside of Asia.

The management team from Nova, formerly the Alberta Pipeline Company, the owner of Grove, consisted of Dora Kwok and Jim Wong. Dora Kwok asked the daughter of the mayor of Shanghai to join them in their visit to the Chinese valve factory, and she agreed.

Louie said, "You have to go to China with Walter. Nova will be sending their management team, and you need to be there. Take Martina along with you if she wants to go."

We flew to Beijing a few days later. When we arrived at the Beijing Airport, the plant manager of the 2,000-person Shenyang Valve Factory met us. He flew down from Shenyang to greet us personally. The daughter of the mayor of Shanghai was also there. No one would let us carry our luggage; the manager of the Shenyang factory personally carried two bags and motioned to several baggage handlers to carry the rest of the luggage.

Martina and I checked into the Beijing Hotel and were scheduled to spend several days in the city as guests of our hosts, visiting notable landmarks. The hotel was the largest in the city, was relatively modern by Chinese standards, and provided us with the best accommodations and service.

Looking down from our fourth-floor balcony, Martina and I saw streams of people on bicycles riding down the boulevard— there were almost no automobiles. Both men and women were wearing drab mufti Mao jackets, loose trousers, and sandals or heavy work shoes; there was almost no colorful garb.

The next day, Martina and I and the Nova group toured a large metal-fabrication shop with our hosts. The freezing shop was heated only by large cans burning oil in the open air, providing little heat but lots of choking smoke.

The next day, Martina and I went shopping for long underwear. She went inside the large Friendship Store while I waited outside and smoked a cigar. After about thirty minutes, I wondered why she was taking so long and went inside the store to find her. I found her in the fur coat department trying on a full-length Siberian red fox coat, which she liked and subsequently purchased.

"Some long-handle underwear," I said.

Martina ignored me—as usual—and asked me for my American Express card to consummate the transaction.

As it turned out, the fur coat was the best thing Martina could have purchased since the cold weather continued. I took a photograph of her in the coat sitting atop a camel on top of the Great Wall on a bone-chilling, sunshiny day. She looked great!

Our hosts invited us to a special dinner in the outskirts of Beijing. We found out later that a renowned carver of flowers from vegetables was called out of retirement to provide his service as the flower chef. The owner opened his restaurant at the request of our host on a day the restaurant traditionally was closed.

It was nighttime when our hosts picked us up in the Lada automobile, its headlights dimmed in cities by law. We drove on semidark, wide streets with very little auto traffic, but hundreds of bicycles. In the dim light, the bicyclists moved like ghostly ballet dancers, their legs on the pedals moving in harmony, up and down, as if choreographed.

We arrived at the restaurant to see a small, nondescript building with a letter missing on the neon sign of the restaurant, but inside it was like a Cinderella land.

The twelve-course dinner was more than excellent. The elegant, flower-sculpted vegetables were a charming and beautiful accompaniment to the food choices.

The next day, we flew to Shenyang, an hour-and-a-half flight northeast of Beijing. We were the only non-Chinese passengers. Looking over the other passengers, who appeared to be Mongolian, I thought they must be workers in transit to work in Shenyang, but I found out later that almost all were businessmen!

When we arrived at Shenyang, our hosts drove us in a Russian Lada sedan, which looked like a pre–World War II Chevrolet, to a large compound with twenty or more large stone dachas built by the Russians several decades earlier.

Our dacha had two stories, servant quarters, kitchen, and dining room on the first floor, and the guest quarters, a large bedroom, sitting room, and bath on the second floor. A servant brought two large thermoses of steaming hot water, a jar of dry tea leaves, mugs, and spoons. We experimented on how to drink a mug of tea without having tea leaves stick to our lips like a mustache. We drank a lot of tea, and we had never felt healthier.

Late one night, I heard a noise and got up. Martina was sleeping soundly, and I did not want to wake her. I heard the sound again and wondered if it were a cry of distress of a beaten or mistreated servant, but it did not seem to be coming from the servant quarters downstairs. I walked over to the windows and opened one to hear where the intermittent sound was coming from.

There was a bright moon, and I could see the snowy land and trees clearly. It was bitter cold; there was a foot or more of sparkling snow on the ground, and a full moon cast its light on the thick woods.

I pulled a chair up to the window and waited. After a while, I heard in the distance someone singing a beautiful song, taken up by someone closer. When the song ended, I heard a piercing, "Yeee-ip!" This provided the answer to where the sounds were coming from, but did not answer what the singing was all about or who was doing it.

Later, I found out that there were military sentry boxes around the dachas, with a sentry at each one. Striking the hour and half hour, a sentry sang a beautiful melody and ended it with the Yeee-ip, a signal for the next sentry to know that he was on his post. Each sentry would pass on the melody, closing with a high, piercing Yeee-ip, on down the line.

The next morning, we had breakfast—and coffee, at last. Our host and his driver picked us up and drove us to the large plant. We toured the facility, examined all the equipment and quality control procedures and test equipment, and returned to our quarters in the early evening.

Our host, the manager of the factory, invited us to a fifteen-course dinner and drinks. There were three glasses of various sizes at each place setting: one for *pijo* (Chinese beer), another for wine, and a third for a powerful liqueur that could blow your head off.

The dinner was splendid; our host, using chopsticks, refilled our plates with additional delicacies as fast as we consumed each morsel. Multiple toasts were made, and the heavyset manager and I got into a contest of toasting each other to see who could drink more of the powerful liqueur. It was a draw; we could both walk out the door on our own power when the dinner was over—barely!

The manager planned a special event for us that evening with the Chinese Ballet at the Orchestra Hall. There were long lines of people waiting to get inside. The plant manager said something to a group of people at the head of the line, and they opened up their line and he escorted us to the front of the line and into the building. Inside the building, he moved a row of people from their choice seats and seated our party in the row with seats to spare. Obviously, the plant manager was high up in the political hierarchy, and everyone else was on the bottom rung.

Rather than a classical ballet, the program was more like a colorful circus, with acrobats, dancers, and piercing high notes of music and song. Martina complained that it was making her deaf.

After a half hour, the food and drink at the banquet made it hard to keep my eyes open, and I eventually nodded off to sleep. I was snoring loudly and Martina was trying to poke me awake, but the plant manager was between us and she had to reach around him to poke me. She finally woke me and whispered between tight-closed lips, "Damn it, Jack, stay awake!" I did—for the rest of the evening.

We concluded our visit the next morning with a meeting in a conference room, where a dozen or so Chinese were seated in chairs on the far wall. The Nova party and Walt, Martina, and I seated ourselves on the opposite side, where chairs were available. The primary topics were quality control and the sale territories to be assigned to the Chinese.

Martina, during the conversations, pulled out her writing journal from her bag and began to write. During the discussion, one of the Chinese men came over to Martina and asked her what she was writing. It is a Communist country, and they are suspicious of foreigners. Martina relieved his mind, telling him that she was writing stories for her university creative writing class, and he returned to his seat semisatisfied.

We returned to San Francisco with a stop in Guangzhou (Canton) and spent a couple of hours in the airport shops. Martina and I tried the thousand-year-old eggs and found them to be duck eggs that had been soaked in tea, salt, ashes, mud, and lime for a hundred days, which created the dark, mottled

---

blackish and greenish translucent colors. The eggs were served in sliced wedges with sweet pickled scallions and vegetables. Neither Martina nor I found them very appetizing, but we ate them anyway.

Our plane, with the fuel tanks topped-off and additional passengers in line, was ready to take off. We boarded the plane and returned to San Francisco.

A month later, a five-person delegation representing the Shenyang operation came to Grove to discuss the open issues of the proposed valve manufacturing and sales license. The primary open issue was where China could sell the Grove-licensed valves. The Chinese adamantly wanted to be able to sell the valves both inside and outside China and Asia, whereas Grove's position was that the Chinese could only sell the Grove-licensed valves inside China and Asia.

Many options came up and were considered, but all fell through at the end. Without agreement, the parties were at an impasse. Louis Mihaly, who chaired the meeting, laid on the table Grove's firm commitment for Chinese sales only within China and Asia and said, "This is nonnegotiable," and the meeting broke up. The Chinese went home without an agreement, after a delicious meal and drinks at the original Trader Vic's in Emeryville, reciprocating the Chinese graciousness during our time in China.

Elandsrand Gold Mine, South Africa

Grove's regulator product line was very marketable; it was very competitive and could be marketed for a wide variety of pipeline applications worldwide. Grove's marketing department joined with Brian Smith, the president of Hydraulic Analysis, a British company, to design and market regulators and surge relievers for specific applications. Hydraulic Analysis provided computer-generated data from which Grove designed and produced the special equipment to control surge problems in the customer pipeline.

One year later, Grove would be suing Hydraulic Analysis and Brian Smith for his refusal to provide Grove with the source code for the hydraulic data provided to, and paid for by, Grove. I would be sitting in the high witness box in London's Old Bailey Court, a scarlet-robed judge with a long white wig down to his shoulders recording the proceeding by hand in a huge journal.

The court barristers wore short wigs on their heads, and our barrister had scars on his face and two fingers missing—the result of a crash in his Spitfire fighter in World War II. The large court building in which the trial was held was constructed of carved stone. The courtroom had a high sloping ceiling, stone balustrades, and a covered walkway ringing the outside of the building.

Unfortunately, we lost the case. However, Brian Smith and his company, Hydraulic Analysis, did provide us with the information we needed.

The customer was the Elandsrand Gold Mine in Far West Rand, South Africa. Hydraulic Analysis provided the computer program, and Grove manufactured and installed the equipment to demonstrate its efficacy in controlling surge in the customer-controlled mine environment.

The South African gold mines offered a unique opportunity for state-of-the-art surge-relief technology and equipment. The gold mines had to provide cooling to the deepest levels of the mines since the temperatures without cooling exceeded 120 degrees in the deepest levels of the mine. The present method of cooling consisted of a water-chilling facility at the surface that piped chilled water to large underground reservoirs cut into the rock at different levels in the mine. Pumps directed the cooled water to the various working locations, providing a mist to cool the work areas.

The Grove surge relievers eliminated the need for these water reservoirs. Grove and Hydraulic Analysis stated that a single fifteen-inch-diameter steel pipe with surge relievers and small auxiliary pipes at each mine level was all that was required to direct the surface cooling water to the various levels of the mine. If the Grove regulators were successful, the result would be a substantial cost saving to the Elandsrand mine and new business for Grove Valve and Regulator Company with both Elandsrand and other South African gold mines.

This was an important potential sale for Grove, and I traveled to South Africa to meet with the mine management and support the Grove team's effort in conducting the demonstration. I asked Martina if she would like to accompany me, and she agreed. Although we were flying business class, it was a long, arduous trip to the southern tip of Africa.

The gold mine was a large facility, but the real action was deep in the mine, where the miners drilled, blasted, and scooped up the gold ore for processing at the surface. On the surface, there was a huge wire cage in the center of a courtyard that held hundreds of yellow canaries. The canaries, carried by the miners into the mine in individual cages, determined the presence of poisonous methane gas in the mine. Canaries have a lower tolerance for the gas, and if the canary died, it was time to get out quickly or probably die from a lethal gas in the mine.

We donned yellow slickers, boots, and helmets with miner lights, and rode the working skip (a large elevator car for the miners) down into the mine. The smaller skip used by supervisors and visitors was not available due to maintenance requirements. About thirty miners and a few visitors crowded into the large skip like sardines. None of the occupants could move until we reached our destination and the door was opened.

The skip descended into the mine at a high speed. It felt as if we were free-falling into a black hole—interrupted by flashes of light as we passed by the various lighted mine levels. We did not go all the way to the bottom—ten thousand feet down, almost two miles—and exited at the 5,500-foot level.

The mine was busy and cramped; we observed crews—mostly black men stripped to their waists—operating the various machinery and equipment. The height of the cramped working areas was only about four feet; the roof was held up by steel or wooden supports.

We completed the tour and met with the mine management and the Grove project team. The initial test of our equipment had been successful, and other tests were scheduled. The mine management was pleased with the test results. Grove's marketing management was in contact with their purchasing manager, and we expected to receive purchase orders for our equipment when the remaining tests were completed.

Artist: Deb Bartelt
Saint Basil's Cathedral, Moscow

Moscow (Mockba)

Machinoimport, the Russian government's purchasing arm for imported machinery, made a tender offer to Grove in 1982. The offer was an invitation for Grove to bid on large, customized surge-relief equipment for a major Russian crude oil pipeline. Grove marketing and engineering reached a preliminary agreement on specifications, contract terms, and pricing with the executives of Machinoimport and the managers of the Russian pipeline.

Machinoimport requested that the president of Grove come to Moscow to finalize and sign the contract. I accepted the invitation and arranged to meet with the Machinoimport *apparatchiks* (officials of the government bureau) in Moscow.

Salvatore, the Moscow-based Italian marketing manager of Grove Italia, made arrangements to meet me at the Moscow airport. Grove Italia, a sister company of Grove, was our agent for the sale of Grove valves and regulators in the USSR.

Joseph Stalin, during his long reign, was a mass murderer of his own citizens, two-thirds of his generals, and millions of common peasants. After Stalin's death, a series of internecine machinations and struggles characterized the turnover of the *Politburo* and premiership of the country.

In late 1982, Yuri Andropov succeeded Leonid Brezhnev as premier. Ronald Reagan was in the White House, and the Cold War was in full effect. Hundreds of intercontinental missiles, carrying multiple nuclear-tipped warheads, were aimed and ready for the command to unleash widespread death and destruction on the cities of both countries.

Our plane arrived at Sheremetyevo International Airport in Moscow in the early evening. It was dark as I deplaned and walked through the slushy snow on the tarmac to the bus that took the passengers to the terminal.

Inside the terminal was a great hall, with a second-story balcony ringing half of the large room. I lined up in a queue for foreign passengers to be processed by Russian immigration and customs.

As I stood in line, I casually, to avoid unnecessary attention, looked around the crowded terminal and balcony and tried to make out the KGB agents. They were relatively easy to spot— they were the men with the black leather jackets reaching almost to their knees and the bulge of a shoulder-holstered Makarov automatic pistol under the jacket. I counted one KGB agent in the balcony and three in the main hall.

When my turn finally came, I stepped up to the window of the glassed-in cubicle, removed my travel documents, and put them on the counter. Inside was a stone-faced, uniformed official with his hat pulled down just above his eyes.

He perused my documents for a moment, laid my passport and other documents down on the counter in front of him, raised his head, and said in English with a heavy Russian accent, "Visa?"

I replied, "They're in the packet with my passport."

He spread the contents of my travel packet, fingered each document, looked up, and said again, "Visa?" in a more urgent— or more threatening—tone.

I raised my hands up in front of me, palms out, and hunched my shoulders, indicating that I was unaware of where the documents could be. He nodded to someone behind me, and I felt the strong grip of a hand on my shoulder. I turned and was face-to-face with a tall, determined Russian soldier in a fur hat, a heavy overcoat, a pistol in a holster on his belt, and a Kalashnikov automatic rifle in his hands. He motioned without any explanation for me to pick up my luggage and gave me a nudge. We proceeded to the exit and onto the dark street, soft lazy snowflakes drifting to the ground. I had no idea where he was taking me.

As we crossed the street, I started to navigate around the piles of slush to keep from filling my street shoes with ice-cold water. The soldier gave me a harder nudge and pointed directly across the street, indicating the direction he expected me to go.

I turned around and pointed to his boots. Although neither of us could speak the other's language, I pointed to my shoes and said, "You have boots on. These are street shoes!"

He slowly got it, nodded, and I picked my way across the street carrying my luggage without the help of nudges from the soldier—a minor victory.

On the other side was a row of buildings that resembled Chicago's three-story apartment buildings. I was marched into one of the buildings and directed up a flight of stairs and down a corridor. As we passed by what looked like a large conference room, I saw a dozen or so uniformed Russian soldiers, apparently off duty, watching a Russian war movie. In the film, it was winter and snow was falling.

We continued down the corridor past a middle-aged man at a desk. I assumed he was the "house father" of this floor, a common surveillance practice in Moscow hotels frequented by foreigners. Continuing on, we reached a door marked 3C. The soldier opened the door, motioned me inside, closed the door, and disappeared—probably to see the rest of the film with his comrades.

After dumping my luggage on the floor, I surveyed the windowless room: a narrow bed made up with sheets, a comforter, and a small table with a pitcher of water, a drinking glass, and a single lightbulb hung from the ceiling. There were no other furnishings in the room; it was not exactly a VIP lounge.

I glanced at my luggage, smiled, and thought to myself, *This is probably the only luggage in Moscow that didn't go through Russian customs or any other inspection.* I could have been carrying any kind of contraband or weapons—even a *Playboy* magazine. I heard that the Russians confiscated *Playboy* because it was popular and they couldn't buy the magazine in Russia.

Since there was no window, I tried the door. It was unlocked, and I opened it and looked out into the hall. There were two young men talking in a doorway down the hall across the passageway: a short black man and a tall young Latin. They were speaking English. An older Filipino couple was inside their room down the hall, door open, looking out, but saying nothing.

I stepped into the hall and said hello to the two young men, who smilingly returned my greeting in English. Robert was outgoing and talkative, wore a watch cap, and looked as if he could be from one of the neighborhoods in west Chicago. As it turned out, he was the son, or said he was, of the minister of education of Sierra Leone. The Ministry of Education, truth be told, was reputed to be a cover for the state secret police of the small African country. The tall, athletic-looking, young Latin told me that he was Cuban and was a dancer with the Ballet National de Cuba in Havana.

The three of us shared our stories of the circumstances that brought about our incarceration. Julio's rucksack—with his passport and identification—was stolen in a stopover in Amsterdam. Robert said that his only problem was that he arrived before his visa date and could not enter the country for three more days.

It was my turn to tell my story, and I told them that I thought that MI-6 lifted my visa at Heathrow Airport for their own purposes when I went through immigration on my stopover.

Robert said jovially, "Those Brits—they do that kind of stuff all the time."

I did not know where he got his information and let it drop. The three of us quickly developed a rapport, and I told them that I had to make a telephone call to the US Embassy to obtain my release. I had an urgent meeting to attend in the morning, and it was now ten thirty Moscow time.

It turned out that Robert spoke Russian, and the three of us walked down the hall to use the house father's telephone. Ivan was a jovial sort and agreed to help us. Robert asked Ivan to call the US Embassy for me. Ivan went through his telephone numbers, found the number, rang the embassy, and handed the telephone to me. I listened to the ringing for about a dozen rings and handed it back to him.

We went through the drill several times, and I decided that I was thirsty and told them that I was going to retrieve a bottle of vodka from my luggage. Robert and Julio had the same thought, and Julio returned with a bottle of Cuban rum and Robert brought a half-full bottle of expensive Scotch whiskey. Ivan provided four more-or-less clean glasses from somewhere, and all four of us were drinking, talking, and taking turns calling the embassy for the next hour and a half. We all got tipsy—as the telephone rang uselessly on the other end.

Around midnight, we decided to call it a night and returned to our respective rooms. I needed a shower and went to the lavatory to see what accommodations there were for a shower in the morning. There was a shower stall with one thin towel, hardly enough to dry off one body. I decided to set my internal alarm clock for five o'clock and take a shower before anyone else was up. I'd dry myself first with the clean towel.

The next morning, after my shower, Robert and Julio stopped by my room, and Robert went to see Ivan about getting something to eat. Ivan called a soldier to take us across the street to the airport cafeteria, and the soldier escorted us. This was the second or third day of detention for Robert and Julio, and they knew the ropes as to what they could do and what they could not. We were obviously being watched.

We were free to roam the mezzanine shops and the cafeteria, but we could not leave the area—including the downstairs main hall—without a military escort. It was unlikely that we would attempt to get to the main hall without an escort because we could easily end up with broken knees in the narrow, iron pipe-fenced security passageway by a guard pulling a lever that activated the opposing bent steel pipe knee-breakers to come crashing together.

At the cafeteria, we picked out our food items from a menu, paid the cashier, took our order number to a table, and sat down. The cashier, who had been operating an abacus instead of a cash register, did not know the exchange rate in rubles for my dollars and refused them as payment. Robert interceded and paid the cashier from a roll of Russian rubles he pulled from his pocket.

I offered to give Robert American dollars in payment for my meal, but he stubbornly refused and said in flawless English, "Forget it. It's on me."

I asked him somewhat facetiously, "Robert, are you sure that you are not an American from Chicago—or maybe a KGB agent spying on us poor, naïve Americanos?"

With a boisterous laugh, he replied in a humorous fake Spanish accent, "You gringos are all alike—you never trust us poor common people. Nope, I am not a Yankee Doodle dandy— or an agent for anyone. I am a Sierra Leonean—educated at Boston University. Let's eat!" His being educated in the United States was news to me, but I guessed quite a few foreigners with rich parents sent their children for an education in America—and he must be one of them.

After breakfast, I asked Robert if he would ask the soldier at the entrance of the mezzanine to call an officer to see me. I had something to tell him. When the soldier got my message, it seemed to activate him immediately. He dialed the telephone and animatedly talked to someone on the other end of the line. We hung around for a while for an answer, but nothing happened. We spent the morning talking together and walking around the area. Robert bought a large bottle of expensive Dom Perignon from one of the shops, appropriated some glasses from the cafeteria, and popped the cork.

We sat at a table—people passing back and forth nearby—and drank champagne as if we were the cognoscenti of the fine grape beverage. We continued our conversation, which was mainly about our families and ourselves, avoiding the subject of politics, whether touching on the Soviet Union, Cuba, Sierra Leone, or the United States.

A Female Russian Colonel

After lunch, a soldier approached me and motioned to me to follow him. He led me to a stern female officer, briskly saluted her, and retired to the background. She wore a uniform with a fur hat, a holstered pistol on her belt, and shoulder boards denoting her rank, which I guessed was at least a colonel. Two soldiers guarding an exit snapped to attention and gave her a crisp military salute as we walked by. She was obviously someone of importance.

She said in British English with a Russian accent and a hint of suspicion, "Sir, I know that you have been detained for lack of proper documents to enter our country, but I want to know why you have come to Moscow and what your purpose is."

I replied, "I have come to Moscow at the invitation of the authorities of Machinoimport to finalize a contract to provide equipment for one of your major oil pipelines. I am president of Grove Valve and Regulator Company in the United States, which will produce the equipment. I need to meet as soon as possible with our Moscow sales agent to review the proposed contract and then meet with the manager of Machinoimport to review and sign the contract."

I handed her the official invitation from Machinoimport.

She read the letter, looked up, and said, "I will see what needs to be done." She waved to the soldier to return me to the mezzanine area, turned on her heel, and left. The soldier snapped to rigid attention as she left.

Robert and Julio had been waiting for me to return, and we finished the bottle of champagne.

An hour or so later, the soldier came back and took me to the colonel, who led me to the waiting room and VIP lounge of the Russian national airline, Aeroflot. To my surprise, Salvatore, the Grove Italia Moscow sales manager, was waiting for me. He had been able, with his Russian connections, to find me and set up this meeting.

Salvatore and I went through the contract, reviewing all the provisions. Our marketing people and Salvatore had done a professional job on the contract, and only minimal changes were necessary. Salvatore left to deliver the contract to the Machinoimport office, and I did not see him again on the trip.

The colonel led me to an office, dictated a short letter to the secretary, signed it, handed it to me along with my passport, and said, "You are no longer a detainee. This letter releases you from further detention, and you are free to go. But first you have to get a plane ticket to leave Moscow in the next twenty-four hours."

There was only one flight available that evening: an Aeroflot flight to Bulgaria, where a notoriously brutal Communist regime was in power. There was, however, a flight to Rome on Aeroflot the next morning.

It was a no-brainer: if I ended up in Bulgaria, I would be in exactly the same predicament, or worse, without a visa, so I decided to stay over in a hotel in Moscow and take the flight to Rome. I could not get a refund or exchange my San Francisco ticket for a ticket to Rome, and I ended up paying twice. I bought a ticket on Aeroflot and charged it to my American Express card. Without the American Express card, I would most certainly have become a street person in Moscow.

That evening, after checking into a hotel close to the airport, I called Louie Mihaly in Rome to brief him on what had happened and get his feedback. He told me that he would have someone meet me at the Rome airport, and he would arrange to obtain a new visa for me in Rome.

I needed only to get some passport pictures taken for the document, and I could return home to San Francisco. It would take a week to ten days to get the visa, and I could return to Rome, pick up the visa, and be on my way back to Moscow. Salvatore had already returned to Rome and would be available to accompany me to Moscow.

The next morning, I caught the flight to Rome. The airliner had multiple windows in the nose of the plane, and it appeared to be a military bomber converted to a civilian airliner. The seat frames and the drop-down dinner trays were plywood.

An hour or so into the flight, the stewardess served fettuccine with *langoustines*, scampi, and scallops, a bottle of Pinot Noir, and a *misa di terra* for desert. The Italian cuisine was delicious.

After finishing my meal, an Italian passenger across the aisle, noting that I was an American, struck up a conversation, possibly to practice his English, which was already very good. He had a two-thirds-full bottle of vodka in a bucket of ice on his drop-down table, much like a wine bottle cooler, that he had charmed the stewardess for. He asked me to join him.

As it turned out, we had two things in common: we both managed manufacturing operations—he was the manager of an Italian industrial instrument manufacturing company in Milan—and we both enjoyed vodka, preferably ice-cold.

I told him about my recent experience in Moscow, and he was not surprised.

He said, "Stranger things than that happen in Moscow all the time." He did not elaborate.

We drank the vodka and munched on crackers topped with Beluga caviar, supplied by the still-enchanted stewardess. We chatted about our respective companies and the problems in selling equipment to the Russians. I spent the rest of the flight enjoying his limitless jokes and ribald stories—some of which were hilarious, others downright carnal—and the time passed quickly.

We finished off the bottle of Stolichnaya as our plane approached Rome.

Salvatore met me at the arrival gate and drove me to the *Esposizione Universale di Roma,* a city built in the late 1930s by Mussolini. The most striking landmark of the EUR was the *Palazzo della Civita Italiana.* Known as the Square Coliseum, it sat on a hill and exhibited twenty-eight large sculptures around the main building.

The upscale residential area also held government offices, foreign embassies, and villas for top government officials. Grove Italia had its headquarters in one of the villas on a hill overlooking Rome about ten kilometers to the north. I met with Louie in his office, and we had lunch together in town.

After lunch, we returned to the villa and reviewed my Grove US Five-Year Strategic Plan. Suddenly, there was an explosive noise; the glass reverberated in the windows facing the courtyard.

I remembered from my first trip to Italy how the Mafia terrorized and controlled much of Sicily. The Brigade *Rosso* (Red Brigade) began a similar—but more organized—terror campaign in Italy in 1970. It grew in strength and began kidnapping special targets. As time went on, they began assassinating their political foes.

The Red Brigade had been bombing, shooting, and kidnapping people in Rome and other Italian cities. On my second visit to Rome in 1978, I visited Louie Mihaly again. Two months before my visit, the Red Brigades kidnapped Aldo Moro, a previous prime minister of Italy, and while I was in Rome, the Italian Carbineer (State Police) discovered Aldo Moro's corpse in a parked car in the heart of the city; he had been assassinated by ten bullets to the head.

These recollections caused me great concern, and I glanced out the windows to see what had caused the explosion. Louie did not give even a casual look to see what was going on and continued reviewing the plan. Louie's office was about a half floor above the parking courtyard and provided an excellent view of it.

All of a sudden, a small, damaged car screamed into the courtyard spouting steam and smoke. A man jumped out and started running, a half-dozen security personnel from the next-door villa chasing him. The security personnel tackled, subdued, and marched the man toward the next-door villa and out of my view. Louie had still not looked up during the whole episode—or made any comment other than about the plan.

A couple of minutes later, there were sharp cracks of a pistol—or pistols—firing ten shots in all by my count, from the direction of the next-door villa, which happened to be the residence of the Italian minister of defense.

I said somewhat facetiously to Louie, who was sitting with his back to a solid block wall while I was sitting in plain sight in front of the windows, "Would you like to change places with me?"

Louie looked up, smiled, leaned back, lit a cigarette with a silver lighter, blew a puff of smoke into the air, and said, "Relax; let's finish this review."

I found out later the story behind the episode I had witnessed.

A bandit had robbed a bank near the Grove Italia office and, while escaping in a stolen car, had smashed into another car at high speed, which was the bomb blast I heard. One of the Grove Italia employee's cars had been involved in the crash while pulling out of a parking space. The guards from the Ministry of Defense in the villa next door captured the fleeing man. As they reached the villa, the man broke loose, made a run for it, and was stopped by a flurry of warning shots fired by the security force.

When we finished our business, the Grove Italia staff had my passport photos. I flew back to San Francisco the next day and arrived home late at night.

I spent the next few days in my office catching up on the accumulated stack of work. Several days later, Salvatore informed me that my visa arrived earlier than expected and I should meet him at the airport for the flight to Moscow. He provided the date and time we should meet and the flight number of the Moscow flight. Salvatore also suggested that I visit the duty-free store and purchase a bottle of perfume to use as a gift at the appropriate time. I figured that I couldn't go too wrong with Chanel No. 5 perfume.

I made airline arrangements and departed the next day—after purchasing the perfume and having it nicely wrapped.

Salvatore

Grove Italia's sales manager met me at the airport, and our flight to Moscow was uneventful. There were no problems with passports or visas, but I was played the fool by a fat female Russian customs inspector.

She had me open my briefcase; she pulled everything out, dumped it back into the case, and slid it back to me.

I was sweating and anxious to get out of the airport. Not realizing that she had not fully closed it, I grabbed the briefcase by the handle and dumped the contents on the floor. As I scrambled to return my belongings to my briefcase, I noticed her with two others, laughing hilariously. I was pissed and murmured under my breath, "Screw you, you fat f--ks."

As we headed for the exit, I noticed several older peasant-type women with babushkas, long dresses, and flat clumpy shoes, pushing wide dry mops up and down the terminal floor. I felt sorry for them and wondered if they were paid for their work or were forced to work as a condition of some social-benefits program. I dismissed the thought from my mind, started to monitor my surroundings, and concentrated on getting out of the airport and to my hotel.

The taxi driver chose the Leningradskoe Highway to the city center. The highway was not exactly modern and clogged up easily as traffic increased. Along the side of the highway, I noticed a few very old houses constructed of logs, rough timbers, and warped wooden shingles, with fences of driven stakes, which appeared as if they had been there well before World War II.

My hotel was near the Kremlin, Red Square, Lenin's tomb, and St. Bazel's Cathedral—dating back to Ivan the Terrible. The Bolshoi Theater and the Moscow Metro were close by, and I decided to visit these sights first thing in the morning.

The Hotel National was the Grande Dame of Moscow hotels, dating back to Czarist times, its Art Deco facade and elaborate furnishings a Moscow landmark. The upstairs hallways were murky; a floor attendant sat at a small desk at the entrance to each floor, keeping watch on all goings-on—and undoubtedly reporting them to his master.

My room was sufficient for my purpose, namely to get a good night's sleep. I went outside for some fresh air and strolled to the underground entrance and down a series of steps to the hall of the *Ploshchad Revolyutsii* Metro station. The marble floor and large bronze sculptures stood along the walls in oval-shaped niches, looking more like a museum than an underground metro.

I walked a few blocks to the Bolshoi Theater to see what it looked like. I thought that I should go to a performance of the world-renowned ballet, but when I returned to the hotel, I was told that there was a waiting list of two weeks.

Back in my room, I looked around and wondered where the hidden microphones—allegedly placed in rooms assigned to foreigners—were. Not being an expert, I did not find any. There was no one but me in the room, and I rarely talk to myself, although I admit that I often murmur to myself.

I spent the evening on my bed sipping from a glass of vodka and reading old issues of the *British News Herald* before I finally went to sleep.

Salvatore met me for an early breakfast at the elegant Moskovsky restaurant in the hotel. After breakfast, we bundled

Jack Watson

up and headed outside to do some sightseeing. I was fortunate to have purchased a Russian fur hat and wore it and my warm Kashmara overcoat, but still wore my regular dress shoes. Salvatore wore his fur hat and overcoat and put on a pair of lined leather gloves.

We crossed over to Red Square, *Krasnaya Ploschad*, with the Kremlin hovering in the background. The wind picked up, and the temperature was close to freezing. Red Square had seen many endless parades with banners and flags festooning the huge square, viewing stand, and soldiers; military vehicles, artillery, and missiles showed off the Soviet Union's military might, with the generals and politicians of the Politburo observing from the grandstand above the square.

I admired the multiple, multicolored, onion-shaped domes of the Bazel Cathedral. Lenin's Mausoleum was closed to visitors, but the mausoleum guards marched crisply back and forth, performing various precision drills with their special-issue rifles.

An ancient automobile displaying a Minister of Commerce placard picked me up at the hotel in the afternoon and drove me to the Machinoimport offices. I met with the managing director and his staff, and we signed a $1.5 million contract and toasted the signing with several rounds of powerful liqueur chased with glasses of cold vodka. This order was very profitable for Grove, with a profit margin of over 65 percent (US $1 million), and represented a breakthrough by Grove into the vast Russian oil and gas pipeline market.

My business finished, Salvatore offered to show me around Moscow, and the next few days involved meeting a number of people. Salvatore drove me through Moscow State University—spread over the Lenin Hills above Moscow—where he had graduated and had learned to speak fluent Russian.

That evening, we went to a restaurant that was overflowing with young Muscovites. Yuri was a slim, flashy, rakishly good-looking young entrepreneur in the electronics industry—or so he said. He was also, according to Salvatore, a gadabout in the Moscow film industry and allegedly had connections to the

KGB. Salvatore invited him to join us for dinner. A stream of young adults and a few middle-aged people stopped at our table and said hello to Yuri. He introduced us to each person who visited our table.

After a fine dinner—and Russian beer, vodka, and wine— Yuri suggested that we meet some of his friends. He drove us to an apartment complex on the edge of the city and entered one of the buildings. Yuri knocked on the door and was invited inside by a young, barely dressed woman.

As we stepped inside the door, Yuri went into the bedroom and came out with a naked young woman over his shoulder who was laughingly kicking and twisting to get loose. Yuri put her down, and she retired to the bedroom. She returned in a one-piece cotton frock, under which she clearly was not wearing anything.

Salvatore had brought beer and a bottle of vodka, and one of the women went to get glasses while the other one loaded discs on the machine to play some music. We had a few drinks, and the two women started dancing together and pulled Yuri and Salvatore onto the small dance area in the center of the room. I was enjoying a glass of vodka, listening to the Russian pop music, and watching the dancers when one of the young women pulled me into the middle of the room and started dancing with me.

Although the Russian women were attractive, sexy, and obviously willing, I had no interest in getting involved. I was happily married—as Johnny Cash sang, "Because you're mine, I walk the line."

After a while, Yuri saw that I was not getting involved with the women and suggested we say good-bye, which we did, to the apparent disappointment of the women.

Our next visit was to an upscale apartment building. A beautiful, sexy, Polish woman in her late twenties opened the door. Her blonde hair was vibrant, and she was dressed in a negligee-type dress of satiny white cloth. Her arms were bare, and a string of pearls around her neck complemented her skin.

I thought, *Is she a budding femme fatale, a seductive Matahari, or what?*

Viviana was Polish, but she spoke Russian and a little English. Yuri and Salvatore chatted with her in Russian while I observed the surroundings. The suite was small and elegantly decorated with paintings and carved furniture upholstered in fine fabrics. There was a silver tea set, miscellaneous silver items, a copper samovar, and a bottle of yellowish liquid and slender drinking glasses in a tall glassed-in cabinet. On one shelf was a display of painted Russian matryoshka dolls, each of which has several smaller dolls nesting inside the larger ones.

Viviana—if that was her real name—made tea for us, and the three of them continued to converse in Russian. After a while, Salvatore told me that he and Yuri needed to see someone for a few minutes in this same building and they would be right back. Before I could open my mouth to protest, they were already out the door.

Viviana sipped her tea slowly and appeared as if she had been through it all before and was waiting for a signal from me. I was uncomfortable and could stand a stiff shot of something alcoholic. I asked her if she had any vodka. She answered, "Niet," then filled two slender glasses from an elegant bottle containing a yellow liqueur.

She made a toast, and we touched glasses. The sweet, syrupy fluid tasted like strong Italian grappa with peaches and apricots. She started a conversation in barely decipherable English, and it became evident after a short while—from her speech and body language—that she was sexually available, but I was not buying it. I sat agitatedly sipping the powerful liqueur, waiting impatiently for Salvatore's return.

Yuri and Salvatore returned a few minutes later, and Salvatore asked me, "Do you want to stay? We can come back for you later."

The question was a no-brainer as far as I was concerned. I was married to a beautiful woman, and I intended to keep it that way. I declined, and after polite good-byes, we left.

However, this was not the last episode.

Anastasia

The next evening, Salvatore drove the three of us—Valentina, Yuri, and me—into a thickly wooded area in the countryside and stopped at a log-cabin restaurant and dance hall. In a strange coincidence, Salvatore's wife in Rome was also named Valentina. It must have been comforting for him to know that if he were to say his Russian girlfriend's name in his sleep with his wife, his wife would think he was talking about her.

Once inside the cavernous log cabin, Salvatore and Yuri introduced us to about two dozen people having conversations and drinking wine, liquors, or vodka with caviar, hard-boiled eggs, and various other accompaniments. A roasted suckling pig on a silver platter sat at the middle of the large dining table, along with platters of sturgeon and salmon, assorted meats, and vegetables and fruit. The settings around the table were china—with silver flatware and several crystal glasses at each table setting.

We were at a birthday party of a young Russian movie actress. The star of the occasion was a charming actress, Anastasia, who was celebrating her twenty-fifth birthday. Most of the guests were involved in the Russian movie industry, including directors, actors, and actresses.

Shortly after our arrival, everyone sat down, and the room buzzed with conversations—mainly in Russian, but also some in Italian and a few in English. A waiter removed the pig to the kitchen and returned with it sliced into small morsels; the platters of food were offered and served to each guest by uniformed waiters.

When the meal was finished, people started to drift to the dance floor, and the orchestra began to play a Russian medley. I took the wrapped perfume to where Anastasia was chatting with several people. As my interpreter, Salvatore introduced me to her. After the social greetings, I offered Anastasia the present. She removed the wrapping and opened the bottle of perfume, applied a few drops to the inside of her wrist, and breathed in the essence—and her face lit up.

She smiled at me and said in halting English, "Thank you very, very much. I love Chanel No. 5."

She asked me, through Salvatore, if I would like to dance. I was trapped like a possum in a tree with the dogs yelping on the ground below and—having no choice—led her to the dance floor. The orchestra was playing a popular Russian song, and I was able to dance to it without completely embarrassing myself. If it had been a simple waltz or a Texas two-step, I might have comported myself a little better.

Valentina

Yuri stayed at the birthday party and said he would catch his own ride home. Salvatore drove his girlfriend and me back to the city and parked on a crowded street about two blocks from her apartment. A light snow was falling, and the faint streetlights caused the snowflakes to sparkle as we walked along the sidewalk. It was quiet, with only a slight buzz from cars on a distant highway.

After talking with Valentina in Russian, Salvatore turned to me and said, "Would you like to sleep with Valentina tonight? She lives alone and is agreeable."

Jesus, I thought. *What next?*

Salvatore continued, "If you would like to stay with her, I could pick you up in the morning and take you back to your hotel."

I collected my thoughts and carefully composed a diplomatic answer. I said, "That is very hospitable of Valentina—and I am sure that she is very nice to sleep with—but my wife, Martina, and I are committed solely to each other, and I must decline your generous offer."

Salvatore accepted my declination with equanimity. However, Valentina's disposition was not quite as genial after my rebuff—no matter how diplomatically it was stated. She appeared surprised and offended at my rejection of Salvatore's offer. She said a terse goodnight, and Salvatore drove me back to the hotel.

Whew, I murmured to myself as the streetlights rolled by. *What next?*

Using one of the few Russian words I had picked up during my stay, I jokingly said, "*spasibo,*" thanking him for his help in obtaining the very profitable Machinoimport order, but I did not bring up recent happenings. We laughed about my use and pronunciation of *spasibo*—and a couple of other Russian words—and said good night and good-bye, since I was leaving for home the next morning,

In retrospect, the thought that comes to mind about all of the peculiar activity in Moscow was that I was being placed in a position to be seduced into compromising sexual situations and entanglements—and possibly set up for blackmail. I believe that it probably had something to do with the KGB. Maybe this was their recruiting method, and I was the recruit.

I do not mean to overplay it, but Moscow was a very strange place for an American to be in the middle of the Cold War in the winter of 1982.

A week after I returned home, two CIA operatives came to my office and questioned—or more like interrogated—me about my trip.

The First Time I Saw Martina Cry

The long flight was more than an hour late due to weather problems. It was late at night as I drove home. Martina was waiting up for me and seemed to be very tired and nervous. I kissed her, told her I loved her, and asked her if she were all right. She said that she had stayed up for me and was really tired. It was almost one o'clock, but I was on a different time zone and it was late morning for me. I felt wide-awake—probably from the jet lag and time difference.

Martina asked about my trip, and with no qualms whatsoever, I told her everything that had happened, including the women with whom Yuri and Salvatore had tried to get me involved.

Martina listened quietly and said nothing. When I completed my story, she screamed, "You bastard, you *fucked* those women—I know you did!"

I was startled and amazed at her accusation. As she stormed to her bedroom, I was seething with rage and anger. *Why would I tell her the whole story—women and all—if I were guilty? It makes absolutely no sense at all! God damn it!*

I clenched my fist and smashed it into the wall. The blow knocked a hole in the drywall, and my fist was bleeding profusely. I reached for a bottle of whiskey and took a hefty snort—and poured the liquor onto my damaged bleeding hand, spilling some of the bloody liquid on the kitchen floor.

I was worried that Martina was so filled with anger that she might leave me. I could not live without her. I prayed to God that she would never leave me.

A few minutes later, Martina came back into the room silently sobbing. I had never seen her cry before during our whole marriage; she was tough and normally kept herself under control.

She brushed away her tears and said, "What's wrong with me? I know you would not do what I said you did. I am sorry!"

Ignoring her question, I took her in my arms and comforted her, kissing her lips and face, brushed away the tears on her cheeks, and said, "Do not worry about it; you were just tired and probably stressed out with my not calling you and my plane being late. I will try to call you next time." I thought, *I am a bastard for not calling her; it's the least I could have done.*

I continued to talk soothingly while I held her in my arms. "Let's forget all about it! And by the way, do we have any regular antiseptic for a smashed bloody fist? I don't want to waste any more of the scotch." We both laughed and knew that we would never part because of a misinformed accusation. We were still in love after ten years.

Capo de Capo—American Style

Bob Blair, the chairman of Nova, reorganized the two valve companies and gave Luigi Fiore, the president of Grove Italia, full authority over both Grove Italia and Grove U.S. In effect, he was the *capo de capo* (boss of all bosses) of both companies.

On assuming authority for the two companies, Fiore issued a directive to the president of Grove U.S.—me—in which he overrode all of my authority to make executive decisions without his specific prior written approval. The essence of his directive was that I would become a puppet on a string, dancing to his tune, without the necessary authority to run the US company. It was a formula for certain failure.

This gave me three choices: kowtow to his wishes, resign, or fight for my authority to manage the company and make unencumbered executive decisions.

I discussed the situation with Louis Mihaly, who was currently a consultant to NOVA, and we agreed that there were many differences in managing an Italian company versus an American company. I responded to Fiore's directive. In my letter to him, I stated the problems with his directive and that I would continue to run the American company the American way, with American customs and laws.

A few weeks later, Bob Blair, the chairman of Nova Corporation, asked me to meet him at a bar in San Francisco.

Smelling a rat in the invitation, I gathered the stack of notes that my staff and I had made over several years of conversations with Nova's management concerning Grove's operations. The stack of yellow tablet sheets was almost three inches thick, and I placed the rubber-banded documents in my satchel to take with me to the meeting. I had a premonition that they would come in handy.

I met Blair in a downtown San Francisco bar and restaurant. Taking seats at a small round table in the bar, he ordered a glass of whiskey, and I ordered a martini on the rocks. We made small talk while Blair—nicknamed Captain Kangaroo—fiddled with his drink, but he did not put it to his lips. It was as if he wanted to show the strength of his will, but it did not work. I finished my drink and ordered another, quietly ignoring him and waiting for him to speak.

He finally said, "I am concerned about Grove U.S., and I told Fiore to make all executive decisions of Grove—and you have contested and disregarded his directive."

I replied, "You are concerned about Grove after the major turnaround and restructuring that we have accomplished in spite of the depressed market? You should be congratulating the Grove management team—and me—who were tireless in our efforts to save the company. We were successful—and saved your goddamn company!"

He did not reply, and we sat silently for a few moments.

I pulled the sheaf of papers from my satchel, removed the rubber bands, and began referring to selected notes. He asked me where the notes had come from. I told him that they were from conversations that we had with Nova executives and managers over the past couple of years.

He replied, "Can I have a copy of them?"

I answered, "Yes, you may—at the appropriate time."

He did not contest my reply, but it was easy to see that he was concerned about the notes regarding the Nova-Grove relationships. He obviously had something to hide.

He said, "There is something that I want to talk to you about—"

I interrupted him, knowing what was coming. I asked him if he knew what the financial legal judgments and settlement amounts were in US executive unlawful termination and age discrimination lawsuits.

He said, "Just generally."

I told him, "California is not like Canada. In the San Francisco Bay Area, judgments for unlawful termination and age discrimination are as high as $500,000 to over a million dollars—particularly for abusive terminations without cause. There is no just-cause basis for my termination, and I am at an age that includes me in the age discrimination law."

He listened, but did not contest my remark. Instead, he thought it over and said, "I am asking for your resignation. Luigi Fiore is here, having flown in from Italy, and he will meet with you on Monday morning at your office to settle the severance issues."

I responded, "That's fine, but make sure that you tell him what I have told you about the potential legal cost of a discriminatory firing. It might save you a lot of money."

I said to myself, *Someone's gonna get hurt*. I felt angry, and for a moment, I thought that I would be justified in shooting him as a warning to other corporate executives who pride themselves in their arrogance, deceive, lie, and trample on those who are powerless. However, the act would be worthless; his type of scum will always be with us.

I have, unfortunately, been associated with too many of these reprehensible characters—and have seen them up close, doing their dirty deeds. These people deserve—and have—my disdain and contempt. These and others of their ilk should be perp-walked out of their corporate offices and retired or jailed before they inflict more harm.

I had the meeting with Luigi Fiore—whom I classified in the same group of despicable individuals.

I believe that my not-so-veiled threat of a lawsuit had the intended effect, and I came out of the negotiation in good stead, with full salary and all benefits until December 31, 1986—more than a year away.

Unknown to me at the time, this was a serendipitous, positive, and pivotal event in my professional career—a change that would lead me to future success!

Chapter 11:
Catching the Brass Ring–NEWFLO

"Neither the condition of your birth nor the circumstances of your life will deny you success—if you persevere." —Jack Watson, 1986

An Acknowledgment

From 1987 through the first half of 1996, I enjoyed the most productive and gratifying period of my professional career. I was offered an opportunity to found NEWFLO Corporation, with an ownership stake, become chairman, president, and CEO—and I succeeded!

I owe this fantastic opportunity to Jay Jordan, founder and managing principal of the Jordan Company, a longtime friend; his belief in me made it possible for me to be successful. And to Jeb Boucher, managing principal of the Jordan Company, for his expertise, valuable assistance, and steadfastness.

I also want to thank all those others of the Jordan Company who helped in many ways to make NEWFLO possible and made NEWFLO Corporation an unqualified success!

NEWFLO Executive Officers

Raymond R. Baker
Senior Vice President;
President Newman's Intl.

Brian W. Warren
Senior Vice President;
President General Valve Co.

John D. Lilla
Vice President
Human Resources &
Risk Management

Robert K. Elders
Senior Vice President;
President Johnston Pump Co.
and PACO Pumps, Inc.

Richard D. Morton
Executive Vice President
& Chief Financial
Officer

J. Jack Watson
Chairman, President
& Chief Executive
Officer

Kathleen Mathews
Vice President
Controller, Chief
Accounting Officer

NEWFLO Corporation

After my termination—or so-called resignation—I left Grove Valve with a severance package of full salary and benefits for a year and a half. In a way, it was serendipitous and was the best thing that could have happened to me. It financed my living expenses and provided me the undivided time and resources to search for, find, and acquire a company.

After leaving Grove Valve and spending a couple of weeks sending out résumés, I decided to start a search for a company to acquire. Dick Morton, my former vice president of finance at Grove Valve, joined me in the search.

It was the ideal time for me to acquire a company. I was as ready as I would ever be. I had worked at—and managed—

eight manufacturing companies with diverse products and manufacturing methods. Products included airplanes and missiles, machinery, pipeline valves, surge relievers, electric motor controls, and others.

All of these companies and products were unique in their manufacturing equipment, processes, materials, methods, and management styles, and I had the opportunity to decide what worked in manufacturing businesses and what did not work.

Overall, my executive positions had allowed me to develop, practice, and perfect my management style and technique. In my management responsibilities, I also visited scores of foreign countries on business—each with its own story. I learned about and absorbed customs, mores, and methods of doing business in the international marketplace.

Martina and I were excited. We sold our home in Kentfield and bought a less expensive home, which provided $300,000 of equity as collateral for financing an acquisition.

Dick Morton and I worked day and night to identify, target, visit, and analyze more than a dozen companies in the Bay Area for acquisition, without finding a suitable company that was within my financial resources.

I decided to call Jay Jordan of the Jordan Company to express my desire to acquire a company, manage it, and have an ownership interest in the acquired company.

Jay, in his usual positive manner, told me, "Jack, just let me know when you find a suitable company."

Over the years, I had maintained contact with Jordan. In 1982, he founded the Jordan Company, an investment-banking firm in New York City, specializing in the acquisition of companies through the leveraged buyout method—and he was highly successful.

Martina and I visited New York and had dinner with Jay. During our conversation, I was amazed at the number and variety of acquisitions in his portfolio. His investment portfolio consisted of a group of thirty or so diverse companies, with total sales of over $2 billion!

Jay Jordan was an early pioneer of the leveraged buyout. Even as a young man, Jay had a certain gravitas, a commanding—yet respectful—sense of important issues, and the communication skill to present his thoughts in a manner that gained credence and respect.

I also met Jay's assistant (now managing principal of the Jordan Company), Jeb Boucher, who was instrumental in providing his expertise in the acquisition of NEWFLO's nine acquisitions and served on the board of directors of NEWFLO Corporation, along with Jay and I and others.

I met Jay at Pressed Steel Tank Company in 1975, when he was a young investment banker with Carl Marks. At the time, he was sporting a very distinguished, full, black beard.

Jay was the investment banker in the sale of the Pressed Steel Company, and he saw fit—in fairness to the value I had built into the business—to allocate to me a piece of the action in warrants exercisable into common stock. Jay closed the purchase of Pressed Steel Tank Company, and the buyer, Jack Rishel, assumed the position of chairman and asked me to stay on as president, which I was happy to do.

In 1985, Jay and I had collaborated on a possible buyout of Grove Valve and Regulator and Grove Italia. At the time, Nova owned both companies.

Jay, Luigi Fiore (the president of Grove Italia), and I met at the Hotel Miramar in Monaco on the Mediterranean Coast. Our plan was to have a management buyout of both companies and integrate their operations worldwide.

Luigi was intractable during our discussions. Unknown to us at the time, he was endeavoring to make a separate management buyout of Grove Italia himself. As a result, we were unable to reach an agreement on our proposed management buyout of the two companies.

After our unsuccessful meeting, Luigi drove us to a small trattoria on the Mediterranean Coast for a late supper. The establishment was closing, and the food choices were slim. We ended up with scanty plates of sardines and asparagus spears. Jay and I were disappointed since we had envisioned a grand assortment of delicious Italian seafood. We finished our insufficient meal and returned to our homes the next day.

PACO Pumps

PACO Pumps, located in Emeryville, California, was to be the first of nine companies making up the NEWFLO Corporation. It was the beginning of a buildup of related companies under the NEWFLO umbrella.

There was a rumor that PACO Pumps was up for sale. PACO, founded as Pacific Pumping Company, provided pumping services to dewater building foundations inundated by the San Francisco earthquake and fire in 1906.

I spent several days following leads to determine who was responsible for selling the company and continued my search until I found the consultant who was in charge of the potential sale. As it turned out, she was a woman—and a bitchy one at that. However, many men have the same problem.

I talked to her several times on the phone, and she always told me, in a condescending manner, "We have several qualified potential buyers, and I will let you know if the circumstances change."

She never did.

I eventually located the owner of PACO Pumps—Amsted Industries in Chicago—and called the president. I told him that I was a credible buyer and had an interest in the possible acquisition of PACO Pumps. He sounded interested, so I told him of my problem in getting any assistance from his consultant. He said that he would call her and instruct her to get in touch with me.

I called Jay Jordan in New York and told him that I had found a company to acquire. He said, "Go ahead and get all the information, and we will talk."

The consultant called me the next day. Over the next month, we began our due diligence of PACO's financial statements and operations. We toured the facilities and talked to the two top managers: Bob Elders, vice president of sales and marketing, and John Terranova, vice president of manufacturing.

We also had meetings with the executive from Amsted who was acting in a part-time role as the temporary president of PACO. Every two weeks, he visited PACO for a few days, had meetings with the PACO staff, made decisions, gave largely ignored directives, and returned to Chicago. There was no manager of finance and accounting at PACO; the financial reports were done by Amsted from information supplied by the bookkeepers and the data processing manager at PACO.

This was no way to run a railroad—or a company!

Elders was upbeat and a helpful, proactive executive. Terranova was negative about the entire thing. I asked Terranova about his issues. He did not believe that our acquisition of PACO was a good thing and could not see any advantage for himself.

I told him, "Sometimes you have to have trust in other people. A good example would be an Outward Bound group in the wilderness, where each person stood on a platform and fell over backward, trusting his associates that they would catch him in his fall."

I asked Terranova what he thought, and he said, "I would not trust you guys to catch me." This statement was a million-dollar loss for him; he would have received over a million dollars had he stayed with the company and done the job right. However, in retrospect, he was not the man for the job.

I serendipitously ran into Brian Warren at the airport. I asked him if he would accept the position of vice president of manufacturing at PACO Pumps. After he thought it over, he accepted the job on the spot.

Brian was no stranger to me; he had worked for me at Grove and was an excellent manager. Both he and Bob Elders did a splendid job in turning around PACO Pumps and later were instrumental in helping to make NEWFLO a resounding success. They—and the other executives of the company—were rewarded for their superior performance when NEWFLO was sold.

Several months later, on September 20, 1987, after financial analysis, due diligence of everything from the accounting to environmental and legal concerns, plus many other matters, we negotiated with the company on the price and terms. The Jordan Company finally had a nonbinding agreement to purchase PACO.

Black Monday

On October 19, 1987, the Jordan Company was making a pitch to several banks for the financing to purchase PACO Pumps. Jeb Boucher invited me to attend, and I flew to New York for the meeting. At the meeting, we had a jolt that could have put the financing of the purchase in severe jeopardy!

In the middle of the meeting, someone opened the conference room door, stuck his head in, and said, "The stock market has crashed! The Dow Jones is down 508 points—a 22.5 percent nosedive." Every face in the conference room seemed to sag on the news, and you could almost hear the ruminations of the attendees.

As it happened, a month later, the banks came around, and the financing of the PACO Pumps acquisition went forward successfully.

On December 23, 1987, the Jordan Company and I acquired PACO Pumps, a seventy-plus-year-old ailing pump company. I assumed the position of president, CEO, chairman, and shareholder.

A Dream Comes to Fruition

PACO, our first acquisition, was the first company in the fluid flow products industry. After the acquisition, the real work began—to make a company that was virtually on the ropes into a highly profitable company.

In my due diligence, I had assessed staffing levels for the various functions, using the personnel metrics of Grove as a rough starting point. I assigned the PACO managers to reduce the payrolls of each of their organizations. It was a difficult job for them. Reducing staff was not in their vocabulary—adding staff was.

After weeks of consultation and gnashing of teeth, we streamlined the organization and eliminated excess staff in both office personnel and shop employees, enough savings to put the company in the black.

We found that the engineering department had full sway over which projects they wanted to work on—with minimal input from sales and marketing.

I instructed sales and marketing to determine what new or enhanced products they could use to increase sales and market share. I assigned them to the engineering department and canceled all existing engineering projects in the engineering backlog—except those needed to resolve problems in the design or quality of the current products.

The marketing department and I were the only ones that initiated any new projects for the engineering department. Because of this change in policy, we substantially reduced the engineering staff until we had approved engineering projects for them to work on.

PACO sales had stayed at about the $30 million sales level over several years before we acquired the company. There was no growth, and the profitability of the company had sunk to an almost breakeven position. I elicited the sales department to examine all product pricing and to make selective price increases that would not cause any significant reduction in market share. I also tasked them to develop and propose new marketing initiatives to increase sales in both the Western Hemisphere and in the Eastern Hemisphere, particularly in Asia.

In a meeting with Jay Jordan just before the completion of the acquisition of PACO Pumps, he asked, "What is the worst scenario for PACO?"

I replied, "The worst scenario for PACO is that it will continue at the same sales level forever, with a minimal profit of no less than $1 million per year. However, I do not expect that to happen on my watch, and I will do my best to make sure the company is successful."

The Ten Operational Principles of NEWFLO's Success

NEWFLO was the parent company of all the operating companies, and all of the company presidents were under the direction of the NEWLO president and CEO.

NEWFLO's success in a large measure was based on ten principles of managing the corporation. The most valuable asset of the company was the experienced, professional, dedicated employees, managers, and executives. The performance of the management team and the employees was a dominant factor in NEWFLO's success.

The focused strategy of NEWFLO substantially increased profitability in the fluid management products industry. Fluid management is the ability to move, control, and measure fluids such as water, water-related liquids, petroleum products, and chemicals that affect almost every aspect of modern global society.

The NEWFLO product groups served a large and diverse market for the chemical, petrochemical, energy, commercial construction, industrial, water resources and municipalities, electric power and cogeneration, agriculture, marine, mining, and original equipment manufacturers, and a number of other industries worldwide

1. Leveraged Buyouts

The Jordan Company was one of the early investment banks to acquire companies using the leveraged buyout method. The acquired company's assets provided a large part of the purchase price, along with bank loans and preferred stock. The remainder was mainly the common stock of NEWFLO invested by the shareholders. This required close management of the cash flow since there were covenants in the bank loans that restricted what the company could do without the possibility of default on the bank loans.

2. Cash Flow Management

The management of NEWFLO regarded cash flow
as the top priority to avoid default on the loans
and to pay down the debt incurred to finance the
acquisitions. Management managed inventory
turnover, accounts receivable, accounts payable,
capital expenditures, and other cash expenditures to
assure optimal cash flow. Cash was king!

3. Buildups

Buildups were the acquisition of companies with
related products to increase the coverage of a
market, such as varieties of valves, pumps, and
flow-measurement instruments. These products
added to the total sales obtained in an undersold
market, as well as increasing NEWFLO's profitability.
The NEWFLO buildups consisted of nine such
acquisitions.

4. Small Corporate Staff

The company maintained a lean staff at the
corporate office to minimize corporate expenses.
NEWFLO achieved this by minimizing the functions
provided by the corporate staff and delegated
maximum authority to the presidents of the
individual companies—with oversight by corporate
management.

5. Retain Preacquisition Owners and Management

When an acquisition was made, every effort was
made to bring into the acquired company those
entrepreneurs and managers who demonstrated
their ability to run their company successfully and

profitably. This policy was an important factor in the overall profit performance of NEWFLO.

6. Measure Performance—Set Goals

NEWFLO management considered it vital that performance measurement of the essential metrics of each company be established and agreed upon. Cash flow, staffing, cost reduction, pricing, quality cost, and other items were included in these metrics. The presidents of each company were held strictly accountable for meeting these metrics—and it was a part of each of their bonus plans. Productivity was the combination of individual work ethic and meeting goals.

7. Tight Control of Staffing

The managers agreed with my assertion that people were the most valuable asset, but also one of the largest costs. The managers recognized that they must have, develop, or hire the most qualified person for each job if they were to have maximum effectiveness, productivity, and profitability.

Organizations tend to get larger and less efficient by adding additional unneeded functions or services and require continual monitoring by top management to eliminate empire building. Every position in the company must be justified.

8. Fair, Firm, and Consistent

These simple words guided the company's human relations: *fair* because people deserve fair treatment; *firm* because the company needs to make a profit to survive and provide jobs; and *consistent* because employees do not like to have management changing their mind on a whim—they want a consistent message from management. The company's excellent results in human relations were from following these guidelines. (No strikes occurred in any NEWFLO Corporation company in the seven years of its existence before it was sold.)

9. Bonuses and Retirement Plans

The company established bonus plans that allowed workers and management to earn extra money by meeting or exceeding realistic goals of productivity, cash flow, and profit improvement. Where a plan already existed, the company modified the plan for maximum results.

Where feasible, the company installed employee retirement plans that gave employees control of their own retirement by choosing their own investments and increasing the value of their portfolio.

401-K retirement plans were installed wherever feasible, with the company matching employee cash contributions.

10. State-of-the-Art Design and High-Quality Products

The engineering department, in close coordination with the sales and marketing department, collaborated to design state-of-the-art products that met or exceeded the customers' requirements and all government standards. Engineering updated their computer programming to provide information to customers that met their needs.

NEWFLO Acquisitions

NEWFLO began a program of increasing profitability through a buildup of compatible fluid management products companies and combined them into our umbrella company, NEWFLO Corporation.

The acquisitions were the result of goodwill, close coordination, and assistance from the Jordan Company, members of our board of directors, the executive management of the company, and the presidents and staffs of the individual companies. Highly qualified and motivated individuals working together as a team can do amazing things together—and did.

NEWFLO's strategy of buildups and management of the acquired companies was to become one of the most profitable fluid-management companies in the industry.

Each of the acquisitions required weeks and months by NEWFLO executives, managers, and staff visiting scores of potential acquisitions, walking through their manufacturing facilities, and talking with their managers. It also required many hours of analyzing their financial statements, environmental problems, safety records, quality control, and other important items.

The Acquisitions

NEWFLO acquired nine companies and sold off one company, Flo-Bend, a subsidiary company of Newman's that did not meet NEWFLO's standard, leaving eight operating companies.

PACO Pumps was NEWFLO's first acquisition. Their pumps sold primarily to the building trade market, but also to other diverse markets and applications worldwide.

NEWFLO also purchased Water Specialties. Dick Huth, an expert in water meter design, started the business in his garage and was very successful. Water Specialties was the first of our acquisitions competing in the fluid measurement market. Water Specialties, although small, was operating at a high gross margin. Their water meters sold mainly for irrigation water measurement.

Dick Huth and his two sons, Steve and Eric, agreed to continue with the company and were welcomed. This met our acquisition profile of keeping intact the management of the acquired company who made it profitable. This proved to be an excellent position for our buildup strategy.

Newman's and Flo-Bend were the third and fourth acquisitions. Newman's had a long-term relationship with established offshore valve manufacturing companies and contracted them to produce valves and fittings for Newman's, which marketed the valves and fittings in the Western Hemisphere. This implemented our strategy to broaden the product line to cover a larger segment of the fluid control products industry and utilize the Newman's extensive sales representatives and distributors worldwide.

Flo-Bend, a subsidiary of Newman's, which manufactured pipe fittings, came along with the purchase of Newman's in 1990. It was quickly spun off and sold, considering its unfavorable position in the highly competitive pipe fittings market with overseas competitors.

NEWFLO acquired the fifth and sixth acquisitions, General Valve and Johnston Pumps, consolidated into a single manufacturing facility in Brookshire, Texas, thirty-five miles west of Houston. We expanded the manufacturing facility and relocated PACO to the same facility.

Moving and consolidating PACO into the Johnston pump-general valve plant increased the profitability of PACO Pumps, primarily from the reduction of labor cost and reduced overhead burden. All three companies shared the overhead and increased their profitability.

General Valve manufactured a line of specialized block-and-bleed valves marketed to airport gasoline-storage facilities and other similar installations all over the world. Johnston Pump produced and marketed a complete line of vertical pumps for agriculture, industrial, and other uses, and provided vertical pumps up to thirty-six inches in bowl diameter.

Penberthy, NEWFLO's seventh acquisition, was an old-line company, with many years of experience in the fluid measurement segment of the industry. The company met the needs of industries that required measurement of liquids for the many large storage tanks used by the liquid storage industry, as well as other industrial fluid measurement applications.

Penberthy had a proven just-in-time manufacturing methodology. The methodology was based on manufacturing cells that performed all the operations on special groups of machines, which reduced moving material from area to area, increased efficiency, and minimized inventories, while improving quality and creating shorter customer lead times (quicker delivery) of its products, giving it an edge over its competitors.

NEWFLO'S eighth acquisition was Techno, a small company in Erie, Pennsylvania, that manufactured and marketed a line of engineered thermoplastic and metal specialty check valves— and was a high gross margin product. These unique valves filled a niche in the market and provided additional coverage and profits from a leading position in this specialty market.

The ninth acquisition was Barber Industries, headquartered in Calgary. The company manufactured and marketed oil and gas wellhead Christmas trees—an assembly of high-pressure valves and fittings that control the pressure of the oil or gas well—and distributed the product from the wellhead to refining or storage facilities. It also produced emergency safety shutoff systems.

Barber, the last company acquired by NEWFLO, was acquired at a bargain price, a low multiple of sales, and was instrumental in increasing the value of NEWFLO, whose sale was in process.

NEWFLO'S Performance

NEWFLO's extraordinary cumulative annual growth rates of sales and profitability made it one of the highest performers in the industry and were a major attraction for interested acquirers of NEWFLO.

NEWFLO's cumulative average growth rate of sales grew at a rate of 23.9 percent per year, while profitability and cash flow (EBITDA—earnings before interest, taxes, depreciation, and amortization) increased at an incredible cumulative average growth rate of 58.3 percent per year.

NEWFLO Sale

In early 1996, the NEWFLO board of directors decided to sell the company. It was highly successful, and it was time for the shareholders to reap the rewards of that success.

NEWFLO selected and engaged Goldman Sachs to spearhead the sale. Goldman produced a list of two dozen companies that might be in the market for an acquisition such as NEWFLO. Of the two dozen companies, eight companies expressed an interest in acquiring NEWFLO at an estimated sale price that would be nonbinding pending a formal purchase contract signed by both parties.

Our first potential buyer candidate was Textron Corporation, the chairman of which was Jim Hardeman. Textron owned the Cessna Company, which built and marketed high-performance quality civilian jet aircraft. Textron offered a price of $280 million.

The final offer, which was accepted by the NEWFLO board of directors, was from Precision Cast Parts Corporation, a manufacturer and marketer of precision castings based in Portland. Chairman Bill McCormack offered $300 million, and the NEWFLO board of directors accepted the offer. The sale was consummated on July 31, 1996.

The $300 million sale price, after all obligations of the company were met, provided NEWFLO shareholders with an average internal rate of return of 58.2 percent. As a frame of reference, the entire stock market generated an average annual return on investment of 10.2 percent that year.

Chapter 12:
Serendipity in a Dream

The results of the NEWFLO sale were unparalleled, and the return on investment for the shareholders was beyond all expectations. We earned the return to the shareholders the hard way—we worked for it! All of the shareholders were a bunch of happy campers.

Although I have not led a religious life, I felt that my faith in God made me a better person and provided spiritual support for me to succeed.

After the sale of NEWFLO, I basked briefly in the euphoria of the moment, reveled in the limelight of my fifteen minutes of fame, and received congratulations and kudos. However, there was something wrong—something was missing. I wished Homer could have been here to see my success and my worth as his son, whom he had abandoned. In reality, however, I had abandoned him.

Over many years, my brother and I separately tried to learn about Homer. We could not verify where he had lived, where he had worked, or when and how he had died. We shared our information over time and found only small snippets of information—not enough in fact or in reality to know much about him.

According to unsubstantiated family legend, Homer was a quarter-breed Cherokee, and his father, Walter, a half-breed.

There was also information that Homer worked on a railroad in Utah and married and had two daughters in Texas. However, we could not verify the information; there were thousands of Watsons in Texas, Oklahoma, and other Southern states, making it difficult to ascertain the facts.

Homer was like a ghost, coming into my life with each fragment of information and leaving again when the information was found wanting of verification.

Serendipity—In a Dream

A dream I experienced several years ago came vividly to my mind. In the dream, I was finally retired and was sitting comfortably in my La-Z Boy lounger at our estate in Montecito, California, watching TV with the sound off, reading the *Wall Street Journal* and listening to Rush on the radio.

All of a sudden, I had a gripping, painful spasm in my chest on my left side. I fell forward from my chair headfirst to the floor, leaving me unconscious.

My eyes opened to find myself in a large, dim room filled with all my relatives looking on, murmuring quietly.

In the far back of the room, I barely made out Homer's silhouette. With a wry grin, he looked at me and silently mouthed the words,

"You – Done – Good, – Son!"

THE END

Epilogue

Martina died on November 17, 2006, after a long, painful, courageous battle with cancer. She was just sixty-three years old, and we had been together and in love for thirty-four years.

I never imagined the possibility that she would pass away before me. I was devastated. It wasn't supposed to be this way. *You are gone, but I shall love you forever.* I hear, in my mind, a haunting refrain of "Heartaches of a Fool" by Willie Nelson: "Started out with the dreams, the plans of a wise man, ended up with the heartaches of a fool."

I hated God for letting Martina die a horrid death, but God works in mysterious ways and I need to accept his will and his love.

On my trips to Oklahoma, Colorado, Utah, and Oregon to research the history of the area and the times, I was fortunate for the help of local residents, historical societies, and museums. Some of the material in this book came from those sources as well as from relatives, friends, associates, and my brother, Perry, whose memory was better than mine in most cases.

When I visited Pittsburg, Oklahoma, to see the place where I was born and to gather facts for this book, I felt like a wild salmon that had swum thousands of miles from its birthplace and had come home to die.

I have had the opportunity while writing this story to visit the Colorado Springs Day Nursery, where my brother and I lived. I visited the day nursery twice, once with my thirteen-year-old granddaughter, Chelsea. The management and staff were wonderful, and I learned the history of the institution and freely spent time visiting all three floors and rooms, including the shower room. I saw and talked with the young children happily immersed in their activities. I am very satisfied that the children are treated with loving care, and I thank each of the people in the administration of the Colorado Springs Day Nursery who made my visits wondrous and satisfying experiences.

Résumé of
J. Jack Watson

POSITIONS HELD:

NEWFLO CORPORATION, Austin, TX, 1988–1996
Chairman, CEO, President, Chairman of the Board
  Company with eight subsidiaries manufacturing and
  marketing valves, fittings, pumps, and meters. 1,900
  personnel.

PACO PUMPS, INC., Oakland, CA, 1986–1988
Presidentand CEO
  Manufacturing and marketing of centrifugal pumps
  and propeller meters. Two plants. 200 personnel.

GROVE VALVE & REGULATOR, Oakland, CA, 1977–1986
President, CEO, Director
  Manufacturing and marketing of pipeline valves and
  regulators and commercial and aerospace regulators.
  Three locations. 900 personnel.

Jack Watson

PRESSED STEEL TANK, Milwaukee, WI, 1973–1977
President, CEO, Director
Manufacturing and sales of compressed gas cylinders
for industrial and commercial markets. Two plants.
750 personnel.

ALLIS CHALMERS, Wichita Falls, TX, 1972–1973
Division General Manager
New start-up division producing and marketing
electrical-mechanical industrial controls. 300
personnel.

MEDALIST INDUSTRIES, Oshkosh, WI, 1968–1972
Vice President, General Manager
Multiplant division manufacturing and marketing
machine tools, special machinery, marine and diesel
engines, pumps and generator sets. Two plants. 350
personnel.

WILTON CORPORATION, Schiller Park, IL, 1965–1968
Manufacturer and marketer of industrial clamping
tools, precision hydraulic products, machine tools
and paper packaging products. 400 personnel.

WALWORTH CORPORATION, Braintree, MA, 1962–1965
Works Manager
Valve and fitting manufacturing and distribution.
Integrated foundry, machining, assembly and
distribution. 700 personnel.

THIOKOL CHEMICAL CORPORATION, Brigham City, UT,
1959–1962
Chief Industrial Planning
Solid rocket engine manufacturer.

BOEING AIRPLANE CO., Seattle, WA, 1950–1959
Industrial Engineer
Aircraft manufacturer. B-52, B-47, B-50, C-97, 707,
KC-135. Bomark, Matador missiles.

EDUCATION:
Bachelor of Science, Industrial Administration.
Oregon State College. 1947–1950 (Honor Roll, 1950).
Inducted into the O.S.C. Engineering Hall of Fame,
2002.